*Evidence of Jesus' Love for Both
Humans and Their Animals*

BLESSED with an Angel and a Rainbow

JAMES ROBERT WAUGH

WESTBOW
P R E S S®
A DIVISION OF THOMAS NELSON
& ZONDERVAN

WestBow Press books may be ordered through booksellers or by contacting:

WestBow Press
A Division of Thomas Nelson & Zondervan
1663 Liberty Drive
Bloomington, IN 47403
www.westbowpress.com
844-714-3454

ISBN: 978-1-9736-1881-2 (sc)
ISBN: 978-1-9736-1883-6 (hc)
ISBN: 978-1-9736-1882-9 (e)

Library of Congress Control Number: 2018901519

Print information available on the last page.

WestBow Press rev. date: 11/07/2023

"RAPTURE SIGNS" RECENTLY FULFILLED!!!

AUGUST 21, 2017 – "THE USA ONLY ECLIPSE" (Only other USA only eclipse was in the year 1776).

SEPTEMBER 23, 2017 – "REVELATION 12 CELESTIAL event:" THE WOMAN, THE CHILD AND THE DRAGON"

LUKE 21: verses (25-28)
REVELATION 3: (verse 10)
REVELATION 7: (verses 9-17)
REVELATION 12: (verses 1-17)
REVELATION 5: (verse 11)
1 CORINTHIANS 15: (verses 50-58)
2 THESSALONIANS 2: (verses 11-12)
JOB 1: (verses 6-22)
REVELATION 21: (verse 8)
EPHESIANS 6: (verses 10-13)

Luke 21

New King James Version

The Widow's Two Mites

21 And He looked up and saw the rich putting their gifts into the treasury, 2 and He saw also a certain poor widow putting in two mites.[a] 3 So He said, "Truly I say to you that this poor widow has put in more than all; 4 for all these out of their abundance have put in offerings [b]for God, but she out of her poverty put in all the livelihood that she had."

Jesus Predicts the Destruction of the Temple

5 Then, as some spoke of the temple, how it was [c]adorned with beautiful stones and donations, He said, 6 "These things which you see—the days will come in which not *one* stone shall be left upon another that shall not be thrown down."

The Signs of the Times and the End of the Age

7 So they asked Him, saying, "Teacher, but when will these things be? And what sign *will there be* when these things are about to take place?"

8 And He said: "Take heed that you not be deceived. For many will come in My name, saying, 'I am *He*,' and, 'The time has drawn near.' [d]Therefore do not [e]go after them. 9 But when you hear of wars and commotions, do not be terrified; for these things must come to pass first, but the end *will* not *come* immediately."

10 Then He said to them, "Nation will rise against nation, and kingdom against kingdom. 11 And there will be great earthquakes

in various places, and famines and pestilences; and there will be fearful sights and great signs from heaven. **12** But before all these things, they will lay their hands on you and persecute *you,* delivering *you* up to the synagogues and prisons. You will be brought before kings and rulers for My name's sake. **13** But it will turn out for you as an occasion for testimony. **14** Therefore settle *it* in your hearts not to meditate beforehand on what you will [f]answer; **15** for I will give you a mouth and wisdom which all your adversaries will not be able to contradict or [g]resist. **16** You will be betrayed even by parents and brothers, relatives and friends; and they will put *some* of you to death. **17** And you will be hated by all for My name's sake. **18** But not a hair of your head shall be lost. **19** By your patience possess your souls.

The Destruction of Jerusalem

20 "But when you see Jerusalem surrounded by armies, then know that its desolation is near. **21** Then let those who are in Judea flee to the mountains, let those who are in the midst of her depart, and let not those who are in the country enter her. **22** For these are the days of vengeance, that all things which are written may be fulfilled. **23** But woe to those who are pregnant and to those who are nursing babies in those days! For there will be great distress in the land and wrath upon this people. **24** And they will fall by the edge of the sword, and be led away captive into all nations. And Jerusalem will be trampled by Gentiles until the times of the Gentiles are fulfilled.

The Coming of the Son of Man

25 "And there will be signs in the sun, in the moon, and in the stars; and on the earth distress of nations, with perplexity, the sea and the waves roaring; 26 men's hearts failing them from fear and the expectation of those things which are coming on the earth, for the powers of the heavens will be shaken. 27 Then they will see the Son of Man coming in a cloud with power and great glory. 28 Now when these things begin to happen, look up and lift up your heads, because your redemption draws near."

The Parable of the Fig Tree

29 Then He spoke to them a parable: "Look at the fig tree, and all the trees. **30** When they are already budding, you see and know for yourselves that summer is now near. **31** So you also, when you see these things happening, know that the kingdom of God is near. **32** Assuredly, I say to you, this generation will by no means pass away till all things take place. **33** Heaven and earth will pass away, but My words will by no means pass away.

The Importance of Watching

34 "But take heed to yourselves, lest your hearts be weighed down with [h]carousing, drunkenness, and cares of this life, and that Day come on you unexpectedly. **35** For it will come as a snare on all those who dwell on the face of the whole earth. **36** Watch therefore, and pray always that you may [i]be counted worthy to escape all these things that will come to pass, and to stand before the Son of Man."

37 And in the daytime He was teaching in the temple, but at night He went out and stayed on the mountain called Olivet. **38** Then early in the morning all the people came to Him in the temple to hear Him.

Footnotes

a. Luke 21:2 Gr. *lepta,* very small copper coins
b. Luke 21:4 NU omits *for God*
c. Luke 21:5 *decorated*
d. Luke 21:8 NU omits *Therefore*
e. Luke 21:8 *follow*
f. Luke 21:14 *say in defense*
g. Luke 21:15 *withstand*
h. Luke 21:34 *dissipation*
i. Luke 21:36 NU *have strength to*

Revelation 3

New King James Version

The Dead Church

3 "And to the [a]angel of the church in Sardis write,

'These things says He who has the seven Spirits of God and the seven stars: "I know your works, that you have a name that you are alive, but you are dead. 2 Be watchful, and strengthen the things which remain, that are ready to die, for I have not found your works perfect before [b] God. 3 Remember therefore how you have received and heard; hold fast and repent. Therefore if you will not watch, I will come upon you as a thief, and you will not know what hour I will come upon you. 4 [c]You have a few names [d]even in Sardis who have not defiled their garments; and they shall walk with Me in white, for they are worthy. 5 He who overcomes shall be clothed in white garments, and I will not blot out his name from the Book of Life; but I will confess his name before My Father and before His angels.

6 "He who has an ear, let him hear what the Spirit says to the churches."'

The Faithful Church

7 "And to the [e]angel of the church in Philadelphia write,

'These things says He who is holy, He who is true, "He who has the key of David, He who opens and no one shuts, and shuts and no one opens": 8 "I know your works. See, I have set before you an open door, [f]and no one can shut it; for you have a little strength, have kept My word, and have not denied My name. 9 Indeed I will make *those* of the synagogue of Satan, who say they are Jews and are not, but lie—indeed I will make them come and worship before your feet, and to know that I have loved you. **10 Because you have kept [g]My command to persevere, I also will keep you from the hour of trial which shall come upon the whole world, to test those who dwell on the earth. 11** [h]Behold, I am coming quickly! Hold fast what you have, that no one may take your crown. **12** He who overcomes, I will make him a pillar in the temple of My God, and he shall go out no more. I will write on him the name of My God and the name of the city of My God, the New Jerusalem, which comes down out of heaven from My God. And *I will write on him* My new name.

13 "He who has an ear, let him hear what the Spirit says to the churches."'

The Lukewarm Church

14 "And to the [i]angel of the church [j]of the Laodiceans write,

'These things says the Amen, the Faithful and True Witness, the Beginning of the creation of God: **15** "I know your works, that you are neither cold nor hot. I could wish you were cold or hot. **16** So then, because you are lukewarm, and neither [k]cold nor hot, I will vomit you out of My mouth. **17** Because you say, 'I am rich, have become wealthy, and have need of nothing'—and do not know that you are wretched, miserable, poor, blind, and naked— **18** I counsel you to buy from Me gold refined in the fire, that you may be rich; and white garments, that you may be clothed, *that* the shame of your nakedness may not be revealed; and anoint your eyes with eye salve, that you may see. **19** As many as I love, I rebuke and chasten. [l] Therefore be [m]zealous and repent. **20** Behold, I stand at the door and knock. If anyone hears My voice and opens the door, I will come in to him and dine with him, and he with Me. **21** To him who overcomes I will grant to sit with Me on My throne, as I also overcame and sat down with My Father on His throne.

22 "He who has an ear, let him hear what the Spirit says to the churches." '"

Footnotes

a. Revelation 3:1 Or *messenger*
b. Revelation 3:2 NU, M *My God*
c. Revelation 3:4 NU, M *Nevertheless you*
d. Revelation 3:4 NU, M omit *even*
e. Revelation 3:7 Or *messenger*
f. Revelation 3:8 NU, M *which no one can shut*
g. Revelation 3:10 Lit. *the word of My patience*
h. Revelation 3:11 NU, M omit *Behold*
i. Revelation 3:14 Or *messenger*
j. Revelation 3:14 NU, M *in Laodicea*
k. Revelation 3:16 NU, M *hot nor cold*
l. Revelation 3:19 *discipline*
m. Revelation 3:19 *eager*

Revelation 7

New King James Version

The Sealed of Israel

7 After these things I saw four angels standing at the four corners of the earth, holding the four winds of the earth, that the wind should not blow on the earth, on the sea, or on any tree. 2 Then I saw another angel ascending from the east, having the seal of the living God. And he cried with a loud voice to the four angels to whom it was granted to harm the earth and the sea, 3 saying, "Do not harm the earth, the sea, or the trees till we have sealed the servants of our God on their foreheads." 4 And I heard the number of those who were sealed. One hundred *and* forty-four thousand of all the tribes of the children of Israel *were* sealed:

5 of the tribe of Judah twelve thousand *were* sealed;
of the tribe of Reuben twelve thousand *were* [a]sealed;
of the tribe of Gad twelve thousand *were* sealed;
6 of the tribe of Asher twelve thousand *were* sealed;
of the tribe of Naphtali twelve thousand *were* sealed;
of the tribe of Manasseh twelve thousand *were* sealed;
7 of the tribe of Simeon twelve thousand *were* sealed;
of the tribe of Levi twelve thousand *were* sealed;
of the tribe of Issachar twelve thousand *were* sealed;
8 of the tribe of Zebulun twelve thousand *were* sealed;
of the tribe of Joseph twelve thousand *were* sealed;
of the tribe of Benjamin twelve thousand *were* sealed.

A Multitude from the Great Tribulation

9 After these things I looked, and behold, a great multitude which no one could number, of all nations, tribes, peoples, and tongues, standing before the throne and before the Lamb, clothed with

white robes, with palm branches in their hands, 10 and crying out with a loud voice, saying, "Salvation *belongs* to our God who sits on the throne, and to the Lamb!" 11 All the angels stood around the throne and the elders and the four living creatures, and fell on their faces before the throne and worshiped God, 12 saying:

"Amen! Blessing and glory and wisdom,
Thanksgiving and honor and power and might,
Be to our God forever and ever.
Amen."

13 Then one of the elders answered, saying to me, "Who are these arrayed in white robes, and where did they come from?"

14 And I said to him, [b]"Sir, you know."

So he said to me, "These are the ones who come out of the great tribulation, and washed their robes and made them white in the blood of the Lamb. 15 Therefore they are before the throne of God, and serve Him day and night in His temple. And He who sits on the throne will dwell among them. 16 They shall neither hunger anymore nor thirst anymore; the sun shall not strike them, nor any heat; 17 for the Lamb who is in the midst of the throne will shepherd them and lead them to [c]living fountains of waters. And God will wipe away every tear from their eyes."

Footnotes

a. Revelation 7:5 NU, M omit *sealed* in vv. 5b–8b.
b. Revelation 7:14 NU, M *My lord*
c. Revelation 7:17 NU, M *fountains of the waters of life*

Revelation 12

New King James Version

The Woman, the Child, and the Dragon

12 Now a great sign appeared in heaven: a woman clothed with the sun, with the moon under her feet, and on her head a garland of twelve stars. 2 Then being with child, she cried out in labor and in pain to give birth.

3 And another sign appeared in heaven: behold, a great, fiery red dragon having seven heads and ten horns, and seven diadems on his heads. 4 His tail drew a third of the stars of heaven and threw them to the earth. And the dragon stood before the woman who was ready to give birth, to devour her Child as soon as it was born. 5 She bore a male Child who was to rule all nations with a rod of iron. And her Child was caught up to God and His throne. 6 Then the woman fled into the wilderness, where she has a place prepared by God, that they should feed her there one thousand two hundred and sixty days.

Satan Thrown Out of Heaven

7 And war broke out in heaven: Michael and his angels fought with the dragon; and the dragon and his angels fought, 8 but they [a]did not prevail, nor was a place found for [b]them in heaven any longer. 9 So the great dragon was cast out, that serpent of old, called the Devil and Satan, who deceives the whole world; he was cast to the earth, and his angels were cast out with him.

10 Then I heard a loud voice saying in heaven, "Now salvation, and strength, and the kingdom of our God, and the power of His Christ have come, for the accuser of our brethren, who accused them before our God day and night, has been cast down. 11 And

they overcame him by the blood of the Lamb and by the word of their testimony, and they did not love their lives to the death. 12 Therefore rejoice, O heavens, and you who dwell in them! Woe to the inhabitants of the earth and the sea! For the devil has come down to you, having great wrath, because he knows that he has a short time."

The Woman Persecuted

13 Now when the dragon saw that he had been cast to the earth, he persecuted the woman who gave birth to the male *Child.* 14 But the woman was given two wings of a great eagle, that she might fly into the wilderness to her place, where she is nourished for a time and times and half a time, from the presence of the serpent. 15 So the serpent spewed water out of his mouth like a flood after the woman, that he might cause her to be carried away by the flood. 16 But the earth helped the woman, and the earth opened its mouth and swallowed up the flood which the dragon had spewed out of his mouth. 17 And the dragon was enraged with the woman, and he went to make war with the rest of her offspring, who keep the commandments of God and have the testimony of Jesus [c]Christ.

Footnotes

a. Revelation 12:8 *were not strong enough*
b. Revelation 12:8 M *him*
c. Revelation 12:17 NU, M omit *Christ*

Revelation 5

New King James Version

The Lamb Takes the Scroll

5 And I saw in the right *hand* of Him who sat on the throne a scroll written inside and on the back, sealed with seven seals. **2** Then I saw a strong angel proclaiming with a loud voice, "Who is worthy to open the scroll and to loose its seals?" **3** And no one in heaven or on the earth or under the earth was able to open the scroll, or to look at it.

4 So I wept much, because no one was found worthy to open [a]and read the scroll, or to look at it. **5** But one of the elders said to me, "Do not weep. Behold, the Lion of the tribe of Judah, the Root of David, has prevailed to open the scroll and [b]to loose its seven seals."

6 And I looked, [c]and behold, in the midst of the throne and of the four living creatures, and in the midst of the elders, stood a Lamb as though it had been slain, having seven horns and seven eyes, which are the seven Spirits of God sent out into all the earth. **7** Then He came and took the scroll out of the right hand of Him who sat on the throne.

Worthy Is the Lamb

8 Now when He had taken the scroll, the four living creatures and the twenty-four elders fell down before the Lamb, each having a harp, and golden bowls full of incense, which are the prayers of the saints. **9** And they sang a new song, saying:

"You are worthy to take the scroll,
And to open its seals;
For You were slain,

And have redeemed us to God by Your blood
Out of every tribe and tongue and people and nation,
10 And have made [d]us kings[e] and priests to our God;
And [f]we shall reign on the earth."

11 Then I looked, and I heard the voice of many angels around the throne, the living creatures, and the elders; and the number of them was ten thousand times ten thousand, and thousands of thousands, 12 saying with a loud voice:

"Worthy is the Lamb who was slain
To receive power and riches and wisdom,
And strength and honor and glory and blessing!"

13 And every creature which is in heaven and on the earth and under the earth and such as are in the sea, and all that are in them, I heard saying:

"Blessing and honor and glory and power
Be to Him who sits on the throne,
And to the Lamb, forever and [g]ever!"

14 Then the four living creatures said, "Amen!" And the [h]twenty-four elders fell down and worshiped [i]Him who lives forever and ever.

Footnotes

a. Revelation 5:4 NU, M omit *and read*
b. Revelation 5:5 NU, M omit *to loose*
c. Revelation 5:6 NU, M *I saw in the midst . . . a Lamb standing*
d. Revelation 5:10 NU, M *them*
e. Revelation 5:10 NU *a kingdom*
f. Revelation 5:10 NU, M *they*
g. Revelation 5:13 M adds *Amen*
h. Revelation 5:14 NU, M omit *twenty-four*
i. Revelation 5:14 NU, M omit *Him who lives forever and ever*

1 Corinthians 15

New King James Version

The Risen Christ, Faith's Reality

15 Moreover, brethren, I declare to you the gospel which I preached to you, which also you received and in which you stand, **2** by which also you are saved, if you hold fast that word which I preached to you—unless you believed in vain.

3 For I delivered to you first of all that which I also received: that Christ died for our sins according to the Scriptures, **4** and that He was buried, and that He rose again the third day according to the Scriptures, **5** and that He was seen by [a]Cephas, then by the twelve. **6** After that He was seen by over five hundred brethren at once, of whom the greater part remain to the present, but some have [b]fallen asleep. **7** After that He was seen by James, then by all the apostles. **8** Then last of all He was seen by me also, as by one born out of due time.

9 For I am the least of the apostles, who am not worthy to be called an apostle, because I persecuted the church of God. **10** But by the grace of God I am what I am, and His grace toward me was not in vain; but I labored more abundantly than they all, yet not I, but the grace of God *which was* with me. **11** Therefore, whether *it was* I or they, so we preach and so you believed.

The Risen Christ, Our Hope

12 Now if Christ is preached that He has been raised from the dead, how do some among you say that there is no resurrection of the dead? **13** But if there is no resurrection of the dead, then Christ is not risen. **14** And if Christ is not risen, then our preaching *is* empty and your faith *is* also empty. **15** Yes, and we are found false witnesses of God, because we have testified of God that He raised up Christ, whom He did not raise up—if in fact the dead do not rise. **16** For if *the* dead do not rise, then Christ is not risen. **17** And if Christ is not risen, your faith *is* futile; you are still in your sins! **18** Then also those who have [c]fallen asleep in Christ have perished. **19** If in this life only we have hope in Christ, we are of all men the most pitiable.

The Last Enemy Destroyed

20 But now Christ is risen from the dead, *and* has become the firstfruits of those who have [d]fallen asleep. **21** For since by man *came* death, by Man also *came* the resurrection of the dead. **22** For as in Adam all die, even so in Christ all shall be made alive. **23** But each one in his own order: Christ the firstfruits, afterward those *who are* Christ's at His coming. **24** Then *comes* the end, when He delivers the kingdom to God the Father, when He puts an end to all rule and all authority and power. **25** For He must reign till He has put all enemies under His feet. **26** The last enemy *that* will be destroyed *is* death. **27** For "He has put all things under His feet." But when He says "all things are put under *Him*," *it is* evident that He who put all things under Him is excepted. **28** Now when all things are made subject to Him, then the Son Himself will also be subject to Him who put all things under Him, that God may be all in all.

Effects of Denying the Resurrection

29 Otherwise, what will they do who are baptized for the dead, if the dead do not rise at all? Why then are they baptized for the dead? **30** And why do we stand in [e]jeopardy every hour? **31** I affirm, by the boasting in you which I have in Christ Jesus our Lord, I die daily. **32** If, in the manner of men, I have fought with beasts at Ephesus, what advantage *is it* to me? If *the* dead do not rise, "Let us eat and drink, for tomorrow we die!"

33 Do not be deceived: "Evil company corrupts good habits." **34** Awake to righteousness, and do not sin; for some do not have the knowledge of God. I speak *this* to your shame.

A Glorious Body

35 But someone will say, "How are the dead raised up? And with what body do they come?" **36** Foolish one, what you sow is not made alive unless it dies. **37** And what you sow, you do not sow that body that shall be, but mere grain—perhaps wheat or some other *grain.* **38** But God gives it a body as He pleases, and to each seed its own body.

39 All flesh *is* not the same flesh, but *there is* one *kind* [f]*of* flesh of men, another flesh of animals, another of fish, *and* another of birds.

40 *There are* also [g]celestial bodies and [h]terrestrial bodies; but the glory of the celestial *is* one, and the *glory* of the terrestrial *is* another. **41** *There is* one glory of the sun, another glory of the moon, and another glory of the stars; for *one* star differs from *another* star in glory.

42 So also *is* the resurrection of the dead. *The body* is sown in corruption, it is raised in incorruption. **43** It is sown in dishonor, it is raised in glory. It is sown in weakness, it is raised in power. **44** It is sown a natural body, it is raised a spiritual body. There is a natural body, and there is a spiritual body. **45** And so it is written, "The first man Adam became a living being." The last Adam *became* a life-giving spirit.

46 However, the spiritual is not first, but the natural, and afterward the spiritual. **47** The first man *was* of the earth, *made*[i] of dust; the second Man *is* [j]the Lord from heaven. **48** As *was* the [k]*man* of dust, so also *are* those *who are made* of dust; and as *is* the heavenly *Man,* so also *are* those *who are* heavenly. **49** And as we have borne the image of the *man* of dust, we[l] shall also bear the image of the heavenly *Man.*

Our Final Victory

50 Now this I say, brethren, that flesh and blood cannot inherit the kingdom of God; nor does corruption inherit incorruption.

51 Behold, I tell you a [m]mystery: We shall not all sleep, but we shall all be changed— 52 in a moment, in the twinkling of an eye, at the last trumpet. For the trumpet will sound, and the dead will be raised incorruptible, and we shall be changed. 53 For this corruptible must put on incorruption, and this mortal *must* put on immortality. 54 So when this corruptible has put on incorruption, and this mortal has put on immortality, then shall be brought to pass the saying that is written: "Death is swallowed up in victory."

55 "O[n] Death, where *is* your sting? O Hades, where *is* your victory?"

56 The sting of death *is* sin, and the strength of sin *is* the law. 57 But thanks *be* to God, who gives us the victory through our Lord Jesus Christ.

58 Therefore, my beloved brethren, be steadfast, immovable, always abounding in the work of the Lord, knowing that your labor is not in vain in the Lord.

Footnotes

a. 1 Corinthians 15:5 Peter
b. 1 Corinthians 15:6 Died
c. 1 Corinthians 15:18 Died
d. 1 Corinthians 15:20 Died
e. 1 Corinthians 15:30 *danger*
f. 1 Corinthians 15:39 NU, M omit *of flesh*
g. 1 Corinthians 15:40 *heavenly*
h. 1 Corinthians 15:40 *earthly*
i. 1 Corinthians 15:47 *earthy*
j. 1 Corinthians 15:47 NU omits *the Lord*
k. 1 Corinthians 15:48 *earthy*
l. 1 Corinthians 15:49 M *let us also bear*
m. 1 Corinthians 15:51 *hidden truth*
n. 1 Corinthians 15:55 NU *O Death, where is your victory? O Death, where is your sting?*

2 Thessalonians 2

New King James Version

The Great Apostasy

2 Now, brethren, concerning the coming of our Lord Jesus Christ and our gathering together to Him, we ask you, **2** not to be soon shaken in mind or troubled, either by spirit or by word or by letter, as if from us, as though the day of [a]Christ had come. **3** Let no one deceive you by any means; for *that Day will not come* unless the falling away comes first, and the man of [b]sin is revealed, the son of perdition, **4** who opposes and exalts himself above all that is called God or that is worshiped, so that he sits [c]as God in the temple of God, showing himself that he is God.

5 Do you not remember that when I was still with you I told you these things? **6** And now you know what is restraining, that he may be revealed in his own time. **7** For the [d]mystery of lawlessness is already at work; only [e]He who now restrains *will do so* until He is taken out of the way. **8** And then the lawless one will be revealed, whom the Lord will consume with the breath of His mouth and destroy with the brightness of His coming. **9 The coming of the lawless one is according to the working of Satan, with all power, signs, and lying wonders, 10 and with all unrighteous deception among those who perish, because they did not receive the love of the truth, that they might be saved. 11 And for this reason God will send them strong delusion, that they should believe the lie, 12 that they all may be condemned who did not believe the truth but had pleasure in unrighteousness.**

Stand Fast

13 But we are [f]bound to give thanks to God always for you, brethren beloved by the Lord, because God from the beginning chose you for salvation through [g]sanctification by the Spirit and belief in the truth, **14** to which He called you by our gospel, for the obtaining of the glory of our Lord Jesus Christ. **15** Therefore, brethren, stand fast and hold the traditions which you were taught, whether by word or our [h]epistle.

16 Now may our Lord Jesus Christ Himself, and our God and Father, who has loved us and given *us* everlasting consolation and good hope by grace, **17** comfort your hearts and [i]establish you in every good word and work.

Footnotes

a. 2 Thessalonians 2:2 NU *the Lord*
b. 2 Thessalonians 2:3 NU *lawlessness*
c. 2 Thessalonians 2:4 NU omits *as God*
d. 2 Thessalonians 2:7 *hidden truth*
e. 2 Thessalonians 2:7 Or *he*
f. 2 Thessalonians 2:13 *under obligation*
g. 2 Thessalonians 2:13 *being set apart by*
h. 2 Thessalonians 2:15 *letter*
i. 2 Thessalonians 2:17 *strengthen*

Job 1

New King James Version

Job and His Family in Uz

1 There was a man in the land of Uz, whose name *was* Job; and that man was blameless and upright, and one who feared God and [a] shunned evil. 2 And seven sons and three daughters were born to him. 3 Also, his possessions were seven thousand sheep, three thousand camels, five hundred yoke of oxen, five hundred female donkeys, and a very large household, so that this man was the greatest of all the [b]people of the East.

4 And his sons would go and feast *in their* houses, each on his *appointed* day, and would send and invite their three sisters to eat and drink with them. 5 So it was, when the days of feasting had run their course, that Job would send and [c]sanctify them, and he would rise early in the morning and offer burnt offerings *according to* the number of them all. For Job said, "It may be that my sons have sinned and cursed[d] God in their hearts." Thus Job did regularly.

Satan Attacks Job's Character

6 Now there was a day when the sons of God came to present themselves before the Lord, and [e]Satan also came among them. 7 And the Lord said to [f]Satan, "From where do you come?"

So Satan answered the Lord and said, "From going to and fro on the earth, and from walking back and forth on it."

8 Then the Lord said to Satan, "Have you [g]considered My servant Job, that there is none like him on the earth, a blameless and upright man, one who fears God and [h]shuns evil?"

9 So Satan answered the Lord and said, "Does Job fear God for nothing? 10 Have You not [i]made a hedge around him, around his household, and around all that he has on every side? You have blessed the work of his hands, and his possessions have increased in the land. 11 But now, stretch out Your hand and touch all that he has, and he will surely curse[j] You to Your face!"

12 And the Lord said to Satan, "Behold, all that he has is in your [k]power; only do not lay a hand on his person."

So Satan went out from the presence of the Lord.

Job Loses His Property and Children

13 Now there was a day when his sons and daughters were eating and drinking wine in their oldest brother's house; 14 and a messenger came to Job and said, "The oxen were plowing and the donkeys feeding beside them, 15 when the [l]Sabeans [m]raided them and took them away—indeed they have killed the servants with the edge of the sword; and I alone have escaped to tell you!"

16 While he was still speaking, another also came and said, "The fire of God fell from heaven and burned up the sheep and the servants, and [n]consumed them; and I alone have escaped to tell you!"

17 While he was still speaking, another also came and said, "The Chaldeans formed three bands, raided the camels and took them away, yes, and killed the servants with the edge of the sword; and I alone have escaped to tell you!"

18 While he was still speaking, another also came and said, "Your sons and daughters were eating and drinking wine in their oldest brother's house, 19 and suddenly a great wind came from [o]across the wilderness and struck the four corners of the house, and it fell on the young people, and they are dead; and I alone have escaped to tell you!"

20 Then Job arose, tore his robe, and shaved his head; and he fell to the ground and worshiped. 21 And he said:

"Naked I came from my mother's womb, And naked shall I return there. The Lord gave, and the Lord has taken away; Blessed be the name of the Lord."

22 In all this Job did not sin nor charge God with wrong.

Footnotes

a. Job 1:1 Lit. *turned away from*
b. Job 1:3 Lit. *sons*
c. Job 1:5 *consecrate*
d. Job 1:5 Lit. *blessed,* but in an evil sense; cf. Job 1:11; 2:5, 9
e. Job 1:6 Lit. *the Adversary*
f. Job 1:7 Lit. *the Adversary*
g. Job 1:8 Lit. *set your heart on*
h. Job 1:8 Lit. *turns away from*
i. Job 1:10 Protected him
j. Job 1:11 Lit. *bless,* but in an evil sense; cf. Job 1:5
k. Job 1:12 Lit. *hand*
l. Job 1:15 Lit. *Sheba;* cf. Job 6:19
m. Job 1:15 Lit. *fell upon*
n. Job 1:16 *destroyed*
o. Job 1:19 LXX omits *across*

New King James Version (NKJV)

Revelation 21

New King James Version

All Things Made New

21 Now I saw a new heaven and a new earth, for the first heaven and the first earth had passed away. Also there was no more sea. **2** Then I, [a]John, saw the holy city, New Jerusalem, coming down out of heaven from God, prepared as a bride adorned for her husband. **3** And I heard a loud voice from heaven saying, "Behold, the tabernacle of God *is* with men, and He will dwell with them, and they shall be His people. God Himself will be with them *and be* their God. **4** And God will wipe away every tear from their eyes; there shall be no more death, nor sorrow, nor crying. There shall be no more pain, for the former things have passed away."

5 Then He who sat on the throne said, "Behold, I make all things new." And He said [b]to me, "Write, for these words are true and faithful."

6 And He said to me, "It[c] is done! I am the Alpha and the Omega, the Beginning and the End. I will give of the fountain of the water of life freely to him who thirsts. **7** He who overcomes [d]shall inherit all things, and I will be his God and he shall be My son. **8 But the cowardly, [e]unbelieving, abominable, murderers, sexually immoral, sorcerers, idolaters, and all liars shall have their part in the lake which burns with fire and brimstone, which is the second death."**

The New Jerusalem

9 Then one of the seven angels who had the seven bowls filled with the seven last plagues came [f]to me and talked with me, saying, "Come, I will show you the [g]bride, the Lamb's wife." **10** And he carried me away in the Spirit to a great and high mountain, and showed me the [h]great city, the [i]holy Jerusalem, descending out of heaven from God, **11** having the glory of God. Her light *was* like a most precious stone, like a jasper stone, clear as crystal. **12** Also she had a great and high wall with twelve gates, and twelve angels at the gates, and names written on them, which are *the names* of the twelve tribes of the children of Israel: **13** three gates on the east, three gates on the north, three gates on the south, and three gates on the west.

14 Now the wall of the city had twelve foundations, and on them were the [j]names of the twelve apostles of the Lamb. **15** And he who talked with me had a gold reed to measure the city, its gates, and its wall. **16** The city is laid out as a square; its length is as great as its breadth. And he measured the city with the reed: twelve thousand [k]furlongs. Its length, breadth, and height are equal. **17** Then he measured its wall: one hundred *and* forty-four cubits, *according* to the measure of a man, that is, of an angel. **18** The construction of its wall was *of* jasper; and the city *was* pure gold, like clear glass. **19** The foundations of the wall of the city *were* adorned with all kinds of precious stones: the first foundation *was* jasper, the second sapphire, the third chalcedony, the fourth emerald, **20** the fifth sardonyx, the sixth sardius, the seventh chrysolite, the eighth beryl, the ninth topaz, the tenth chrysoprase, the eleventh jacinth, and the twelfth amethyst. **21** The twelve gates *were* twelve pearls: each individual gate was of one pearl. And the street of the city *was* pure gold, like transparent glass.

The Glory of the New Jerusalem

22 But I saw no temple in it, for the Lord God Almighty and the Lamb are its temple. **23** The city had no need of the sun or of the moon to shine [l]in it, for the [m]glory of God illuminated it. The Lamb *is* its light. **24** And the nations [n]of those who are saved shall walk in its light, and the kings of the earth bring their glory and honor [o]into it. **25** Its gates shall not be shut at all by day (there shall be no night there). **26** And they shall bring the glory and the honor of the nations into [p]it. **27** But there shall by no means enter it anything

[q]that defiles, or causes an abomination or a lie, but only those who are written in the Lamb's Book of Life.

Footnotes

a. <u>Revelation 21:2</u> NU, M omit *John*
b. <u>Revelation 21:5</u> NU, M omit *to me*
c. <u>Revelation 21:6</u> M omits *It is done*
d. <u>Revelation 21:7</u> M *I shall give him these things*
e. <u>Revelation 21:8</u> M adds *and sinners,*
f. <u>Revelation 21:9</u> NU, M omit *to me*
g. <u>Revelation 21:9</u> M *woman, the Lamb's bride*
h. <u>Revelation 21:10</u> NU, M omit *great*
i. <u>Revelation 21:10</u> NU, M *holy city, Jerusalem*
j. <u>Revelation 21:14</u> NU, M *twelve names*
k. <u>Revelation 21:16</u> Lit. *stadia,* about 1,380 miles in all
l. <u>Revelation 21:23</u> NU, M omit *in it*
m. <u>Revelation 21:23</u> M *very glory*
n. <u>Revelation 21:24</u> NU, M omit *of those who are saved*
o. <u>Revelation 21:24</u> M *of the nations to Him*
p. <u>Revelation 21:26</u> M adds *that they may enter in.*
q. <u>Revelation 21:27</u> NU, M *profane, nor one who causes*

Ephesians 6

New King James Version

Children and Parents

6 Children, obey your parents in the Lord, for this is right. 2 "Honor your father and mother," which is the first commandment with promise: 3 "that it may be well with you and you may live long on the earth."

4 And you, fathers, do not provoke your children to wrath, but bring them up in the training and admonition of the Lord.

Bondservants and Masters

5 Bondservants, be obedient to those who are your masters according to the flesh, with fear and trembling, in sincerity of heart, as to Christ; 6 not with eyeservice, as men-pleasers, but as bondservants of Christ, doing the will of God from the heart, 7 with goodwill doing service, as to the Lord, and not to men, 8 knowing that whatever good anyone does, he will receive the same from the Lord, whether *he is* a slave or free.

9 And you, masters, do the same things to them, giving up threatening, knowing that [a]your own Master also is in heaven, and there is no partiality with Him.

The Whole Armor of God

10 Finally, my brethren, be strong in the Lord and in the power of His might. 11 Put on the whole armor of God, that you may be able to stand against the [b]wiles of the devil. 12 For we do not wrestle against flesh and blood, but against principalities, against powers,

against the rulers of [c]the darkness of this age, against spiritual *hosts* of wickedness in the heavenly *places.* **13 Therefore take up the whole armor of God, that you may be able to withstand in the evil day, and having done all, to stand.**

14 Stand therefore, having girded your waist with truth, having put on the breastplate of righteousness, **15** and having shod your feet with the preparation of the gospel of peace; **16** above all, taking the shield of faith with which you will be able to quench all the fiery darts of the wicked one. **17** And take the helmet of salvation, and the sword of the Spirit, which is the word of God; **18** praying always with all prayer and supplication in the Spirit, being watchful to this end with all perseverance and supplication for all the saints— **19** and for me, that utterance may be given to me, that I may open my mouth boldly to make known the mystery of the gospel, **20** for which I am an ambassador in chains; that in it I may speak boldly, as I ought to speak.

A Gracious Greeting

21 But that you also may know my affairs *and* how I am doing, Tychicus, a beloved brother and faithful minister in the Lord, will make all things known to you; **22** whom I have sent to you for this very purpose, that you may know our affairs, and *that* he may comfort your hearts.

23 Peace to the brethren, and love with faith, from God the Father and the Lord Jesus Christ. **24** Grace *be* with all those who love our Lord Jesus Christ in sincerity. Amen.

Footnotes

a. Ephesians 6:9 NU *He who is both their Master and yours is*
b. Ephesians 6:11 *schemings*
c. Ephesians 6:12 NU *this darkness,*

Critical Background Information

Around the year 1972, I was in our living room at **"184"** *Kent Drive, Pittsburgh, Pennsylvania.* One of my closest high school friends had been visiting and was mostly speaking with my mother about political topics which I don't specifically remember. It was around eleven o'clock at night and we were all sitting in the living room. My friend went home, and my mother retired for the night. Although she went upstairs to bed, she had left the radio on. I remember hearing on the radio the late-night talk show that my mother had listened to for many years. I do remember the guest on the show and his conversation with the radio show host. His topic was the Bible, and more specifically The Book of Revelation. I believe the television was off, so I was focused on the things that the guest was saying regarding the prophecy of The Book of Revelation. The guest seemed to be giving a pretty detailed description of the prophecy. I was able to find our Bible. I opened it up and found The Book of Revelation. At that time, I was not very familiar with the Bible. At some point I was in Chapter 22, (not sure why), and read about the warnings that are in Chapter 22. In that chapter, there are warnings about "adding to" or "subtracting from" the words of the prophecy. I remember the guest giving what seemed like detailed descriptions that I thought might be his own personal interpretations of the Book of Revelation prophecy. I decided to call the guest and see if he was aware of the warnings of "adding to", or "subtracting from", the prophecy. The call screener took my call and put me thru to ask my question. I asked my question to the guest. Basically, I was just interested in seeing if he was aware of the warnings. If he was aware, then I would assume that he knew the parts he was describing were more common knowledge and less interpretation. Interesting how I ended up in **Chapter 22 (verses 18 and 19) of the Book of Revelation, where these warnings are given.** The only reason I mention this time in my life, is that years later, after my mother's funeral, my concern for the accuracy of this prophecy dramatically affected me.

The following is Chapter 22 of The Book of Revelation:

Revelation 22 (NKJV)
The River of Life

22 And he showed me a pure[a] river of water of life, clear as crystal, proceeding from the throne of God and of the Lamb. ²In the middle of its street, and on either side of the river, *was* the tree of life, which bore twelve fruits, each *tree* yielding its fruit every month. The leaves of the tree *were* for the healing of the nations. ³And there shall be no more curse, but the throne of God and of the Lamb shall be in it, and His servants shall serve Him. ⁴They shall see His face, and His name *shall be* on their foreheads. ⁵There shall be no night there: They need no lamp nor light of the sun, for the Lord God gives them light. And they shall reign forever and ever.

The Time Is Near

⁶Then he said to me, "These words *are* faithful and true." And the Lord God of the holy[b] prophets sent His angel to show His servants the things which must shortly take place.

⁷"Behold, I am coming quickly! Blessed *is* he who keeps the words of the prophecy of this book."

⁸Now I, John, saw and heard[c] these things. And when I heard and saw, I fell down to worship before the feet of the angel who showed me these things.

⁹Then he said to me, "See *that you do* not *do that.* For[d] I am your fellow servant, and of your brethren the prophets, and of those who keep the words of this book. Worship God." ¹⁰And he said to me, "Do not seal the words of the prophecy of this book, for the time is at hand. ¹¹He who is unjust, let him be unjust still; he who is filthy, let him be filthy still; he who is righteous, let him be righteous[e] still; he who is holy, let him be holy still."

Jesus Testifies to the Churches

[12] "And behold, I am coming quickly, and My reward *is* with Me, to give to every one according to his work. [13] I am the Alpha and the Omega, *the* Beginning and *the* End, the First and the Last."[f]

[14] Blessed *are* those who do His commandments,[g] that they may have the right to the tree of life, and may enter through the gates into the city. [15] But[h] outside *are* dogs and sorcerers and sexually immoral and murderers and idolaters, and whoever loves and practices a lie.

[16] "I, Jesus, have sent My angel to testify to you these things in the churches. I am the Root and the Offspring of David, the Bright and Morning Star."

[17] And the Spirit and the bride say, "Come!" And let him who hears say, "Come!" And let him who thirsts come. Whoever desires, let him take the water of life freely.

A Warning

[18] For[i] I testify to everyone who hears the words of the prophecy of this book: If anyone adds to these things, God will add[j] to him the plagues that are written in this book; [19] and if anyone takes away from the words of the book of this prophecy, God shall take away[k] his part from the Book[l] of Life, from the holy city, and *from* the things which are written in this book.

I Am Coming Quickly

[20] He who testifies to these things says, "Surely I am coming quickly."

Amen. Even so, come, Lord Jesus!

[21] The grace of our Lord Jesus Christ *be* with you all.[m] Amen.

Footnotes:

1. Revelation 22:1 NU-Text and M-Text omit *pure*.
2. Revelation 22:6 NU-Text and M-Text read *spirits of the prophets*.
3. Revelation 22:8 NU-Text and M-Text read *am the one who heard and saw*.
4. Revelation 22:9 NU-Text and M-Text omit *For*.
5. Revelation 22:11 NU-Text and M-Text read *do right*.
6. Revelation 22:13 NU-Text and M-Text read *the First and the Last, the Beginning and the End*.
7. Revelation 22:14 NU-Text reads *wash their robes*.
8. Revelation 22:15 NU-Text and M-Text omit *But*.
9. Revelation 22:18 NU-Text and M-Text omit *For*.
10. Revelation 22:18 M-Text reads *may God add*.
11. Revelation 22:19 M-Text reads *may God take away*.
12. Revelation 22:19 NU-Text and M-Text read *tree of life*.
13. Revelation 22:21 NU-Text reads *with all*; M-Text reads *with all the saints*.

(NKJV)

CHAPTER – 1

CHILDHOOD ALLERGIES:

ALLERGIC TO MANY MEDICATIONS

I vividly remember, when I was about twelve years old, my mother taking me to our doctor. I think I had gotten a puncture wound. My mother was explaining to the doctor how allergic I was to penicillin. I had a very bad reaction to that drug in the past. The doctor said he understood our concern for my allergies and informed my mother that we are only going to give your son a third of a tenth of a "cc" of a different drug. I don't recall what the drug was that he gave me. The doctor assured us that nobody could ever be allergic to that small a dosage of the drug. We left the doctor's office sometime in the early afternoon and were back getting an antidote for the drug that very night around midnight. The doctor had to leave home and open his office just because of me. I had developed hives in my throat. When we were leaving, I recall hearing the doctor saying inquisitively, **"This would have to be considered one for the medical books."**

BAD ASTHMA FROM BIRTH UNTIL 47 YEARS OLD: I was always catching bronchitis as a kid. My mother would inform me that when I was a baby, she would have to stay in my bedroom and run a humidifier at night. She would do this, so my asthma would be controlled. As I got a little older, I realized that I was allergic to almost every smell on the planet. Flowers, trees, dust, molds, spores, pollens, smoke, freshly cut grass, animal fur, etc. etc., were all allergens that threatened my breathing. If it wasn't pure air, then it was a potential asthma problem for me. I often joked that I was not meant to live on this planet, but on some other planet. Living in Pittsburgh, we had many cold, snowy winters. The house would be closed and the heating system (furnace) would carry the heat through the ducts to each room of the house. With the heat, it also carried allergens from room to room as well. If it was a very cold day, my dad would try to smoke in the garage while working on one of our cars. The smoke would be drawn into the heating ducts and carry up into all the other rooms of the house, including my bedroom. I would have to close off my air vent and then freeze in my room, or else leave the vent open and smell some of the second-hand cigarette smoke. It was a diluted smoke, but nevertheless my bronchial tubes would tighten up because they somehow knew that this **was not pure fresh air**. After they would tighten-up, there was always the chance of me getting a bad case of bronchitis. Actually, there was no such thing as getting a good case of bronchitis. In all my years having bronchitis, there was never one that was easy to get rid of quickly. Bronchitis almost always took ten days to two weeks to get over. My mother would always try to protect me and my breathing. She would tell my dad to either put out the cigarette, or take the car outdoors and work on it there. I had a hard time telling my dad that his cigarette smoke was giving me asthma, as I didn't think he could relate to my condition. If I told him directly, I felt he would think of me as either imagining my asthma (psychosomatic), or just being a strange kid and not normal. If that happened, I would probably end up feeling weird about myself. I didn't think I was weird, just incredibly allergic to things. I would hear my dad yell back up from the garage defiantly shouting, "It's impossible for my smoking to be bothering Jay (what my family called me instead of James), two stories up in his bedroom!" I might hear the word "crazy" mentioned too, as far as his thoughts concerning the situation. Most people would probably have reacted the same way my dad did. After-all, he was on the basement level working in a garage with the garage doors open, and I was still getting enough smoke from the furnace two stories up to come down with an asthma attack. It almost sounds comical now, but at the time these types of situations were extremely serious to me. That little amount of smoke was a very critical thing that I had to avoid. Thanks again to my mother,

I was able to avoid the smoke and a lot of other allergens that the family would on occasion bring into our home.

MY KNIGHT IN SHINING ARMOR:

My mother was **my Knight in Shining Armor, as far as protecting me from allergens brought into the house by other family members.** She just understood that from a baby, I had breathing problems due to allergies. When one of my brothers would try to use cologne or have some other smell in the house, she would take charge and have them get rid of the substance. She would ask them to wash it off immediately. I remember my grandmother staying with us and she was wearing baby powder (a powder product), which really set my mother off. She told her she could not wear the powder and would have to wash it off. My grandmother objected some by stating that, "In my day, there was no such thing as allergies." She still had to wash off the powder. Coincidently, my grandmother was complaining of having problems with migraine headaches. We both said that the powder may be the thing that is causing those migraines. After all, she was inhaling the baby powder into her sinuses and her lungs. My grandmother's generation did not believe in allergies, but one might think that breathing a powder into their sinuses might have a negative reaction to the person's general health. My grandmother was about 75 years old and wearing baby powder. (Maybe it made her feel young again.) I could not be objective when it came to an allergen that might affect my breathing. To most people, the powder may have smelled good. To someone that is allergic to it, however, the powder is a smell, (an enemy to be avoided), definitely not a fragrance. I could never consider putting a powder, cologne, or any other smell on my body. I had a specific soap to bathe with and a specific brand of detergent that I used to wash my clothing. Any other brand would usually cause a type of allergic reaction with my asthma, or even an allergic reaction on my skin. I remember playing touch football and suddenly having my back start to itch uncontrollably. The combination of me sweating and something about the shirt I was wearing, were causing me real discomfort. It turned out the detergent that my shirt was washed in, was the culprit. I had my mother go back to using the one detergent that best worked for my allergies. My dad would do most of the chores that I could not do, because of the smells of certain chemicals, etc. I did do a lot of the cooking for my mother, and on occasion, I would cut the grass. The smell of freshly cut grass would make me sneeze (affected my sinuses), usually three times in a row, then I would continue cutting the grass, hoping that the spores I inhaled would not give me breathing problems. For the most part, I tried not to deep breathe anything but clean fresh air, which was an impossible goal to obtain. When my brothers would have to do work in or outside of the house, they would ask my mother why I wasn't helping. On occasion, I would get criticized by one of my brothers. One brother would sometimes say, "Maybe he should be living in a bubble." I thought that would be something that might help my asthma, but I would not want to be confined to that level. Besides, I am also claustrophobic. I could not stay in the bubble if I had one. It would have to be a giant bubble for me not to feel claustrophobic. I never took the bubble comment seriously as I was able to live a pretty healthy life by avoiding allergens. I had a real legitimate excuse why I could not help in certain chores, but they did not always see it that way.

EXERCISING WITH ASTHMA:

Sometimes I would get on a healthy exercise program and jog around the streets in our neighborhood. If I ran in the summertime, I would deep breathe the fresh airborne pollen spores into my lungs, which would then trigger my asthma. Once the asthma was triggered (tight breathing with swollen bronchial tubes that reduced the amount of oxygen flow into my lungs), I was then very likely to get a case of bronchitis. If I jogged in the colder months, the chimney smoke of the neighbor's homes would trigger me to have the same asthma (tight breathing), and by the next day, I would have caught bronchitis. As an athletic child, this was very frustrating. I figured if we did not have any animals (allergic to the dander on their fur), then I might be better, if not much better. The trouble with that idea is that I was the one who brought at least one of our cats home with me. If I saw a stray kitten on the way home from school, I would feel sorry for it and bring it home. I was possibly my own worst enemy.

How could I tell my mother we needed to get rid of the cats when I was the one responsible for bringing a stray or two home with me. Not only that, I loved our cats and so did my mother.

USING THE DRUG CALLED TEDRAL SA (PRESCRIPTION DRUG) TO HELP MY BREATHING:

At one point I did get help with the breathing by taking a prescription drug called Tedral SA. The SA meant slow-acting. The medicine was in the form of a pill. It would improve my breathing by giving me more oxygen in my blood (expanding my red blood cells). It really helped me to get through the bouts of bronchitis, often-times keeping me from having to be taken to the hospital. I kept taking the Tedral SA when I had bad breathing. The drug did not do anything to prevent the asthma or bronchitis, but it did make the situations more bearable. I felt better because I had more oxygen in my entire bloodstream.

10 YEARS LATER TRYING ALLERGY SHOTS FOR HELP WITH ASTHMA AND BRONCHITIS:

I did not experience any help in preventing my asthma, as I did not want to take allergy shots. I did not understand how being injected with the same allergens that I was tested allergic to, could go into my blood and somehow make me more tolerant of those allergens.

When I was about twenty-two years old, I did finally go in for allergy shots. I think I was told how they helped a relative of ours. Anyway, the doctor gave me the skin prick allergen test to see which foods, molds, etc. might be causing my asthma and bronchitis. I remember the doctor explaining to me and my mother that if the skin showed a swelling (like a mosquito bite), then that meant that my body was allergic to whatever it was that was in the serum. I also remember the doctor sounding bewildered instructing my mother to come closer and observe. He said to her, "Look at this, even with just the prick of the needle, without any allergen injected under the skin, your son's body has a positive reaction. Look how large the swelling is. It is as if he is allergic to just the needle prick itself." He did seem very confused over my skin reacting to just a needle prick. I received an allergy shot that was made up of some of the allergens I tested allergic to, which would be a shot with almost every allergen I was tested for, not counting the needle that was used to give me the serum. I went home and immediately started playing basketball at the side of the house. I probably should have just stayed calm and rested at home, but that was not my normal behavior. After running around for nearly an hour, my breathing started to tighten-up even more than without the allergy shot. I gave up on the allergy shots immediately. I knew injecting myself with the allergens that I was allergic to would be a bad idea. To be fair to the allergy shot, I probably should not have played basketball after returning home.

GROWING UP WITH ANIMALS, MOSTLY CATS:

On occasion, I would make my mother feel guilty for having the cats that affected my breathing problems. My mother would insist that if we did give the cats up, I would quite possibly still have the same breathing problems from other allergens. Then she would return the guilt to me by asking me if I was willing to give up the cats. Then she would ask me which cat we should give up first. I just couldn't imagine saying yes to giving up one, let alone all of the cats. I loved our cats * and after-all it was my problem, not theirs. (* I think my mother was the one who put that thought in my mind at an earlier time.) It was true however, because I seemed allergic to many things. It was not the cats that were allergic, they were just fine. It was me that had the problem being allergic to the cats. I think if I had said I was willing to, my mother would have gotten rid of all the cats, even if it broke her heart to do so. After-all, she did realize her son was more important to the family than the cats; at least I think she did. It never actually got to that point however, as I could not break her heart, or my heart for that matter, to actually get rid of the cats. I could not even see naming one or two to be the ones that would have to go first. I think by now anyone reading this would realize my asthma was possibly going to be around even without any cats. I would have considered it a disaster if we had given up one or more of the cats because of me, and I was no better. My mother and I loved all animals, especially fur bearing animals. We were not much for spiders or snakes. She believed in not killing small spiders in the house however. We lived in a residential area in Pittsburgh where there were not many snakes. I knew then that my asthma was always going to be a concern.

Eye problem related to rubbing my right eye after petting a friend's cat: When I was about 7 years old, I had pet a friend's orange colored cat and ended up rubbing my right eye. My friend's mother called my mother and had her drive over to take me home. My eye was extremely swollen. Just me rubbing my eye, with the cat dander on my fingers, resulted in me having to be picked up and driven home. When we arrived home, my mother gave me an ice pack to put on my eye. I laid on the living room couch for about an hour till the swelling went down. I felt somewhat embarrassed, wondering what my friend and his mother might have thought about what had occurred.

CHAPTER - 2

LIVING WITH MY PARENTS AND TWO OF MY BROTHERS AT THE "184" KENT DRIVE ADDRESS IN PITTSBURGH, PENSYLVANIA:

I lived with my parents at the **184 Kent Drive** residence until I graduated from college (both undergraduate and graduate school). I participated in high school football but did not play my senior year. I was somehow able to make it through my freshman, sophomore and junior years. Many times, I would have tight breathing, but I just kept pushing myself. I fought through the tight breathing, as- long as it did not turn into bronchitis. The football practice field and game field were not around trees and plants, which greatly helped my breathing. However, I always seemed to catch bronchitis whenever I went out for the tennis team (tennis courts were located next to a very wooded area which gave off pollens from flowers and trees for me to inhale into my lungs). I had gone away to college twice, only to return home each time and end up going to a college in Pittsburgh, for the remainder of my education. By the time I was about thirty-one years old, I had graduated from the master's program in taxation and was still living at home at the 184 Kent Drive address. I was living there with my parents, and approximately five cats. My mother's hope was for her and my dad to move to California, once my dad retired from his job. They already had three sons living in Southern California, and a few years later a fourth son would also move to California. **That fourth son would be me.**

Mother was a very strong influence on my morals:

One example which illustrates the influence that my mother had on my morals was when I had learned from one of my weightlifting friends at college that he had taken a steroid that promoted size and strength. I remember thinking that I could never take steroids as the disappointment I would cause my mother would be just so devastating. It might destroy the trust she always had in me to do the right thing. Steroids to me were plain cheating. I would also be disappointed in myself if I took steroids, as I always considered myself to be a good person who accepted and believed in Jesus Christ as my Lord and Savior.

My dad was also a great role model to me. He was a hard worker and did not force any real expectations on us. He was extremely honest as was my mother. Christmas was wonderful as they kept Santa going far beyond what most parents did. I remember being at the home of one of my neighbor friends, and his mother was confirming with my friend that Santa Claus was not real. I went home and told my mother what his mother had told me. My mother immediately called my friend's mother to correct her. My mother said my neighbor wanted me to come back to their house. When I went back to my friend's house, my friend's mother assured me that there was a Santa Claus. I remember my friend, just sitting there looking so bewildered by what his mother was saying. He did not say anything but looked like his world was really being shaken. His lower jaw just dropped, and he kept staring at his mother like she was betraying her own son. I was sure Santa was real the first time I visited my friend and his mother. I was not swayed by my friend's mother's comments. After-all, she corrected what she had said. That is how much my mother cared about my childhood and preserving the innocence of Christmas and Santa Claus. I usually had a nice relationship with my parents and I enjoyed their company growing up. They usually let us make our own choices but would not allow us to make a bad decision. I really, really wanted a motorcycle my senior year in high school, but neither parent would allow it to happen. Too dangerous was the reason they gave me, and looking back many years later, I certainly appreciate their stopping me from getting one. Even to this day, after maturing many years past the age of eighteen years old, I still have never had one. Why, because I truly believe they are too dangerous. My mother was very supportive and created a moral expectation that I would not want to disappoint. I knew if my grades were bad, it would be disappointing to both of my parents. I also knew that before anything else, I always wanted to be a good son. I believe my parents appreciated that fact, and that I had their respect for not being a trouble maker as a kid. If I did get into trouble, my mother would immediately come to my defense. She would assume that I would not have done anything wrong intentionally. If I was in some-kind-of trouble, she would assume that I had a good reason. My mother was a huge football fan and we enjoyed watching both college and pro football games together. My dad also enjoyed watching and we all were Ohio State fans. My dad and oldest brother had both graduated from Ohio State. If I didn't like a team, then my mother would also root with me for the other team. She was really-fun to watch games with, and I really miss having her watching and routing with me. She really understood football and constantly complained about how small the camera view was of the football field. She must have been right, because years later, the football cameras have greatly expanded the view to even include a sky camera. My father would watch games that involved the family alma mater team (Ohio State), and the Pittsburgh Steelers games, but he was generally too busy working on the cars and other handyman chores that could only be done by him on the weekends.

RELIGIOUS INFLUENCE OF MY MOTHER

My mother greatly influenced me as far as my religious beliefs. She would tell me to call on the power of Jesus Christ if I needed help. I remember her telling me about an experience she had with the laying of hands ceremony. A minister laid hands on her and she experienced a great warmth and love.

We went to a Christian Church, mostly just on holidays, but that did not mean we did not have constant faith and belief in Jesus Christ. I commented when I was about fourteen years old, as we were leaving the church, how quickly people changed once they were out of Church. I remember upon leaving the church, the person in the car behind us who was honking his or her horn at other church goers. They were in an apparent hurry to get out of the church parking lot. I remember this impacting how I felt about attending church. I knew that it seemed like some people go to church, but then change back to their regular ways of behavior once they leave church. This was probably an exaggeration, but it did make me think twice about some of the people who go to church.

THE MOVIE "JESUS OF NAZARETH"

I remember watching the movie *"Jesus of Nazareth"*, when it was shown nationwide on Palm Sunday (Part One), and then Easter (Part Two), in the year 1977. It was such a long movie that it was shown in these two parts. I remember my mother saying to me, "You are really enjoying this movie, aren't you?" I think the reason she made this comment was that she was sitting closer to the television than I was, and she was staring directly at me for a while without me even noticing. I was concentrating totally on the movie. I thought her comment was a little unusual, but I knew she meant it to be a positive observation.

CHAPTER - 3

MY PARENTS RETIRE AND MOVE TO CALIFORNIA:

By the time my parents were ready to retire to Southern California, I had already moved there and been working there for close to five years. I originally lived in the city of Psalms with my next oldest brother. After that I moved to an apartment in the city of Brentwood. After Brentwood, I moved to an apartment in Playa Del Rey. My parents then moved to Simi Valley, California, and they purchased a home there.

I believe it was a few years after my parents came to California that I got my first inhaler for asthma. The drug in the inhaler was called Albuteral, and it worked miracles for my breathing problems. It was not a steroid, as I shunned anything with steroids, because of their potential for long-term harm. Now, if I inhaled an allergen into my lungs and my bronchial tubes started to swell shut, just one puff of the inhaler would relax my bronchial tube muscles, thereby allowing them to expand again restoring the full flow of oxygen to my lungs. The swelling would go away within seconds. I would, almost instantly, have a normal amount of air flow through my bronchial tubes. Also, the mucus that would normally go into my lungs to coat and suffocate the allergens, would no longer drain down the back of my throat into my lungs. The prevention of mucus would keep my lungs dry, and that would prevent me from catching bronchitis. There has never been a better product for my breathing problems (asthma and bronchitis) than albuterol. This drug allowed me to feel like I was like other humans, meant to live on this planet.

I had always been a total prisoner to allergens. Now, I finally had something that allowed me to fight back against the allergens (the foreign particles that my body's defense system considers something like alien pods that want to take over my body). Most people just breathe these same allergen particles into their lungs and their defense systems accept them as harmless. My defense system sounds more exciting, but really made my life difficult. Now with albuterol, I could almost think of myself as normal.

CHAPTER - 4

LIVING WITH MY PARENTS IN SIMI VALLEY AT THE FINCH COURT ADDRESS – ("THE 118" IS KNOWN AS THE *SIMI VALLEY FREEWAY*):

I made the decision to move in with my parents, rather than continuing to live in my apartment in Playa Del Rey. The agreement that I made with them was that the money I would save by living with them, and not having to pay rent for an apartment, would instead go towards the purchase of expensive exercise machines. I would have their garage to put these expensive machines in. I would usually have to go to the gym to use this equipment, but now owned the machines and did not have to leave their home to exercise on them. I allowed my dad to control my money. My dad was always generous to us sons, and I totally trusted him with my money. They had given us so much at their own expense, that I had hoped my dad would use some of my money for themselves. I left it entirely up to him, knowing he was a better money handler and budgeter than myself. I knew he would pay my bills timely, which was something I was not very adept at doing.

I trusted him to the point where I knew he would probably end up giving me money from their savings. He and my mother were better (more generous) to us kids, than they were to themselves.

I bought these expensive machines from a company that was located not more than about 20 miles from their home. My dad and I delivered them into my parent's garage and they let me have full use of the garage for exercising. I had about ten exercise machines and was in heaven owning them and using them. I was still hoping to be a competitive bodybuilder, but always had problems developing my chest and shoulders. They were good size, but not in proportion to my arms. My arms were twenty-two inches around and very impressive. Then I discovered my own secret for the development of my chest and shoulders, which I was very proud of, and it really worked great! I loved exercising in the garage because the indoor air was not as likely to trigger my asthma. This is the reason I gave up active sports years before. I could not stay healthy in a sport where I had to deep breathe the outdoor air. The smells, pollens and spores would be inhaled deeply and would then set off my asthma. If I caught bronchitis, I would then have to either keep practicing and playing with the team, or try to recoup at home, hoping not to get kicked off the team for being out. Anyone reading this by now must realize what a great burden my asthma continued to be in my life. One situation at the Simi Valley residence was that my bedroom had an orange blossom tree about ten yards from my bedroom's window. I was having some breathing problems and had traced it to the orange tree. I had to ask my parents if I could get rid of the tree. They were at first hesitant, but quickly agreed because they knew it was possibly affecting my breathing. They realized that once I had targeted the orange tree as the culprit, I would not stop bringing it up until it was alleviated. The trouble with allergies is sometimes no one else is affected by what you are affected by, which means the non-allergic person has a hard time understanding and relating to your allergy problems. We were well past this issue with me, as they knew I had more allergies than anyone they knew of, or heard of, or read of, or even dreamed that they could imagine anyone having such bad allergies. My mother did have asthma too, but nowhere near to the extent I did. She could relate to my breathing problems more than my father could.

CHAPTER – 5

THE DAY THE THIRD CO-WORKER SHOWED UP WITH THE OTHER MASONRY WORKERS - (THE SIMI VALLEY HOME)

Special day when a "third co-worker" shows up with the other masonry workers:

In the year **1995**, my next oldest brother was the family representative that dealt with the masonry contractor who was doing incredible brick and concrete block improvements to our front yard. Using bricks, he built a castle for our mailbox, an incredible lantern, and a planter with bull-nose brick around the large olive tree. Using blocks, he built a beautiful retaining wall around the front and side yard. One day, my next oldest brother noticed that the masonry worker and his co-worker had brought a third co-worker. The third co-worker was noticeably shorter than the other workers. Size did not make a difference, as this worker had a huge heart and a built-in determination to be a permanent part of a team. This worker had black fur and a little white patch under his neck area. This is how my next oldest brother affectionately described the day the kitten showed up at my mother's home. The team he was meant to join was our family, not the masonry team. This wonderful day was the day when Wheatie showed up and instantly became one of my mother's cats. My mother accepted the kitten as she already had four cats, and she and I were always pushovers for furry animals. When the issue of naming the cat came up, I said to my mother it was hard to come up with a name. I said that we already had so many cats that most names were already taken. This was obviously not true, but during my lifetime we did have nearly thirty cats and dogs. The name that came to me naturally was Sweety, but that was not a macho name for a male cat. I said we could call him "Wheatie". The formal name for him later became "Wheatie-Boy", but he was really named after the word Sweety. I would tell people he was named after a breakfast cereal, but I knew otherwise. I didn't want to make him feel like a sissy by saying he was named after the word Sweety. It was the perfect name for him as he was the sweetest cat I could ever have known. He was my "pal" and my "buddy". When my mother passed, I inherited Wheatie-Boy and her other cats.

THE "118" SIMI VALLEY FREEWAY:

I was about thirty-nine years old when I was living with my parents in Simi Valley. I would drive the Simi Valley freeway every weekday for work and often on weekends for going back and forth to do other personal things. The **"118"** is known as the **"Simi Valley Freeway"**. (Reminder: When my parents retired to California, I had already been living and working in California for about five years. I had lived with them for about 34 years growing up in Pittsburgh.) After my dad passed, my mother sold the home in Simi Valley and she and I moved to Yorba Linda, California.

When my father had died in the Simi Valley Hospital, I remember holding his hand and telling him what a great father he had been to us. He had passed just before I had told him this, but I believe he knew how much we loved and admired him. He had a great calmness about him which kept the family grounded. Our family would go through very emotional times. My father's strong refusal to become emotional, kept logic as our family's foundation for making important decisions.

CHAPTER - 6

A COUPLE MONTHS BEFORE MOVING INTO THE YORBA LINDA HOME:

After my father died, my mother purchased a home in Mission Viejo, California. Upon moving in, we found that both of us had breathing problems (asthma attacks). This was just after the first day of moving in. My mother had to call the realtor and cancel the deal. The reason for our asthma we concluded was due to the lakes that were in the area. The lakes may have had mold growing, due to stagnant water. At least this is the explanation we gave for the possible reason of our breathing difficulties. The home we moved into was on a golf course. The home had a pool table in the living room, which was used by the prior owner. The second thought of an allergen was the chalk used on the pool cues. Could this chalk be on the inside walls of the living room? Most people would think a person could not be affected to this extent by allergens, but that actually was one of my thoughts for a second allergen that could have affected our breathing.

CHAPTER - 7

LIVING WITH MY MOTHER IN YORBA LINDA AFTER MY FATHER HAD PASSED.

My mother and I lived in Yorba Linda and I would try to help take care of her. I would be gone during the day to my professional tax job. My next oldest brother would come over and cook her dinner during the week, so she usually had someone at home to help her. At one point she had a stroke and was not as well as she once had been. It was nice of my next oldest brother to come over and help her while I was at work. He was not employed at the time, so it worked out better for my mother and for me.

As my mother got older, she also developed a more problematic asthma. She also had an inhaler, with albuterol. I took my inhaler about 12 times a day, sometimes more. My lungs were constantly under attack from allergens, but the albuterol would restore my breathing every time. The doctor would recommend me using something stronger, but neither my mother nor myself wanted to start using steroids to treat our asthma.

One night my mother was getting ready to go to bed and was having a problem with her breathing tightening-up. My brother suggested, almost insisted really, that I take her favorite cat ("Baby"), that always slept on her bed, and instead put the cat in the garage for the night. Our intent was to help her breathing by removing the cat. I did what my brother suggested. My brother and I had good intentions, and we hoped that the removal of her favorite cat "Baby" would result in her tight breathing improving. The next day however, I found Baby lying on the garage floor, dead. The cat was very light when I carried him into the garage, but there had not been any signs of sickness that we knew of before he died. Also, the garage did have some smell in it. We could not use a cat pan, so having a cat pan was **not** something we did well. We preferred the cats to do their business outside, rather than inside with a cat pan. Cat pans were never fun things since both my mother and I had breathing problems related to cat pan smells. I could not even breathe the kitty litter substance, let alone the smells of the cat's urine. What a horrible situation with Baby dying. I may have lost some of my mother's respect over the death of her favorite cat, but she did not express it. She did show signs of depression now, because of the closeness of her feelings for her cat. She still had other cats, but Baby was definitely her <u>favorite</u>. She was becoming very lonesome at home, with me at work and the cat not around to comfort her anymore. Baby was her companion. At the time I did not realize the amount of joy and companionship an animal can give to a human. There was some kind of mutual respect and love that was present daily, and she no longer had that companionship anymore. Not every person and animal will have as great a bond, but there are animals and humans that can form this bond of total trust and love for each other. All that was left in her life were two sons that took one action to help her, which resulted in the loss of her closest animal companion. I had to bury Baby. Mother hid most of her emotions of losing her loyal friend. I could tell this truly devastated her. I heard her speaking out loud stating that she is the only one left of all her friends. My dad had passed, and she thought she was outliving the others in her life. After hearing her, I was getting the impression that she was starting to feel as if it was nearing her time to also pass on. I was sure the passing of her favorite cat was having a big impact on her feeling elderly and detached from this world. She stated to me that maybe her being around was keeping me from having my own life. I tried to reassure her that she was not keeping me from having my own life, but I knew she was really getting depressed. My father had died a few years before at age 77, and my mother was now 79 years old.

CHAPTER - 8

MY MOTHERS BREATHING ATTACK:

I don't think it was more than a couple of weeks of hearing my mother state these words, that she had a more serious breathing attack. She was having a shortness of breath, but her albuterol inhaler medicine was not giving her any relief. My mother decided I should call 911 and have them come to the house. The paramedics showed up and ended up putting her into their ambulance. I watched as they put her into the back of the ambulance, but I decided not to go in the ambulance. I stared into the back of the ambulance, and because I have a fear of enclosed places, I decided not to go. I somewhat rationalized to myself that she would be okay. I knew that she had recovered from breathing problems in the past. I received a phone call within a half hour after they had left for the Yorba/Placentia Hospital. The hospital representative stated that my mother was still having breathing problems, and it appeared to be very serious. I said I would leave immediately. I arrived shortly after they had called me. We lived only about 5 minutes from the hospital. Instead of directly seeing my mother however, I had to answer some basic questions for an emergency room employee. I kept looking to my right at one of the hospital beds where my mother was lying. I was hoping the questions could be finished quickly so I could go see how she was doing. After finishing the hospital questions, it took only seconds for me to get to the foot of her bed. There were three medical people (doctors I assume, maybe one nurse), immediately to my right. I was mostly focused on my mother and not as much the doctors or nurse. I started talking to my mother, but I could not see any response. It was only a few seconds from the time I got to be with her, that the monitor showed her heart stopping. The lines on the monitor showed she had just passed. The monitor was just a flat line with no pulse showing. This is where the name **"Miracle of the Hospital"** was coined by the patient administrator, who was responsible for all the patients at the hospital. I wrote a poem several years later describing what followed next at the hospital. The Poem is called *"My Mothers Gift from Jesus for Me."*

James Robert Waugh

My Mother's Gift from Jesus for Me

Mother passed three times that day,
that's what their monitors said;
The first time in the emergency room,
the doctors thought her dead.

I kept looking at my mother's eyes,
this miracle I must share.
I kept repeating the same 5 words,
"Blink if you are there."

I also felt my selfish need,
to keep my mother with me.
She'd lived her life and raised four boys,
some might say to let her be.

But not this selfish, selfish son,
not this son at all.
For my mother and I were quite a team,
from before I learned to crawl.

I stared and stared to catch a blink,
though the doctors had given up.
I asked her to blink, to blink her eyes;
I was hoping she'd look up.

I realized it was not up to me,
not my decision to make.

It was up to someone MUCH greater than I,
Jesus held her fate.

I asked my mother to come back,
I wanted my mother to stay.
I asked my mother to come back,
"if Jesus says it's okay."

I was very aware of the doctors,
probably thinking of something to say.
Thinking of something to assure me,
there was no reason to stay.

My mother was sometimes disappointed,
because we did not always agree.
But when it came to doctors,
she protected us, especially me.

I decided not to leave her,
not until I knew she had passed.
I grew even more determined,
to be loyal to her to the last.

Then I thought that I had seen movement,
her right eye had partially blinked.
I informed the doctors beside me,
they seemed doubtful, in disbelief.

I kept asking my mother to come back,
to blink again I continued to say.

And I continued to ad to my statement,
as-long-as Jesus says it's okay.

She blinked! I proclaimed to the doctors,
this time I said it with zest,
The doctors were still disbelieving,
but one asked another to test.

The test used checked for a heartbeat,
they thought my observance was false.
Then one of the doctors exclaimed,
I THINK I'M GETTING A PULSE!

They confirmed my mother was with us,
and I was relieved to hear the good news.
It could not have been more than a minute,
they had whisked her to ICU.

Then I heard over the speakers,
the words "code blue ICU".
I asked for needed directions,
was buzzed in and went to her room.

They said my mother had passed,
and a nurse said I did not belong.
But one of the others said "No",
he speaks to her, and she seems to respond.

I repeated the words as before,
said the words without any delay.

Come back and blink your eyes mother,
<u>if Jesus says it's okay</u>.

After this she passed one more time,
after this third time was back to stay.
Only for a week in the hospital,
but in that week, we all had our say.

My brothers all got to see her,
she was able to speak and seemed fine.
But after she spoke to my brothers,
she passed for the very last time.

I was home when the hospital called me,
that night of the very same day,
that all of us were able to see her,
to share words we wanted to say.

That night when I touched my mother,
I returned to find her skin tight.
This time I said to my mother,
mother, go to the light!

I will always be thankful to Jesus,
for allowing my mother's return.
Four times she passed from this world,
to another we'll all someday learn.

_____

FLASH FORWARD TO THE YEAR 2017:

I woke up one day questioning whether the last two lines of my poem were good enough for the ending of the poem. I remember writing a poem in my teenage years and it had a great ending. I was thinking most poems had a catchy ending to them. The whole purpose of a poem, it seemed to me, was to build a concluding message that was expressed in the last few lines of the poem. I went outside that day and saw a relative of one of my neighbor's working in my neighbor's front yard. I mentioned to him about my mother's passing three times in the hospital the first day she went in. I said to him that we did not question her to learn what she may have experienced, having passed three times. My neighbor's relative said the following words back to me. "Someday I guess we'll all know." I instantly realized this was a message to me that the words at the end of the poem were acceptable to the Lord. I left the poem alone and never questioned the words again. The poem explains my mother's death from when I stood at her bedside asking her to come back, "If Jesus says it's okay", to the time she died, several days later. Not everything that transpired is in the poem, because a poem only covers so much.

FLASHBACK TO THE TIME MY MOTHER WAS ALIVE IN THE HOSPITAL:

One critical thing that took place while my mother was in the hospital was that I had brought her a stuffed cat that I had purchased from the hospital's gift shop. I then gave it to her to have until she came home to see her real cats. As soon as I showed it to her, the first thing she asked me was, "where are the cats?" I told her Blackie was in the garage. She quickly interrupted me and instructed me by saying, "Make sure that the first thing you do when you get home is let Blackie out of the garage." I said I would. Then she asked me, "Where are the rest of the cats?" I told her that the rest of the cats were in the house. That was fine with her. My mother had a fear of the garage after her cat's death, and I knew immediately that her intension was not to let any of the other cats ever be shut in the garage.

CHAPTER - 9

ANGEL IN THE INTENSIVE CARE UNIT:

After leaving my mother's room, where this time she had passed, I went out into the hallway. I was in such a daze from concentrating on my mother's passing, that I only remember walking out of her room. I don't remember where I went next. I just remember being in the hallway. Then, to my immediate right, I noticed a nurse sitting behind a very beautiful light brown colored wooden desk. There was a matching set of wooden rails around the front and sides of the desk, like a wooden fence. The desk was set back a short distance from the rails. The nurse that was sitting behind the desk informed me that my mother had a question that she wanted to know before she died. I asked what it was. She said that my mother wanted to know if I had let the black cat out of the garage. I don't remember if she specifically said black cat, or just cat. I knew she was talking about "Blackie", our black cat that had white fur in areas that made him look like he was wearing a tuxedo. I said to the nurse that I had let the black cat out of the garage. I noticed that the nurse had large forearms, and I remember thinking to myself that she must be a big boned woman with forearms more like those of a man. I also noticed that her hair color had a shade of brownish orange tint to it, which made me think she was of the Mexican heritage. I think her uniform was blue and white, but I cannot remember anything about her face, other than her hair color. At the time, I really wasn't trying to analyze what she looked like, because I had answered my mother's question that my mother had given to the nurse. After this, I went back to the area where my mother had been in the Intensive Care Unit. When I saw the main nurse in charge of my mother, I thanked her for taking care of my mother. I then told her that I wanted to thank the nurse that had the question from my mother about whether I had let the black cat out of the garage. She then asked me for a description of the nurse. I explained that I believed she was Mexican. She went away and huddled with the other Intensive Care Unit nurses. She came back and said that there is no Mexican person working in the ICU. Then she said, "And besides, I can guarantee you Mr. Waugh, that your mother did not leave any last question with any of the nurses in the I.C.U." To this day, I believe that the nurse was an angel. I believe that my mother, having passed three times the first day in the hospital, and being allowed to return each time, showed that she was not ready to leave this world that day. She had too many things still on her mind, as well as me calling her back if Jesus says it's okay. The fact that she was granted the blessing of returning three times, probably made the fourth time even more important. I imagine the angel, or relative that came for her may have asked something like, "Okay Eleanor, (or Elle as she liked to be called generally), are you ready this time to pass on, or do you have things weighing on your heart or mind that are not yet settled?" I believe she had said all that she needed to her sons that day. That final passing, I think she told the angel, or relative that came for her, that she had one very important question that she needed to know had been taken care of. I think that she had nothing more on her mind but for one critically important concern, and that was whether a black cat that she had not asked me about since the first day I spoke with her in the hospital, was no longer shut in the garage. I believe that the angel got the answer directly from me and was going to relay the answer directly to my mother. Having gotten the answer in person from me, that would have made my mother content. I believe my mother received the news from this angel, and that would have made her relieved and at peace. Especially after the fate of her cat Baby, which I know was on her mind. She knew that she was going to pass that very night. Just as some of her sons, including me, were leaving her that evening, she mentioned a pain she was having in her right side. She insisted she was going to die that night. She was informing us, not in a worry-some fashion, but just stating it as a fact. I told her that it was probably just from leaning on her right side for a while. Her nurse overheard me and said that she agreed with me. As it turned out, my mother was right, as she usually was on critically important things. I start to tear up when I tell people about the angel, because I think of Jesus treating my mother's concern with such great importance, that He would have an angel be sent to get the answer directly from me. All this, so that my mother would be able to pass with comfort, knowing that one of her cats "Blackie", was out of what she felt was possibly a dangerous situation. Most people would probably feel that a person passing, whose only concern is over the welfare of a cat, would not be a very significant issue that needed to be resolved. To Jesus Christ however, it obviously was ***extremely important.*** Worthy enough to send an angel to get the answer, and then to have the angel directly give the answer to the person passing. Most would probably think that an angel had better things to do. Even now, reliving this part of my mother's death is making me tear up again. I tear up when I think of how much Jesus cares about us, and the concern that we have for the welfare of our animals; the pets that we love and were given dominion over.

THANK YOU AND PRAISE YOU LORD JESUS!

CHAPTER - 10

PREPARING FOR MY MOTHER'S FUNERAL:

My oldest brother arranged to have my mother's funeral held at his church with his minister. After my mother had passed three times and returned three times the first day she went into the hospital, she had mentioned something very special to my next oldest brother. I could hear her telling him the very special thing that she saw. The words were, "Once you see the ?, it's always there." When I prepared my mother's eulogy, I took this special message she gave my brother and researched it on the internet. I described what she had witnessed when I gave the eulogy. I quit telling people what it was that she had seen, when my eyes started burning. I had second thoughts now believing that this may have been information between my mother and the spirit world, that was not to be shared with people in this world. She had volunteered this other information to my brother. She could not get the object she saw out of her mind's eye, because she was still only back, as it turned out, for a temporary amount of time. **Living on borrowed time** is an old phrase and one that aptly applied. We were curious of what experiences my mother may have had in passing three times, however, we did not want to ask her, knowing that the realization of passing three times may have sent her into cardiac arrest. Unfortunately, that strategy became irrelevant when we noticed that the hospital's patient administrator was across the room, apparently explaining to my mother the things that had happened to her that initial day in the hospital. I could hear her describing to my mother something about her son, so, she must have been relaying what the doctors had told her about my mother's returning three times. She was talking to her at a distance across the large room, so I don't know exactly what was being said, just what little I heard. I remember the administrator excitingly doing all the talking while my mother just listened. This is the same administrator that was telling us that they were calling my mother **"The Miracle of the Hospital."** I think my mother must have known some of what happened to her. After-all, she did mention something she saw to my next oldest brother. She must have been aware that the object she was saying she could not forget seeing, was not of this world. Regardless of what she knew from the other world, she was back to share her last days with her sons, and to wrap up anything that weighed on her heart or mind.

At mother's funeral I gave my eulogy based on what I believed was a description of current Heaven. I was determined to give the listeners information that described the religious experience my mother had gone through in the hospital. I was going on about what my mother had seen and then started describing how it related to Heaven. As I spoke, I was describing things in Heaven that I had read in the article from the internet. I realized later that I was describing the new Jerusalem that is coming to the earth and not necessarily current heaven. I was very emotional about my mother's death and was almost preaching to our friends and relatives in the church pews. Then, suddenly my left wrist was grabbed sharply and very aggressively by the minister. I did not even realize he was standing beside me. He held my wrist strongly for a couple of seconds and gave me the impression that I had spoken long enough. **He may have thought it an innocent action, but this too would soon be an <u>extremely significant moment in my life</u>.**

CHAPTER - 11

MY EYES START BURNING AND I GET A PINGUECULA ON MY RIGHT EYE:

After my mother was buried, I went back to work. I decided to keep living in the same house and continue to care for my mother's cats. I inherited the cats and accepted them as my responsibility. I knew they would probably miss my mother, but I was not prepared for the degree that the cats would miss her. I could not have conceived of them being so mentally attached to my mother. Within the first couple of months, only one cat had survived my mother's death. Two of the four cats died quickly from cancer. The only survivor was Wheatie-Boy, and his fate was going to be decided soon for another reason. I had developed a pinguecula on my right eye (in the white area) and needed to see an ophthalmologist. My next oldest brother knew of an ophthalmologist who was a close friend of his. I had also met this eye doctor at a couple of Christmas parties in Pasadena. They would invite my brother, our parents and myself to see the New Year's Rose Bowl Parade floats that passed by their home the night before the Rose Bowl Parade. I went to him and he gave me an eye drop prescription drug to take overnight. He set up an appointment for me to return the next day. I took the drops and afterwards felt that I had a headache from taking the drops. I saw on the prescription that one of the side-effects of the drug was a headache. It said only 4% or less of the people that had taken the drug had reported a headache. When I explained to the eye doctor that I had a headache after taking the drops, he looked stunned. He said he thought that the people who reported a headache only reported it as a placebo effect (imagined their headaches). He wanted to have my tear ducts plugged to see if this would help my dry eyes, pinguecula, as well as burning eyes. At that early time of my eye problems, I passed on having my tear ducts plugged. My reasoning was that it seemed extreme and unnatural. The process was to insert a plug into each eye's tear duct (located on the inside of each lower eyelid), thereby preventing the tears in the eyes from leaving the eye. In other words, he wanted to plug up my eyes natural drainage system. I did not at that time feel the need for this, but as my eye problems worsened, I later changed my mind. I was having eye problems that no one in my family had ever experienced. I had a pinguecula on my right eye (what a horrible name for something on the eye. A name that is meant to scare the willies out of someone like myself, who had never heard of the crazy sounding word).

CHAPTER - 12

I LOSE MY JOB OF 5 YEARS:

I was told by the eye doctor that putting "over the counter" drops (liquid tears) in my eyes was the answer to my dry eye problems. I went to work after getting the drops. I worked in a company that developed tax software and had worked with the same group of individuals for almost 10 years (5 years at this company and 5 years with my last company). Now, when using the computer, I was to use the liquid tears as much as necessary. These over-the-counter drops were supposed to have just a mild amount of chemicals. They were purchased without even needing a prescription. I put the drops in my eyes and the cool liquid felt very good in my eyes. I started using the computer and stared at the terminal as everyone does. I found my eyes feeling great for about 10-20 minutes, then they started to burn worse than without using the drops. It was a nightmare. I could not be on the computer long enough to get any work done. The liquid tears would allow me to have some relief for a maximum of 20 or so minutes, then my eyes would start to feel like the liquid tears were turning to glue. I would have to rinse the liquid tears out of my eyes. By now, they had changed into a sticky glue-like substance (because of my body attacking (rejecting) the artificial tears). My eyes were having an allergic reaction, even to these extremely mild chemicals.

My associates that I had been working with over the years did everything they could to help me survive with the company. They accommodated me by allowing me to move my office to the other side of the building. The hope was that maybe the air was cleaner there. The change of environment had no effect on my eyes getting better. I lost my job about a week later and had to be fired. They were really upset to lose me, but what could they do?

CHAPTER - 13

ISOLATING THE ALLERGENS FROM MY ENVIRONMENT:

When my eye problems started, my asthma (lung problems) virtually disappeared. I would go out and run in the neighborhood in the daytime finding that my asthma was almost gone. I tested myself by going to the beach at night. I would drive down to the beach to where they had barrels burning. I think the barrels were burning to keep people on the beach warm at night. I would breathe the smoke from the barrels deeply into my lungs. My asthma did not kick in at all. My bronchial tubes would not react to the smoke at all. They did not tighten up or do anything they had done since I was a baby. In the daytime, I got the lawnmower out of the garage and started cutting a small patch of grass. I was testing my asthma and sinuses by breathing in the freshly cut grass. The smell of fresh cut grass was a certain sneezing attack. I would sneeze at least three times, if not more. Now, nothing was happening! I did not sneeze even once! I put the freshly cut grass right up to my face (which had a very strong smell) and inhaled it as deeply into my lungs as I could, but nothing happened. I was deep breathing something (freshly cut grass) that always triggered my sinuses causing me to sneeze. When my sinuses did not cause me to sneeze even once, I began to be concerned that my saliva glands may have been damaged. I figured maybe damage to the saliva glands was keeping me from sneezing, and maybe causing my eyes to become so dry they were burning. Somehow, as my eye problems got worse, my asthma was virtually gone. I figured maybe damage to my saliva glands was affecting my asthma, but in a good way. As far as my breathing, it was as if I was somehow transported to the planet that I was always meant to live on.

CHAPTER - 14

CONCERN OVER THE BOOK OF REVELATION WARNINGS:

I then stayed at home and tried to figure out what could be affecting my eyes so badly. My eyes were now burning worse, and I figured that, like my lungs growing up, that something in the environment, some allergen must be affecting them. This did not seem like the typical dry eye syndrome described to me by the ophthalmologists. I began to think about my mother's funeral and the eulogy I gave regarding a description of current heaven. I remembered the warnings of Revelation. After-all, I called the late-night radio program years ago and made sure the guest was aware of the warnings. I began to worry that my eye problems may be in some way related to those same warnings. If I accidently "added to" the prophecy, then maybe my right eye having a growing pinguecula, and the fact that both eyes were burning, seemed to be unusual enough to wonder if it was somehow related. I began to think maybe that was the real reason the minister grabbed my wrist so aggressively. Maybe he grabbed my wrist because he knew I was saying something wrong. This started to weigh more heavily on my mind after losing my job. Not being able to work on a computer because of burning eyes seemed strange, even to me, someone with many asthma and bronchitis breathing problems growing up.

CHAPTER - 15

AVOIDING THE CAT TO TEST IF HIS FUR WAS AFFECTING MY EYES:

I would leave the house at night and drive down to a motel where they had an available outdoor pool. I would dunk my head in the chlorinated water with my eyes wide open. Somehow the chlorine would give me relief from the dryness of my eyes and the burning. This would last about 2-4 hours and then slowly the burning feeling would return. What a nightmare.

After losing my job, I needed financial help from my oldest brother. When I became needy, my oldest brother recalled my history of being allergic to cats. Everyone in the family knew of my allergies. We made an agreement that I would have to get rid of the cat "Wheatie-Boy", before he would help me financially. I of course, did not know if the cat was the problem or not. Wheatie was the only reasonable answer, but I did not know for sure.

I could not let the cat go unless I was positive. My brother instructed me to take the cat down to the local pet store and stand on the front steps. I was to hand him off to a stranger. I could not do this unless I was positive my eye problems were related to the cat. I started my own testing to see if the cat was the problem. The testing involved avoiding the cat entirely. I would leave the home during the day and stay at a motel near the beach at night. I would come home during the day just long enough to feed the cat. When I entered the home, I would put on a pair of totally protective eyewear (goggles). The goggles would hopefully keep the cat's fur dander from entering or affecting my eyes. Wheatie would see me setting out food and water. He would come running to meet me, but I would quickly finish and run out without petting him or even speaking to him. I did not speak to him because I was trying to hold my breath, so I did not breathe in any of his dander. I did not stay more than a minute. The cat was certainly lonely and surely realized that I was avoiding him. I was **avoiding him like he had an infectious disease.** It was breaking my heart and probably the cat's too. I felt like a **cruel jerk.** I may have been a cruel jerk, but I was desperately trying to solve my dry and burning eye problems. I could not be around the cat if in fact he was my problem. My oldest brother would call after each weekend to see if I had given the cat away. I would have to lie and explain that I did take him down to the pet store steps, but that no-one wanted him. I began to think that the cat might not be the problem, but I still wasn't sure. I could not see myself giving up the cat unless I was positive. I had been out of the house in the daytime and stayed at a motel at night. This went on for over a week. I was really feeling guilty about the feelings of the poor cat (at this point he was still one of the cats I inherited from my mother). This entire time I did not feel any noticeable improvement. I continued to go to a chlorinated pool and dunk my eyes in the water to get a few hours of relief. It seemed strange that getting my eyes in chlorinated water would help my burning dry eye condition, but it did. I began to turn my allergen suspect from the cat to the Yorba Linda lake.

TURNING MY FOCUS FROM THE CAT TO AIR-BORN LAKE MOLDS:

I started reasoning that maybe the fact that the chlorine was making my eyes feel better was because chlorine kills molds, and maybe I was getting airborne mold spores in my eyes. After-all, that is what we concluded when my mother and I both had breathing problems in the Mission Viejo home. My mother had to back out of buying the Mission Viejo home. This made sense to me, but I thought anyone else would think it almost insane. Then my sanity was validated by the second ophthalmologist I had seen. He came up with his own hypothesis. He said that if it was air-borne mold spores from the lake, then I needed to have a giant net that would filter out the mold before it got to my house and into my eyes. I thought at first that he was putting me on. After a little more discussion, I realized he was extremely serious. I was becoming very impressed with this doctor. This is the kind of eye doctor (ophthalmologist) that really understood the importance of avoiding airborne allergens. He seemed to know that even common allergens can be dangerous to some of us whose immune systems treat these allergens as sinister forces meant to do our bodies irreparable harm. He took the importance of preventing the contact of these mold allergens to a new level, a level not reached by even most allergy doctors that I had seen in the past. Wow, he thought I needed a giant net to filter out the airborne mold spores that were blowing toward my house, where they would eventually end up in my eyes. I did not pursue that idea with him, as I knew that such a net did not exist. I was very impressed with this doctor. A giant net that would filter out allergens was something I thought only I ever imagined. As a kid, I may have mentioned a potential cure for breathing air-born allergens to my mother with a similar solution. I believe this eye doctor really understood my war against allergens. He was taking solutions for allergens, molds in this case, to a prevention level I thought only I could imagine as a possible solution. When a doctor started coming up with ideas that most people would think crazy, or totally ridiculous, but that made perfect sense to me, then this was the doctor I knew I wanted to have help me with my allergies. He apparently knew very well the terrible reactions that some people have towards molds. Even if he could not solve my eye problems, at least he validated my air-born mold concern of the lakes in Mission Viejo and Yorba Linda. In his mind, he probably also was thinking that this person would be better off to volunteer for space travel to another planet, in-order-to escape the allergens that are present on this planet.

UNKNOWN CURE FOR ASTHMA SEEMS TO BE GETTING, BURNING DRY EYES

I explained to every ophthalmologist I had seen that when my eyes got dry, my asthma virtually disappeared. All but one of the twelve or more ophthalmologists I had gone to informed me that getting dry eye syndrome does not cause asthma to just go away. They did agree that my eyes showed a lot of irritation due to allergies in them, but they could not explain why allergies now affecting my eyes would cause my asthma to virtually go away.

The ophthalmologists would all say that getting dry eye syndrome was much preferable to having asthma. This was easy for them to say. I had pretty much learned how to control most allergens by just avoiding them. I had an inhaler which contained albuterol. The inhaler worked miracles controlling my breathing problems. I could now take my inhaler containing albuterol and get almost instant relief. My bronchial tubes would relax allowing me to breathe normally without catching bronchitis. Now, I was facing this new nightmare where my allergies that were present in my lungs had somehow now moved into my eyes. In other words, my overly protective immune system (which in its opinion had been protecting my lungs for over 47 years), had now been neutralized by the formidable ally of the airborne allergens called albuterol. My defense system apparently made a tactical maneuver to surrender the lungs to the albuterol drug and instead go protect my eyes. This must have been an incredible defeat for my defense system. My defense system must have retreated to my eyes and set up a new base there. That way they could overreact to the common allergens that had always been able to invade my eyes without any resistance. Now they could fight against the same allergens without having to face the drug called "albuterol". Now my eyes were to be the new battleground of my defense system. **I had absolutely no idea how to stop this new predicament.** One ophthalmologist informed me that no eye doctor could look into my eyes and tell me how much they were burning me. Maybe that is why they would comment that dry eyes were better than having asthma. My entire life before this, I never had to worry about allergies affecting my eyes. If I pet a cat and then transferred fur dander directly into my eye by rubbing my eye, I could get a very swollen eye; but all the allergens that affected my breathing such as smoke, pollens, molds etc. never affected my eyes. Now, instead of getting tight breathing, I would instead have to experience constantly burning eyes. Only I would know how much they were burning. The cure for asthma, constantly burning eyes, would be even worse than the asthma disease itself.

The only ophthalmologist that had a possible explanation as to why my asthma virtually disappeared, was the second ophthalmologist I had seen. He is the eye doctor that had the giant net idea for catching molds. He hypothesized to me stating, "Maybe the body's immune system protects the eyes at a higher urgency level than the lungs. In other words, my eyes were considered more important to the body than the lungs. Therefore, the body's defense system switches its attention to the eyes instead of the lungs." He may have had a hypothesis that the other ophthalmologists had not come up with, but to me it made me feel more comfortable that at least he had a medical reason for me now having my allergies in my eyes. I don't know why my asthma was better, but the second ophthalmologist seemed at least to have a brilliant hypothesis. It made some sense to me, but I don't know if he was right. People going to doctors want explanations for their health conditions, **not the doctor saying, "Gee that's weird, that really makes no sense medically."**

CHAPTER - 16

OLDEST BROTHER'S "BRILLIANT IDEA" TO SEND WHEATIE-BOY TO MY COUSIN'S HOME IN VIRGINIA:

My eyes did not seem better by staying away from the cat. That actually made me feel better, because I knew then that I was not going to get rid of the cat. Then my oldest brother came up with the **greatest idea imaginable!** He suggested I call my cousin in Virginia and ask him if he would take the cat at his house. I remembered how beautiful my cousin's area was, and how wonderful his backyard was for animals. When my brother suggested my cousin in Virginia, I was elated. I could only hope that the next step would be for me to later join my cat at my cousin's house. I was excited for the cat, knowing that in Virginia, he would be safe from the very dangerous coyotes that roamed much of Yorba Linda and Southern California in general. The coyotes are the reasons many pets end up missing from their yards. I called my cousin and asked him if he would take the cat. He agreed and said that he would be happy to take the cat. Then I asked if it would be okay for me to come out a few weeks later and stay with him too. My cousin's quick response was a very inviting, "Of course!"

I drove Wheatie-Boy to the airport in his large cat carrier. I always buy an oversized carrier in case the animal is claustrophobic like myself. The baggage carrier scooped Wheatie up in his cat carrier and whisked him off before I had a chance to officially say goodbye to the cat. The porter was in a hurry to get Wheatie to the plane, and I certainly did not want him to miss his flight. I figured

49

I was going to re-unite with my cat in a month or so anyways. Wheatie was no longer my mother's inherited cat. I had grown close to Wheatie because I felt so badly having ignored him for so long, while isolating his dander from my eyes. Wheatie had been one of my mother's cats, but since I realized that my eye problems were not related to his fur, he was now **my cat.** He was for the moment going to be my cousin's cat, but hopefully only until I was able to join him at my cousin's house. Going from a dry air state like California, to a humid state like Virginia, gave me some hope that the dry and burning sensations I was experiencing with my eyes would improve. Growing up in Pittsburgh, I was used to the change of seasons, as well as the beautiful trees and grasses that California usually lacked. Now that my asthma was virtually gone and certainly under control, I could only imagine the huge difference in not having to worry about asthma or bronchitis this time. The big question is how my eyes would react to the very hot, really humid, Virginia air. I figured they couldn't get much worse.

AFTER WHEATIE-BOY WAS GONE TO MY COUSIN'S:

After Wheatie-Boy flew to Virginia, I started expanding the other allergen possibilities. I had eliminated the cat from my eye problems and wasn't sure how to test for lake mold. Another consideration was the glue smell used when the house was changed to all wood flooring, instead of carpeting. We put the wood flooring in thinking it would be better for our allergies to have wood. There was an article on the internet stating that some people were allergic to some of the glues used with the hardwood floors. To test, I stayed in the garage all week avoiding going into the main part of the house. If I did go into the main part of the house, I would wear the protective eyewear goggles. I did not wear the goggles in the garage, but I did wear them whenever I went into the main part of the home. I also wore them when I left the house and drove past the lake. Even when I went the opposite direction of the lake I would wear the goggles until I got farther down the road. Can the reader see how nuts this was getting? Worrying about mold from the lakes, while testing the wood glue smells of the six-month old hardwood flooring. I spent the next few weeks staying both day and night in the garage. I slept in my recliner chair. After about two weeks of living mostly in the garage, I was not seeing any improvement. I concluded that the glues used to bond the wood to the concrete were not causing my eye problems. I continued to go to a pool to get relief from my eyes burning. I would go to the nearby hotel and walk in the open pool gated area, then dunk my head in the pool water. I kept my eyes wide open in the pool water, so the water would hit every part of my eyes. Then I would go home to the garage and feel better for about 2 to 4 hours. I started taking pool water home with me in a large drinking cup to use in the garage. Having ruled out the cat and the wood flooring glue, I finally decided to see about selling the house. If my eye problems were from air-borne lake spores, then I could not continue to live there. I did not have a giant net to filter out the mold spores, and besides, if I did have such a net, the Homeowner's Association would certainly have ruled against me being allowed to use it. I planned on going to Virginia to stay with my cousin for a time. I figured I would buy a house there if the very high Virginia humidity helped my eyes.

CHAPTER - 17

DRIVING CROSS COUNTRY TO VIRGINIA:

When I drove to Virginia, I drove across country in my Pontiac Firebird Trans-Am. I enjoyed driving the car and I was praying that this trip would result in my eyes getting better. When I drove across country, I remember being in a higher elevated area in Missouri with lots of trees. I noticed that my eyes were not burning as much. They seemed slightly better in that area of the country. Then I drove across the rest of the country and my eyes went back to burning at the same intensity as when I left California. The most wonderful feeling in the world for me was experienced when I began crossing some bridges in Virginia. I was getting very near the James River Bridge, which was within twenty minutes of my cousin's home. I noticed that my eyes started to "itch", not burn. I remember thinking how much better my itchy eyes felt, as compared to them burning. I knew this was a giant improvement. It was the opposite of what I had been experiencing. Itching, not burning, was a wonderful feeling! I remember saying to myself, "I'll take itching eyes over burning eyes any day." Just another hour to my cousin's home and my new itching eye condition. Itching was pleasant compared to burning. As you can imagine, I was thrilled and somewhat relieved. The itching to me was a wonderful sign that I had hope in the state of Virginia, and the possibility of my eyes not burning anymore.

ARRIVING AT MY COUSINS HOUSE IN VIRGINIA:

After seeing my cousin, I asked him about Wheatie-Boy. My cousin said he was fine and was somewhere around the house. He explained that when he first got the cat home from the airport, he went through some difficult nights. They would lock Wheatie in the back bedroom and he would let out a blood curdling scream that would keep them from sleeping. My cousin said he never heard such a scream from a cat. He said it was like having Big-Foot trapped in the back bedroom. He had to leave the cat there until Wheatie got used to eating and staying at his house. I don't know if Wheatie was calling for me or if he just wanted out of this strange bedroom. (Let's just say it was because he missed me so much!) It makes me feel good to think he was trying to cry out loud enough for me to hear his cry, all the way to California. I don't know if somehow my subconscious mind could hear his cry, but it certainly may have, because I certainly missed him. My cousin really came through for me and Wheatie. When I saw Wheatie, he was hesitant to greet me at first. After-all, the last time he saw me he must have felt I was having him shipped off to get rid of him. Before that, I had been avoiding him, to see if I was allergic to the dander on his fur. Once I began talking to him, I could tell he recognized me. I also noticed that Wheatie did exactly what he did in California. He used to go out to the street curb and put his face into the front grill of the cars that were parked there. This is how he would recognize one car from another. I think this may have also been his way of associating people with their cars. My cousin has a very large front yard. Later that day, I noticed Wheatie was standing in front of my Firebird which was parked in the street. He was looking in the grill of my Pontiac Firebird. Maybe he was checking my car because that was one of his favorites. He must have been checking to see which car I drove to Virginia. I had another red sports car (a red Chevy Camaro SS), and that car was shipped later to Virginia. He definitely recognized my car. He spent about fifteen minutes poking his head into different holes in the grill area of the car. He had a natural interest in car shapes, especially the front grill area. I think if Wheatie-Boy was born a human, he would have been an automobile designer.

CHAPTER - 18

BUYING A HOME NEAR MY COUSIN:

After several months, I bought a home around the block from my cousin's home. I was reunited with my cat at our new home. This time I knew his fur was not bothering my eyes. This time we were united for good, as-long-as God willed it.

When I started working in Virginia, I decided that I should go into some type of sales. I picked sales because sales relied less on the use of a computer, and more on personality. Human interaction and a minimum of computer interaction was my goal. I chose car sales because I knew that I would not have to be staring at a computer screen for very long. At first, the car salespeople did almost nothing on the computer. We did have to document a few things on the computer, but it took only a few minutes. Then they later had us using E-mail, which resulted in more computer time. After a year in car sales, I took a job indoors selling furniture. I figured it might help me to get out of the sun. I found out that the sales in furniture involved more computer time than car sales. I was told that they wanted us to get help for a month or two, by utilizing the more experienced agents when it came to typing-in the sales on the computer. Long after the two months of help I was to ask for, I continued to split my sale with another salesperson. I was more than happy to split my sales. I would let another agent assist me by asking them to write up the sale on the computer. The salesperson could make more money if they did the whole transaction themselves, but I preferred asking for someone else to do the computer part of the sale. I would lose half the commission, but at least I still had a job. In this way, I did not have to be on the computer worrying if my pinguecula was getting any larger; or suffering because my eyes were burning. My eyes seemed to actually be getting stronger, but my pinguecula kept getting irritated (red), and then growing more. I was aware that if the pinguecula gets to the point of growing over the color part of the eye, there would be the need to remove it. It is considered a "callous" on the eye. To remove it they would freeze the callous and then peel it off the eye. Some special drugs would then be used to help heal the eye. I figured I better not get to that point, because I would most assuredly be allergic to the healing medication. This possibility obviously frightened me to the extent that I did everything I could to minimize the growth of the pinguecula. I continued to avoid the computer in my profession. After about three years, I started using a computer at home somewhat sparingly. I began to have more confidence staring at the monitor light. I took a job selling timeshares after my last car sales job. There was no computer work in this job at all. The job required sales training in a classroom atmosphere. Then we would meet potential buyers and sit with them for about an hour asking them to buy a timeshare. This job was the perfect job for me with my eye condition. I did not have to use my eyes staring at the computer at all. After the timeshare job, I began feeling somewhat better about my eyes. I had been using a computer at home and seemed to be doing much better.

WENT TO SEE YET ANOTHER OPTHALMOLOGIST IN NEWPORT NEWS:

I went to another ophthalmologist located in Newport News, that upon pulling down my lower eyelids, said that he was astonished at what he saw. He said I had tremendous allergies in my eyes. He said my lower inner eyelids were bright red, and that he wanted to put extremely strong steroids in my eyes if I would agree to his suggestion. I knew that the insides of my lower eyelids were red. I had seen them in a slightly magnified mirror I purchased for use at home. I also knew that steroids had bad side-effects. I recognized too that the eye doctor was suggesting something none of the other eye doctors had suggested. Yes, the other ophthalmologists seemed to agree that I had many allergies in my eyes, but none suggested the use of extra strong steroids. I did not go back to this eye doctor, and only saw him on this one occasion. If I look at the inside of my lower lids today, they look red and irritated, but do not feel as badly as they look. I think my lower inner eyelids always show redness, even when they feel okay. I'm glad I did not let him experiment on me. I did have a situation later where an ophthalmologist did put what he said was a mild steroid drop in each of my eyes. My eyes reacted by having the white areas turn "beet red." When I looked in the mirror I frightened myself. It was the perfect Halloween face (bright red eyes), but it was not Halloween. I wore sunglasses to work trying to avoid getting much attention. Wearing sunglasses to an indoor meeting did not help to avoid attention. If I had let this other doctor put in the extra strong steroids he wanted me to agree to, I think my eyes would have exploded.

DECIDED TO GET MY TEAR DUCTS PLUGGED:

I finally decided to see if getting my tear ducts plugged would make my eyes feel less dry. I went to a building in Newport News that had a group of ophthalmologists working there. One suggested, like my brother's friend in California, that I have my eyes plugged. He plugged the tear ducts in a simple procedure and I left the building feeling like I had a very unnatural thing done to my eyes. I think my immune system was downloading the negative analysis (thoughts) from my brain. I decided to use my new eyes and go walking to see how they would feel. After walking for over a mile, I noticed them starting to lightly burn. The more I walked the more the burn intensified. I left the trail and went straight back to the doctor's office. I asked to have the plugs removed. The ophthalmologist that did the procedure for me (or to me, if you take my immune system's version of what happened) had gone home. I complained enough about the burning intensifying that they got another doctor to reverse the procedure (remove the plugs from each tear duct). At least I gave the procedure a try. My immune system obviously could not see it as a solution to my dry eyes, but instead thought of it as a frontal attack directly to my eyes. Somehow, it analyzed the procedure as an enemy that somehow snuck into a very vulnerable organ (my eyes), and had entrenched themselves so deep, that they were shutting off my eye's very necessary drainage system. This brought my overactive immune system to full alert, and it targeted these little tiny pieces of plastic that were the cause of the drainage system being jammed up. My overreactive immune system acted in the only way it knows, mass aggression. It sent strong signals to my brain that if these plugs were not taken out, the result would be endless burning. My brain got the message and I had the plugs removed. To an overactive immune system this must certainly have been considered a fantastic victory. A time to celebrate the defeat of the tiny plastic plug invaders. Mission accomplished overreactive immune system. The drainage system has been freed from the foreign invaders!

SUCCESS WORKING IN SALES JOBS THAT DID NOT REQUIRE EXTENSIVE USE OF THE COMPUTER:

I was able to survive about seven years of car sales at dealerships, three years of furniture sales and over one year of timeshare sales. I did my best not to put anything in my eyes, no drops or drugs. I would only put water in them if they became overly irritated. An exception to this strategy came when I went from selling furniture back to selling cars. The next week's weather forecast predicted that the temperature would go over 100 degrees. I felt that I would have to put something in my eyes to help them. I would certainly have to be outdoors in the car lot that next week. I went back to the original ophthalmologist that I had first seen when I came to Virginia. He had an excellent reputation. He gave me some drops that I planned to use if I had to be in the car lot in over 100 degrees of heat. When I went outside that next week, I waited to see how my eyes were doing in the heat. I could tell they needed the drops, as the heat was really making them feel uncomfortable. I put a drop of what the ophthalmologist gave me in each eye. The heat outside had reached, as predicted, over 100 degrees. After putting the drops in my eyes, they felt very cool and moist. In about fifteen minutes that all changed. My eyes suddenly started to burn like they were on fire. The burning was intense. The sun was very bright, and I thought I was going to have a real possibility of suffering permanent eye damage. I needed to go to a water fountain and rinse them immediately. Suddenly, something happened. I felt a large trough of tears start draining down my cheeks. It felt good. It was as if I was crying. My tears seemed to be flushing the chemicals out of my eyes. I was astonished. I quickly realized that this did not make a lot of sense. I questioned myself as to how I could be suffering from Dry Eye Syndrome and have all these tears draining down my cheeks. I called the triage of the ophthalmologist and told her about my experience. I had spoken with her in the past about some bad reactions I had due to medicine or drops that the doctor had given me. She always listened to me. Then she would respond to me by saying "the doctor would not give you anything that would be harmful to your eyes." I guess she never believed my eye reactions that I had described to her on other occasions. I explained what had happened on the car lot with a temperature of over 100 degrees. I asked her if there is a reservoir of tears that the eyes use in an emergency. This time she was speechless for about thirty seconds on the phone. When she finally spoke, I will always remember what she told me. She said **"Mr. Waugh, you have eyes from a different planet."** That was obviously the last time I went to that ophthalmologist. Looking back, maybe she was the real eye expert. She could not explain my eyes reaction but may have been exactly correct with her diagnosis. I decided at that moment not to go to any more ophthalmologists. Obviously, they could not figure out my eye problems. It seemed that the more I went to ophthalmologists, the worse my eyes became. I kept coming back to the Bible "warnings", as the possible explanation for what I had been experiencing since my mother's funeral.

CHAPTER - 19

TRYING TO SHOW GOD THAT IF I HAD SAID SOMETHING WRONG IN MY MOTHER'S EULOGY, IT WAS NOT INTENTIONAL:

I had become so worried about the Bible prophecy that **I decided I would start memorizing "The Book of Revelation". In this way I could** <u>show my loyalty by proving to Him that I did not intentionally "add to" or "subtract from" the Revelation prophecy.</u> I was very emotional over my mother passing three times and with her returning to this world. I decided to memorize as much of the Book of Revelation as I could. I started in Chapter 1 and would try to go farther each time. I would memorize a part and then say the words aloud. I realized that I could not "add to" or "subtract from" the words. I used the New King James version of the Bible. I vividly remember an experience I had when walking the Noland Trail. The Noland Trail is a walking trail that goes around the Mariner's Museum in Newport News, VA. The museum has many small lakes and the trail goes around the lakes and around the museum. My asthma was much better than it had ever been in my life. I was able (for the first time in my life living in the Eastern side of the United States again) to breathe the lake molds, tree and plant pollens and spores, etc., without any allergic reactions in my bronchial tubes and lungs. The trail runs for almost five miles. One day, as I was not yet half way around the trail, I was memorizing and reciting Revelation Chapter 1. As I was walking along the trail, I suddenly noticed a huge, **and I do mean huge,** black snake about ten feet long. I say huge also because of the **size of the snake's enormous head.** It was moving slowly, traveling straight down one of the giant trees, head pointed straight down to the ground and tail pointing straight up to the sky. The tree was one of the trees that lined the trail's pathway. I had not seen a snake with a head that large in the wild. I stopped and observed it. I would not go past the tree with the snake so near. I was a good fifteen yards from the tree and the snake. I was thinking how I had been doing my reciting and that the snake was there, as he was in the Garden of Eden. As I stood and watched the snake, I was not feeling less uncomfortable. I suddenly was passed by an oriental family. They ignored me and walked straight over to the snake. Then, to my surprise and relief, they started taking pictures of the snake. They got within a few yards of the snake and that is when I decided to make my move. I went around the tree and the snake getting off the path and then returning on the other side of the tree. The family continued taking the snake's pictures, as if it was inside a cage, not within easy striking distance. It was as if they knew the snake was not harmful. They were not speaking English to each other and they seemed fascinated by the huge snake. To my knowledge, I was not even sure a snake that big is found too many places in North America. Maybe they were visiting and touring the museum, as it is a very well-known tourist attraction. When I think back now, maybe they were just tourists. Maybe they thought the snake was a normal reptile commonly seen at the trail. I had been around the Noland trail over 100 times and never seen even one snake, except for this monster snake. Possibly the Oriental family and I were witnessing the reason I have never seen any other snakes on the trail, because this one ate all the others. I never saw that huge black snake on the trail again, and come to think of it, I never saw the oriental family again either.

CHAPTER - 20

THE MESSAGE OF THE CLOUD
THAT WENT OVER MY HOUSE:

The concern of mine over my eyes and the Book of Revelation warnings lasted until one divine evening. I received a sign from the Lord in the shape of a cloud that passed directly over my front porch. It crossed over my porch area and went straight down my rather long driveway. I had asked for a sign about current happenings in today's world. I was given a sign, but the sign I was given was personal, and it put my heart and mind at peace over my concerns about the warnings in The Book of Revelation. I wish not to share the cloud's shape and message. I consider it to be personal. For the same reason, I wish not to share the description of the object that my mother volunteered when she commented "Once you see the (?), it's always there." Apparently, after returning to this world, she could not forget seeing the object.

After the cloud passed over my porch and down my driveway, it crossed over the street located in front of my house. Because of this cloud, I believe my porch and driveway are blessed. It then traveled over the elementary school, which is across the street. From there, it would have passed over some extremely tall trees that tower beyond the elementary school. Then, the blessed cloud would have gone towards The Mariners Museum area.

CHAPTER - 21

EYES STRONGER AND WELL ENOUGH TO WORK SOME ON THE COMPUTER:

I was able to get back into my tax profession and work on the computer again. I am currently, as of January 2018, able to work on the computer. The proof is I am typing this book. I am typing and do suffer a little from dry eyes, but I do not have the burning eyes I used to have. I just keep going and do not put anything in my eyes. Occasionally, if they get too dry, I may throw a little water in them.

My right eye with the pinguecula has many more floaters than the left eye. I still carry an inhaler for asthma, however I take it only once every few days. I used to take it more than a dozen times a day. I cannot remember getting a case of bronchitis for many years. It seems that when my eyes became stronger again, that a little bit of my asthma did come back. Maybe the second ophthalmologist was correct in his hypothesis. Now that my body's overreactive immune system was less concerned for the safety of my eyes, the balance of my overreactive immune defense system went partly back to my lungs.

CHAPTER - 22

WHEATIE MAY BE ON HIS LAST CAT LIFE:

I had lived with Wheatie-Boy for over 15 years in our house in Virginia. I say our house because he was instrumental in making me feel at home with his loving presence. I would tell Wheatie that my job was to pay for the house, and his job was to protect the house. No matter how long I was gone during the day or night, I would find him in the driveway loyally waiting for me to return home. After nearly 15 years of sharing our home, I was now facing a difficult situation with Wheatie. He was not eating and was hanging out in a corner of the dining room not acting himself. I knew I needed to get him to the veterinarian.

The veterinarian said he would need to take blood tests to find out more about the cat's condition. I took Wheatie in on a Saturday. The doctor looked at him and stated that Wheatie looked like he should last until Monday, the day the blood tests were due back. When the tests came back it was on Tuesday. A female veterinarian gave me his blood test results. She started out by saying, "Wheatie-Boy has probably seen his better days." He had three major diseases and she thought he should be starting medications right away. Later, after speaking with the doctor, I had been on the computer and somehow ended up in what I believed to be the Bible. I say I thought I was in the Bible. The message I had read said "Compliments are Medicinal". Instead of starting Wheatie on medication, I decided to follow the informative phrase that I believed came from the Bible. I did not know how expensive Wheatie's medications would be. I also had no idea how effective the medications would be. If she had started the blood results by saying that Wheatie is in bad health and needs the medication, which will allow him to live a long time, rather than saying he has seen his better days; then I might have thought more about giving him the medicine she was advocating. I decided to go with what I believed was guidance from the Bible. I started complimenting Wheatie-Boy immediately, telling him how beautiful he was. I told him his fur was beautiful, just gorgeous. Whenever I saw him, I complimented him repeatedly. It was about a week that I noticed him eating more normally. Then his fur started looking less dry. He was getting his natural black fur back again. After a month or so his fur was actually-looking kind of "silky" black.

FLASH FORWARD TO TODAY: I never have been able to find these words in the Bible again. I feel that the Bible is where I found them originally, and for about two more years I continually told Wheatie how beautiful he was, and how gorgeous his fur looked. Imagine if we as humans had someone telling us how wonderful and beautiful we are, endless times a day. Well we do have someone telling us, if we would all just listen to Him. The closest thing to "Compliments are Medicinal" that I could find is Proverbs 17 Verse 22, which follows:

Proverbs 17 - (NKJV)

[22] **A merry heart does good, *like* medicine,[b]
But a broken spirit dries the bones.**

(NKJV) Scripture taken from the New King James Version®. Copyright © 1982 by Thomas Nelson. Used by permission. All rights reserved.

Public Domain

I was told by a Christian neighbor that the Lord can change the wording in the mind of the reader, sometimes to make it more understandable to the person reading the scripture.

This is about as close to **"Compliments are Medicinal"** as one can get. The **compliments** would give Wheatie a **merry heart** and that would act as a **medicine** for his health.

CHAPTER – 23

COMPLIMENTS ARE MEDICINAL SEEMED TO BE WORKING AND HELPING WHEATIE REGAIN MUCH, TO SEEMINGLY ALL-OF HIS HEALTH.

As-a-result of the compliments I gave him, his health had returned; and he was actually-getting a healthier looking coat of fur than he had in many years of his earlier life. He always had problems with fleas, and they had a bad effect on the condition of his fur. He would go nuts sometimes when the fleas were biting him. As he got older, it seemed he would have severe seizure-like attacks, due to flea bites. He had terrible reactions to fleas. When he had a flea attack he would flip himself upside down on his back, scratching and biting uncontrollably. He would go crazy when this happened. If he had a flea attack and he was on something where he was elevated off the ground, he would just forget everything and fall off the table or bed onto his back when he hit the floor. There were times when he would fall onto his back hard enough to possibly break a bone or disc in his back, but somehow, he'd be okay. One time, I was carrying him to the house and he suddenly went berserk, turning himself upside down and biting to the point that I had to drop him onto the driveway. He fell on his back on the driveway and I about went nuts too, thinking he might have a permanent injury to his back from me dropping him on the concrete. I felt just horribly, but he would be just fine. Remember I wrote earlier that I believe my driveway is blessed, because of the special cloud that passed over and down my driveway. I was so relieved. I thanked

God he was not hurt. I began anticipating his seizure type reactions. I started shaving his back for fleas, and he knew that it was helping his flea problems. He would actually-come over to me when I got out the electric clippers. I really didn't have to even call him. He would see the clippers and just come straight over. You could tell he hated having his fur cut off, but you could also see he preferred the haircut to the fleas. The fleas would not hang out on his lower back where he was shaved. They were exposed and left for greener pastures, or at least longer (uncut), black fur. This did not guarantee he would not have more seizure type responses to fleas in other areas of his body, so I undertook other ways to protect him from falling from heights that might get him hurt. I started putting up shelving in the bedroom where I slept. I would put up a ramp where he could climb into metal shelving and sleep in a nicely padded area. I would duct tape window screens to the sides of the shelving, so Wheatie-Boy could see out easily, and I also put duct tape around the shelving so there was no way he could fall out. If he had a flea type seizure, he would uncontrollably flip himself onto his back, trying desperately to bite and scratch the fleas, but he could not fall out of the shelving. I really think he knew what I had done to protect him from falling during his flea seizures. There were times after a flea seizure that he would make eye contact with me, staring as if he was thanking me and acknowledging that he understood what I had built for him. I was so happy with the shelving idea that I did the same for any chair he might lie in. He just seemed so appreciative of what I had done for him. Some may not think cats are smart, but Wheatie knew that I was preventing him from hurting himself. After-all he was over 105 years old in people years, so he had to have a lot of wisdom by that age. He probably was wiser than I was since I was only a little over half his age. I always called him "my pal" or "my buddy". He never wanted to be treated as if he was less than myself (human); but he never wanted to be treated better than me either. Just being treated as an equal was just right for him and for me. I'm crying as I type this because he was so much more to me than just an animal that lived with me. He truly was **my buddy** and **my pal.**

CHAPTER - 24

NOW THINGS GET REALLY INTERESTING:

I woke up on a Sunday and had recently started attending a different Christian Church (Baptist). I had gotten up with the intention to go to the church. I was up and, as always, began getting my keys and inhaler from where I put them on the bed the night before. This time was different, however. I found my car keys, but there was something extremely different about my inhaler. The inside canister was missing from the outside plastic holder. I truly was saying to myself "how in the world could this happen?" In the twenty or more years of having a bronchial inhaler, I could not recall ever having this happen. I was lifting the mattress saying to myself, "This is crazy, it never comes out of the plastic holder. I don't ever remember this happening." I also said to myself, "This makes no sense." I was beside myself. I went to look in the pocket of the pants I wore the night before, but it was not there.

I could not even guess where it was because it just never came out on its own. Even pulling it out on purpose takes a good grip and some force to pull it out.

When I went into the back bedroom, I saw it lying on the floor. I picked it up from the floor and checked the number of inhalations left, to make sure it was the correct inhaler. I checked the number of inhalations left on the meter. The meter starts at a maximum of 204 inhalations. The number on the meter showed I had "**184**" inhalations left, before the canister was considered empty. I was happy to find it and I pressed it back into the plastic holder. I went about 3 steps and suddenly realized something. "**184**" is the address I grew up at in Pittsburgh most of my life, from 6 years old to about

34 years old. I thought strongly that there was a possibility that this was a sign that something bad, or possibly good, was going to happen to one of my two brothers, or to myself since we all grew up in that house. My oldest brother did not grow up at the "184" address, as he was several years older and grew up at our previous residence. I called my oldest brother later in the day and explained the unusual thing that happened to me. I told him that maybe something bad or maybe good was going to happen due to the **184 Kent Drive** number. My parents were both buried in California for over 16 years. My brother had hung up on me, as he must have thought the **"184"** was just a coincidence. He must have been skeptical and thought I was making too much of the situation. I immediately went out front and was going to sit in the car and relax. I started thinking about all the hedge trimmings I had cut, and I was wondering what I was going to do to get rid of these trimmings. That was when it hit me like a giant bombshell, this was **Mother's Day.** This was not a warning, but a message from my mother, my dad, or both, that they were thinking of us, me and my brothers, on Mother's Day. I called my oldest brother back instantly and left him a voice mail. I explained that this is not a sign of anything bad or good that was going to happen to one of our brothers or myself. It was a message from our parents on Mother's Day.

ABOUT FOUR MONTHS AFTER THE "184" WAS FOUND WHEATIE WAS NOW DYING

Wheatie-Boy had lived around two more years in good health having those three diseases that did not get him down. The "compliments are medicinal" seemed to have added nearly two more years of good health to my cat's life. I was asked by the veterinarian if I wanted to keep the cat going. Naturally I said, "Yes, I want to keep him going." After the veterinarian left the room, I was presented with what it would take to keep Wheatie going. The bill was for nearly $600, for the one-time overnight testing. I said I could not afford the bill, and I honestly could not have. The veterinarian never came back in the examining room to see me or my cat. I told the young women that presented me with the invoice, that even if Wheatie had all these tests done, he is still going to show he has the 3 major diseases that we have already known about for almost two years. I felt strangely that day when I was leaving. Outside of the high-priced testing, they did not offer any treatment for my cat. The doctor did not even give Wheatie a hydration (fluid) shot for dehydration.

My next oldest brother called me, and I asked him if he would speak to Wheatie on my cell phone. My brother liked talking to the cat in the past and Wheatie always knew his voice from knowing my brother in California. I went looking for Wheatie around the house as he was looking for some kind of privacy because of his ill-health. I found him in the back bedroom, right at the very same spot where I had found the inhaler canister that had the number "**184**" on it. He was lying in the same exact place. I thought it kind of a coincidence that he would be in that back room at that very spot. I laid the phone down next to Wheatie's ear and he seemed to be listening to my next oldest brother's voice. Wheatie then stood up and seemed to be leaving. Instead, his body just collapsed into a position that had one of his ears even closer to the phone than he was before. It looked like he was really interested in hearing my brother's voice. Suddenly, crash! boom! objects were crashing on my lower back. I was bent forward looking at the cat and the phone. I was really perplexed. I looked to see what had crashed on me and it was a couple of large plastic laundry bins (thankfully empty, but still had some weight to them nonetheless). I had set them up on some shelving about a week earlier. I looked to surmise how they could have fallen so far from the shelving (distance-wise), to be able to land on me. They were actually-several feet to the right of where I was standing, and there was nothing that I could observe that would explain how I could have triggered the bin avalanche. I picked up the phone from the floor and told my brother that maybe we should not be talking to Wheatie. Maybe the bins crashing on me is a sign to leave him alone, and to let him pass on. Maybe what we were doing was keeping him longer in this world. I started thinking that maybe, just maybe, the spot where I found the canister was a blessed spot in the house. Now another thing had happened there, at that same spot on the bedroom floor, the bins crashing on my lower back.

One of the hardest things I have ever done was saying to Wheatie that it was okay for him to go on. I told him he had done everything in this world that he could do for me. All the love and support from Wheatie meant he was going to be a very missed kitty. His death was almost overwhelming to me. I knew that I was going to get past his death because of the signs the Lord had given me up to then. I also knew that the Lord had given me an extra two years or so to be with my cat that we would not have had otherwise (by we, I mean Wheatie and me). I truly believe God gave him this extra time and I really, really, appreciated God's love and help. I later started to associate the blessed spot on the floor with a place where Wheatie was being prepared mentally and physically for passing. Could an angel have knocked off those laundry bins?

CHAPTER - 25

THE DAY WHEATIE PASSED, HE PASSED AT THE SPOT ON THE FLOOR WHERE THE INHALER CANISTER WITH THE "184" ADDRESS WAS FOUND:

There was a lot of action the night before and the morning that Wheatie passed. I purposely laid Wheatie down on the floor where I found the "184" canister. That morning I called to Wheatie to see if he had passed on. I saw him move and realized he was still hanging on for me. This was very tough for me, hoping he would pass, so that he would not be in any pain. I took Wheatie in the carrier to the veterinarian's office that I felt had not been fully helpful to me. On this later visit, I discovered the high- priced testing would not have been worthwhile, as the veterinarian told me that Wheatie's body is old and his kidneys and other organs are just shutting down. It made me wonder what the purpose of the high-priced testing was for, if in truth, his body was shutting down regardless. Maybe the almost $600 bill was to clone Wheatie-Boy, because outside of that, it did not make any sense to me. That is the reason Wheatie and I made a huge scene at the doctor's office the morning Wheatie died. I walked in that Saturday morning with a full waiting room of concerned animal lovers with their pets. I came into the waiting room with Wheatie lying in the lower half of the cat carrier, fully exposed to everyone as he had no energy to move off the carrier. I walked in almost in tears asking, (so that everyone could hear me) "Am I just supposed to sit around my house for days or weeks and watch my 23-year-old cat die of starvation and dehydration? You could tell that the ears of the people in the waiting room really were at attention. They were all tuned in to the frequency channel of the emotional guy and his 23-year-old cat. They knew his age because I stated it to give Wheatie and myself even more sympathy and compassion. The waiting room eyes (animals included) were all on Wheatie-Boy, and myself. The office women quickly reacted and took me into the examining room farthest from the waiting room. The veterinarian came in shortly afterward and said to me, "You need to relax and calm down." This message from a veterinarian who didn't even give my cat a dehydration shot to even temporarily help my cat the first time we came in. I asked him the same question that I asked upon entering the waiting room. That is when Wheatie's true diagnosis was given to me, that his body was just shutting down. I think if he had just told me that during my original visit, I would have understood and not made such a scene (huge stink) that day. I guess most people would have been able to afford the big bill testing, then after being given the real truth, would have realized their animal was beyond help anyways. If Wheatie-Boy had any doubts how much I loved him, I can guarantee you he had none after we left that doctor's office that morning. It would have been nice if our righteous indignation would have added another cat life to Wheatie-Boy, but I was just thankful he was given the extra time with me that we did receive. I even asked the veterinarian for the name of another veterinarian. When I was leaving we went past the waiting room again. I saw a woman nodding to me, giving her approval for me to take Wheatie to another veterinarian. I bet after we left, some of the other pet owners were having second thoughts about letting their beloved pet be seen by this animal doctor. Wheatie and I went to another vet just to get another opinion. I knew by now his full prognosis. I felt good taking him to another vet anyways. I had my hand on him to comfort him as I drove. Maybe in reality, it was his body touching my hand which was giving me comfort. I called my cousin and he told me of a veterinarian not far away. I drove Wheatie to the parking spot nearest the veterinarian's office. I went in without him. After speaking with them, I got the impression they cared more about the money than the ill-health of my cat. The lady vet said she could not see Wheatie until noon. As it turned out, Wheatie had passed that morning before noon. When I went back out to the car to see Wheatie, I noticed horses in an enclosed fence area nearby. I lifted Wheatie off the bottom of the cat carrier and carried him over to see if he could see the horses. The closest horse was about twenty yards away. I sensed that maybe he was not well enough to observe the horse. I pulled Wheatie back to me. I looked into Wheatie's eyes to see if he was able to see the horse. I will never forget the look I saw in his eyes. His eyes looked at me expressing total love and trust. These are the words that came to my thoughts. I could tell from his eyes that all he cared about was that I had him in my arms. He seemed so relaxed and content. I felt I had just been shown a great lesson by the Lord. The lesson to me was that we should all have these same feelings, thoughts and emotions for the Lord. We should have total love and trust in our Lord and Savior Jesus Christ, as He holds us in His loving arms. I took Wheatie home as he was still holding on to this world to be with me. I went into the back bedroom carrying him in the bottom half of the carrier. I laid the carrier as close to where I found the inhaler canister as I remembered finding it. I had to go to the pawn shop to get money, and by the time I returned, Wheatie-Boy had passed. I was so thankful that he had passed. I could hardly watch him and think of him not eating or drinking and suffering in pain. The main thing that helped me cope with the severity of my cat's suffering, was that in actuality, he never really seemed to be in any pain. That seemed remarkable to me. Even when I lifted him up from the bottom half of the cat carrier, to show him the horse, he did not even make one sound. He was weak certainly, but he did not seem to mind me picking him up or holding him. I wondered if some-how he was getting some help for the pain from an angel at the blessed spot in the bedroom.

CHAPTER – 26

THE DAY WHEATIE-BOY PASSED: *GOLD TREES, LIGHT RAIN AND A RAINBOW*

On the evening of Wheatie-Boy's death, my cousin and I were sitting in folding chairs in the driveway. We both went in the house so that my cousin could see the cat. He stared at Wheatie, who was in the bottom half of the cat carrier which was on the bedroom floor. Wheatie was still in the blessed spot on the bedroom floor where he had passed. My cousin said that he looked like he had passed content and happy. I asked him if he could really tell that he passed happy. My cousin said he could. When I looked at how Wheatie was in the carrier, I noticed how his head and chin were held very high. Wheatie's chest was jutting out in a very proud manner, just like a military person standing at attention, head held high and chest sticking out. When we came out of the house after seeing the cat, we sat in the folding chairs again. I complimented my cousin for accepting Wheatie-Boy at his home and picking him up at the airport. I told my cousin that he had extended Wheatie's life by many years. I told him he was responsible for getting him out of coyote country. As I was thanking my cousin, he interrupted me by exclaiming, "Look at the color of the trees!" The top one-third of the towering trees that are beyond the elementary school **turned from green to gold in color.** Then, within minutes, **a comforting rain fell.** It was a very comforting rain because the humidity was very high. The rain started a couple of minutes after the trees had turned gold. Then within a couple more minutes, my cousin again shouted at me saying, **"Look at the Rainbow!"** A beautiful rainbow started from the ground, just to the right of the trees that turned gold. It arched up over those same trees. **After seeing the rainbow, I immediately informed my cousin that this was a sign that my Wheatie-Boy had a blessed passing.** *This all occurred in the same direction that the blessed cloud had gone the night it flew over my house. (I feel my porch and driveway are blessed.)*

ANOTHER SIGN RELATED TO WHEATIE'S DEATH:

The next few days were consistent with being unusual. I did not bury Wheatie for about 3 days. On the days after Wheatie passed, the front yard motion alarm would go off for absolutely no reason. This alarm was attached to the main tree in the front yard. This alarm had always been as dependable as any I have ever had, and in the past, it would only go off when there really was something that would set it off. It is a motion alarm, and I had it for over two years without false activations. Now, since the day after Wheatie's death, it was going off every 10-15 minutes. It would go off four or five times each day, in the morning or afternoon. Something must have been setting it off that the human eye could not see.

FLASH FORWARD TO TODAY WRITING THIS BOOK: Now eight months have gone by since Wheatie was buried, and not one false alarm has occurred.

THE "TWO DEER" THAT SHOWED UP ON MOTHER'S DAY:

There are deer that sometimes appear in the backyard, but not so often in the front yard. On the day of my "Mother's Day **184**" blessing, the motion alarm attached to the tree went off that evening. When I opened the door, there were **two deer** standing side by side (motionless), staring directly at me. They just stood there staring. I just stared back finally saying, "Whaaaat?" I didn't know what they wanted, but I did throw them some bread.

THE "ONE DEER" THAT SHOWED UP THE DAY
WHEATIE-BOY PASSED

Wheatie had died a few months later, in the same year (2017) as the "184" address found on the inhaler on Mother's Day. I was talking with my cousin and he was going to come over to see Wheatie's body. As the call with my cousin ended, the motion alarm went off that is on my tree out front. The same motion alarm that went off when the two deer were staring at me on Mother's Day. I opened the front door, and there was a single deer standing motionless, just staring at me. I asked it what it wanted (as if it could talk), but it just stood there staring at me like the other two deer had stared at me. I think I threw it some bread like I did the other two deer. It did seem strange that it was in the exact spot as the two deer that stood there looking at me on the evening of Mother's Day.

CHAPTER – 27

THE DAY AFTER WHEATIE'S DEATH

"Wheatie-Boy", had passed on Saturday and I went to church the very next day. After the church service was over, I spoke to the minister and I mentioned that my twenty-three-year old, or possibly twenty-four-year old cat had passed away the day before. When I went out to the lobby of the church, I saw two older women that apparently were friends. I stated that my twenty-three-year old cat had passed away yesterday. One of the ladies that I told it to quickly turned to me making direct eye contact. She said, **"The only good cat is a dead cat."** She said this with a grin as if she was very proud of her statement. I asked her why she thought that way. She said she had allergies to cats. I told her that I could understand, and since she was allergic, she probably would not like cats. I walked out the side door of the church with these two older women and commented about Tim Tebow and the Halo over the football play-off game with the Pittsburgh Steelers. They listened a little, and then I got the impression they might not be wanting to hear more about the game. I asked what would happen to her if she was around a cat. She said her neck would swell up. "Wow" I said, "that would be bad." Then she repeated her mean words, "The only good cat is a dead cat." Maybe she was showing off for her friend. Maybe she was just a woman with an I'm-better-than-you attitude about herself, with a self-centered ego (spoiled little rich girl trapped in a withering body whose insults are no longer considered cute). I thought about her reaction again and realized the insensitivity of the woman. I took her insult more personally this time, inferring to me that if I like cats, then there must be something wrong with me. Just because she was allergic to cats, the whole world was supposed to hate cats. After-all, I had severe allergies my whole life to many things, including cats. I still could not hate an entire animal species just because I was allergic to them. Remembering what my mother had told me as a child, it was not the cats that had the problem, they were just fine. It was me that was allergic to the cats. I was the one with the problem. The woman walked to her car in the opposite direction of her friend. I quickly decided this time that I was not going to let the second insult of my cat pass, especially since Wheatie-Boy gave me twenty-three years of loyalty, love and companionship. My close friend was not going to be disrespected again. I fired back to them by addressing her friend first. I shouted at her stating, "What that lady said was sick!" I continued, "My cat was twenty- three years old and that what she said was sick!" Then I shouted some more, "What an awful thing to say to someone who lost their 23 year-old-cat." Then I kept going with my insults. I called to the lady that hated cats stating, "Just because you dress up and go to church, doesn't mean you are going to heaven." Then I said, "What you said was sick, it was the devil speaking through you." Then I called every phone number (minister included), that was listed on the church flyer. I left messages about what the lady had said to me. It was about two hours later that I saw the same woman at the end of my driveway. I was just pulling out and she yelled to me. She had a card signed asking to be forgiven. I told her that I would forgive her. It made me think again about people who dress up to go to church and really are not what they portray themselves to be in church. The next time I went back to this church the minister said we should go say greetings to each other. The lady did not come to me to say she was happy to see me, or any words at all. I figured she could apologize when no one was around, but when she was in church with her friends, she did not make any gesture to me. I felt good however, that I had caused her embarrassment over the cruel and evil words she had spoken regarding my cat's death. I let it go the first time, but when she said it again in the parking lot, that just didn't seem right at all. A Christian is to have compassion and her comments were just the opposite.

CHAPTER - 28

THE RAINBOW WAS SPECIAL ACCORDING TO OTHERS THAT SAW IT:

I went into a Christian shop to get a little Christian cross to bury with my cat. I explained to the lady behind the desk what I was looking for. She said to browse and see if I could find a cross or something else that might work. I heard the lady conversing with an employee and she wanted to know if he had seen the rainbow on Saturday. At first, I thought that Saturday didn't sound like the day Wheatie had passed. Then I remembered the morning going to the veterinarian's office and that was definitely-Saturday when he passed. When I left the store, I asked the lady if the Rainbow looked like anything unusual. She exclaimed, **"It was Huge!"** A couple of days later, after Wheatie was buried, I went to pay my real estate taxes. I told the lady that took my payment about my cat, the trees turning gold, the light comfortable rain, and the rainbow. She informed me that some people in the office were talking about a rainbow that happened over the weekend. Newport News has plenty of rainbows, so this one had to be very special. I asked the lady if she knew why they were talking about the rainbow. She said, **"because it was so beautiful."** Almost a month had passed when I walked into my grocery store and saw a friend that had a cat that was having health problems. I told him about my cat and the rainbow, hoping to encourage him by letting him know how much Jesus loves us and our animals. The cashier that oversees the self-serve checkout lanes had overheard us talking. He offered that he too had seen a fantastic rainbow. I explained that the rainbow related to my cat happened about a month ago. He said that the rainbow he remembered was nearly a month ago. I told him it was on a Saturday. He thought for a moment and then stated that, "Yes, it was on a Saturday." I was astounded. It was a rainbow that he had seen almost a month ago, and he still remembered it as special. A day or two after Wheatie was buried, I was standing at the end of my driveway. I was nearest the area where my cousin and I had seen the trees turning gold (top 1/3 of the trees) and the rainbow had occurred. I was giving thanks in my mind to Jesus, Yahweh and The Holy Ghost for showing me a blessed sign that my Wheatie-Boy had passed okay. I knew this was a very significant spiritual moment, so I decided to look at my inhaler. In my mind I told myself that there probably wouldn't be any meaningful number, but when I checked it, I saw that the number on the inhaler was "**118**". It took no more than two or three seconds to understand the great significance of the number "**118**". The freeway where my parents and I lived together in Simi Valley California was, and still is, called the "**118 Freeway**". This was the only other house where I lived with my parents since living at the "**184 Kent Drive**" address in Upper St. Clair, Pittsburgh.

Thank you Jesus for the signs You gave to me that turned tragic times to blessed times. I know I'll see my parents someday as they were Christians. I was not sure if animals go to heaven, but now I know that there is a great chance I will see my Wheatie-Boy again as well, now that I know how much You care about people who have a special loving bond with their animals.

PRAISE JESUS, YAHWEH, AND THE HOLY GHOST

CHAPTER - 29

PARENT'S GRAVESTONE MARKER:

My parents are both buried in the same cemetery in California. They are buried next to each other, as my oldest brother and his wife had purchased both burial plots at the time my dad passed away.

I wrote out a poem at home while I was beginning to have eye trouble.

I wrote the following wording for their shared gravestone. My brothers and other relatives did not object to the poem. **The following poem is engraved on their headstone:**

A TRUE STORY OF LOVE AT FIRST SIGHT

TWO CHRISTIANS WHO WERE FULL OF LIFE,
    FULL OF FAITH, AS MAN AND WIFE.
TWO CHRISTIANS WHO WERE FULL OF LOVE,
    WHO LIVE AGAIN, IN HEAVEN ABOVE.

TWO PARENTS KNOWN AS MOM AND DAD,
    WHO GAVE THEIR KIDS ALL THEY HAD.
TWO PARENTS FULL OF LAUGHTER AND FUN,
    WHO RAISED FOUR BOYS, THEIR WORK WAS DONE.

BUT EVEN THOUGH THEIR WORK IS DONE,
    AND THEY'VE GONE TO THEIR REWARD;
IN OUR HEARTS AND MINDS, WE'RE STILL AS ONE,
    UNITED THRU THE LORD.

There is a picture of them (cameo) in the center of the monument.

On my dad's side of the monument it states he was a Civil Engineer, and WW II Veteran, U.S. Army Corps of Engineers, along with Grandfather and Great Grandfather. My mother's side says she was a Homemaker, Lover and Defender of Animals, along with Grandmother and Great Grandmother. Each was born in different cities in Ohio, my dad in Columbus and my mother in Youngstown. Each died in separate cities in California, my dad in Simi Valley and my mother in Yorba Linda.

PRAISE JESUS, YAHWEH, AND THE HOLY GHOST

The following pictures are of:

My parents 50th wedding anniversary

My parents cameo on their grave marker

My Wheatie-Boy (age 23 or 24 years old)

Wheatie-Boy with his back shaven for fleas – (please note that part of his tail was bitten off by a barn owl in California. I always told Wheatie that the barn owl did him a favor, as it gave him an even cuter look, because he had the shape of a small bear.)

A picture of Wheatie-Boy in his youth.

A picture of my cousin's cat "Murphy", who took Wheatie
under his wing to protect him from the Siamese neighbor cat.

A picture of the garage where I stayed and slept in the recliner chair, while testing to see if the wood flooring glues were affecting my eyes.

A picture of the back porch, where I slept at night in the recliner chair while testing for certain indoor allergens, to see if they were affecting my eyes.

Closeup of where one deer was standing on one occasion and where two deer were standing on another occasion. They stood immediately to the right of the tree that lies just behind the white bench. They were facing me while I stood at my front door.

A deer in my backyard with the same kind of stare I was getting from the deer in the front yard on those two occasions described earlier in the book.

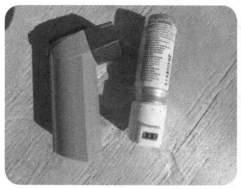

My asthma inhaler with the canister out of the plastic holder

My asthma inhaler with the canister inside the plastic holder

This is my inhaler showing the "184 Kent Drive" home address as it appeared on Mother's Day in the year 2017.

This is my inhaler showing the "118" Simi Valley Freeway number at time I was giving thanks for the gold trees, light rain, and the spectacular rainbow that appeared the evening of Wheatie's death.

A picture of me posing in the Yorba Linda
home showing my 22 inch arms.

A picture of my Pontiac Trans-Am parked in front of my
cousin's home. Wheatie was out looking in the front grill
of the car on the day I arrived at my cousin's house.

VERSES IN THE BIBLE THAT SHOW GOD LOVES US AND OUR ANIMALS:

Genesis 1 (NKJV)

[26] Then God said, "Let Us make man in Our image, according to Our likeness; let them have dominion over the fish of the sea, over the birds of the air, and over the cattle, over all[b] the earth and over every creeping thing that creeps on the earth." [27] So God created man in His *own* image; in the image of God He created him; male and female He created them. [28] Then God blessed them, and God said to them, "Be fruitful and multiply; fill the earth and subdue it; have dominion over the fish of the sea, over the birds of the air, and over every living thing that moves on the earth."

My thoughts:

[The words "dominion over" means ownership. **With ownership comes responsibility.** We own our pets and are expected to treat them well and not abuse them. They were created for us to experience unconditional love. How we treat them back is a reflection of our own soul. How can we be trusted to do good, if we aren't compassionate enough to appreciate one of God's gifts to mankind, pets that are born with one goal, to love us. **This message is expressed in the following Bible passage:**

Proverbs 12 (NKJV)

[10] A righteous *man* regards the life of his animal,
But the tender mercies of the wicked *are* cruel.

Psalm 84 (NKJV)

[3] Even the sparrow has found a home,
And the swallow a nest for herself,
Where she may lay her young—
Even Your altars, O Lᴏʀᴅ of hosts,
My King and my God.

Luke 12 (NKJV)

[6] "Are not five sparrows sold for two copper coins?[a] And not one of them is forgotten before God. [7] But the very hairs of your head are all numbered. Do not fear therefore; you are of more value than many sparrows.

Revelation 4 (NKJV)

The Throne Room of Heaven

4 After these things I looked, and behold, a door *standing* open in heaven. And the first voice which I heard *was* like a trumpet speaking with me, saying, "Come up here, and I will show you things which must take place after this."

[2] Immediately I was in the Spirit; and behold, a throne set in heaven, and *One* sat on the throne. [3] And He who sat there was[a] like a jasper and a sardius stone in appearance; and *there was* a rainbow around the throne, in appearance like an emerald. [4] Around the throne *were* twenty-four thrones, and on the thrones I saw twenty-four elders sitting, clothed in white robes; and they had crowns[b] of gold on their heads. [5] And from the throne proceeded lightnings, thunderings, and voices.[c] Seven lamps of fire *were* burning before the throne, which are the[d] seven Spirits of God.

[6] **Before the throne *there was*[e] a sea of glass, like crystal. And in the midst of the throne, and around the throne, *were* four living creatures full of eyes in front and in back.** [7] **The first living creature *was* like a lion, the second living creature like a calf, the third living creature had a face like a man, and the fourth living creature *was* like a flying eagle.** [8] ***The* four living creatures, each having six wings, were full of eyes around and within. And they do not rest day or night, saying:**

"Holy, holy, holy,[f]
Lord God Almighty,
Who was and is and is to come!"

[9] **Whenever the living creatures give glory and honor and thanks to Him who sits on the throne, who lives forever and ever,** [10] **the twenty-four elders fall down before Him who sits on the throne and worship Him who lives forever and ever, and cast their crowns before the throne, saying:**

[11] "You are worthy, O Lord,[g]
To receive glory and honor and power;
For You created all things,
And by Your will they exist[h] and were created."

Footnotes:

1. Revelation 4:3 M-Text omits *And He who sat there was* (which makes the description in verse 3 modify the throne rather than God).
2. Revelation 4:4 NU-Text and M-Text read *robes, with crowns.*
3. Revelation 4:5 NU-Text and M-Text read *voices, and thunderings.*
4. Revelation 4:5 M-Text omits *the.*
5. Revelation 4:6 NU-Text and M-Text add *something like.*
6. Revelation 4:8 M-Text has *holy* nine times.
7. Revelation 4:11 NU-Text and M-Text read *our Lord and God.*
8. Revelation 4:11 NU-Text and M-Text read *existed.*

New King James Version (NKJV)

James Robert Waugh

A Warning To The People of Earth

People of earth please Awaken,
your souls are under attack.
The devil and all of his angels,
are making certain of that.

People of earth these were angels,
cast down from their heavenly perch.
Now they have only one mission,
to deny to the world Jesus birth.

They'll tell you there isn't a Jesus,
tell you right to your face.
Do all they can to deceive you,
they despise the whole human race.

They say Satan was a great angel,
obsessed with his beauty and pride.
Then when God created two humans,
he sinned and told Eve a "big lie".

People of earth we must focus,
on the things we know true in our heart,
that the devil is here to divide us,
trying to "tear us apart".

So protect your most valuable asset,
the devil's most sought after prize.
Stay strong in the words of Lord Jesus,
your soul will always survive.

Say no to Satan's distractions,
he'll lead you astray every time.
Say yes to the teachings of Jesus,
who took water and turned it to wine.

People of earth we were cursed,
for the actions of Adam and Eve.
From then it became very clear,
the devil will always deceive.

Jesus for-told of His Kingdom,
which soon will be coming to earth.
He described some traits of the bless-ed,
like *those* <u>who are last shall be first</u>.

Remember the love of Lord Jesus,
who died so our souls could be saved.
And just like He promised His brethren,
on the third day He rose from the grave.

Our King has accomplished His mission,
has the keys of both Hades and Death,
Reconciled <u>us all</u> to The Father,
did all to show we are <u>Blessed</u>.

So if you are not a Christian,
or not sure of your own Christian way;
Then the devil is going to get you,
He'll turn you into his slave.

The Books of the Old and New Testaments

Old Testament	New Testament
• Genesis	• Matthew
• Exodus	• Mark
• Leviticus	• Luke
• Numbers	• John
• Deuteronomy	• Acts
• Joshua	• Romans
• Judges	• 1 Corinthians
• Ruth	• 2 Corinthians
• 1 Samuel	• Galatians
• 2 Samuel	• Ephesians
• 1 Kings	• Philippians
• 2 Kings	• Colossians
• 1 Chronicles	• 1 Thessalonians
• 2 Chronicles	• 2 Thessalonians
• Ezra	• 1 Timothy
• Nehemiah	• 2 Timothy
• Esther	• Titus
• Job	• Philemon
• Psalm	• Hebrews
• Proverbs	• James
• Ecclesiastes	• 1 Peter
• Song of Solomon	• 2 Peter
• Isaiah	• 1 John
• Jeremiah	• 2 John
• Lamentations	• 3 John
• Ezekiel	• Jude
• Daniel	• Revelation
• Hosea	
• Joel	

- Amos
- Obadiah
- Jonah
- Micah
- Nahum
- Habakkuk
- Zephaniah
- Haggai
- Zechariah
- Malachi

(1)   The Rapture
(2)   The Invisible World
(3)   Perilous Times in the Last Days
(4)   Satan and his angels are cast down to the Earth
(5)   The Rise of the Anti-Christ
(6)   The Second Beast
(7)   The Destruction of The Holy People
(8)   Six Things the Lord Hates, 7 are an Abomination
(9)   A Country's Borders
(10)   Elevating A Sin
(11)   The Transgressors
(12)   No One Comes to the Father Except thru Jesus
(13)   A House Divided
(14)   The Ten Commandments
(15)   Jesus to be Born and Jesus to return again
(16)   Fear him Who can destroy both Body and Soul
(17)   The Unrighteous who will not inherit the Kingdom of Heaven
(18)   Unlawful sexual relationships; warning that the land will vomit out its inhabitants
(19)   Blood Moons
(20)   Curses for not Behaving God's Laws
(21)   Commandment from God to Israel
(22)   Homosexuality

CURRENT BIBLE TOPICS:

The topics here are intended to strengthen
your "CHRISTIAN ARMOR"
so that you are shielded from Satan's
lies and misinformation.

Get the information <u>directly from the</u>
<u>Bible</u> so others cannot distract you from

"THE TRUTH".

(1) The Rapture

Daniel 12 – Old Testament
1 Thessalonians 4 - New Testament
1 Corinthians 15 – New Testament
John 5 – New Testament
Revelation 18– New Testament
Revelation 19– New Testament
Revelation 7– New Testament

(2) The Invisible World

2 Corinthians 4 – New Testament
Colossians 1 – New Testament
1 John 2 – New Testament

(3) Perilous times in the last days

2 Timothy 3 – New Testament

(4) Satan and his angels cast down and then deceive the nations

Revelation 12 – New Testament
Revelation 20 – New Testament

(5) The Rise of the Anti-Christ

Daniel 8 – Old Testament
Revelation 13 – New Testament

(6) Mark of the Beast

Revelation 13 – New Testament
Revelation 14 – New Testament

(7) Destruction of the Holy people (Saints and Prophets)

Daniel 8 – Old Testament
Daniel 12 – Old Testament
Revelation 17 – New Testament

Revelation 18 – New Testament
Revelation 19 – New Testament

(8) Six things the Lord hates, seven are an abomination to Him

Proverbs 6 – Old Testament

(9) A Country's Borders

Genesis 22:17 – Old Testament
Genesis 24:59 – Old Testament
Deuteronomy 28 – Old Testament

(10) Elevating a Sin

Matthew 5 – New Testament

(11) The Transgressors

Isaiah 1 – Old Testament

Isaiah 46 – Old Testament
Isaiah 48 – Old Testament
Isaiah 53 – Old Testament
Daniel 8 – Old Testament
Psalm 37 – Old Testament

(12) No one comes to the Father except through Jesus.

John 14 – New Testament

(13) A House Divided

Matthew 12 – New Testament
Jude – New Testament

(14) The Ten Commandments

Exodus 20 – Old Testament

(15) Jesus to be born and Jesus to return

Isaiah 52 – Old Testament – Prophecy of a Messiah to be born
Isaiah 53 – Old Testament – Prophecy of a Messiah to be born.
Daniel 7 - Old Testament – Jesus coming with clouds
Revelation 1– New Testament – Jesus coming with clouds

(16) Fear Him who can destroy both body and soul

Matthew 10 – New Testament

(17) The unrighteous who will not inherit the Kingdom of Heaven.

---

1 Corinthians 6 – New Testament
1 Timothy 1 – New Testament
Revelation 21 – New Testament

James Robert Waugh

(18) Unlawful sexual relationships; warning that land will vomit out its inhabitants.

Leviticus 18 – Old Testament

(19) Blood Moons

Joel 2 – Old Testament
Acts 2 – New Testament
Revelation 6 – New Testament

(20) Curses for Not Behaving God's Laws

Deuteronomy 28 – Old Testament

(21) Commandment from God to Israel

Deuteronomy 6 – Old Testament

(22) Homosexuality

Leviticus 18 – Old Testament
Leviticus 20 – Old Testament
Romans 1 – New Testament
Mark 10 - New Testament
1 Corinthians 6 – New Testament
1 Timothy 1 - New Testament
Revelation 21 – New Testament

James Robert Waugh

(1) The Rapture

Daniel 12 – Old Testament
1 Thessalonians 4 - New Testament
1 Corinthians 15 – New Testament
John 5 – New Testament
Revelation 18– New Testament
Revelation 19– New Testament
Revelation 7– New Testament

Daniel 12 (NKJV)

Prophecy of the End Time

12 "At that time Michael shall stand up,
The great prince who stands *watch* over the sons of your people;
And there shall be a time of trouble,
Such as never was since there was a nation,
Even to that time.
And at that time your people shall be delivered,
Every one who is found written in the book.
² And many of those who sleep in the dust of the earth shall
awake,
Some to everlasting life,
Some to shame *and* everlasting contempt.
³ Those who are wise shall shine
Like the brightness of the firmament,
And those who turn many to righteousness
Like the stars forever and ever.

⁴ "But you, Daniel, shut up the words, and seal the book until the
time of the end; many shall run to and fro, and knowledge shall
increase."

⁵ Then I, Daniel, looked; and there stood two others, one on this
riverbank and the other on that riverbank. ⁶ And *one* said to the man
clothed in linen, who *was* above the waters of the river, "How long
shall the fulfillment of these wonders *be?*"

⁷ Then I heard the man clothed in linen, who *was* above the waters of
the river, when he held up his right hand and his left hand to heaven,
and swore by Him who lives forever, that *it shall be* for a time, times,
and half *a time;* and when the power of the holy people has been
completely shattered, all these *things* shall be finished.

⁸ Although I heard, I did not understand. Then I said, "My lord, what
shall be the end of these *things?*"

[9] And he said, "Go *your way*, Daniel, for the words *are* closed up and sealed till the time of the end. [10] Many shall be purified, made white, and refined, but the wicked shall do wickedly; and none of the wicked shall understand, but the wise shall understand.

[11] "And from the time *that* the daily *sacrifice* is taken away, and the abomination of desolation is set up, *there shall be* one thousand two hundred and ninety days. [12] Blessed *is* he who waits, and comes to the one thousand three hundred and thirty-five days.

[13] "But you, go *your way* till the end; for you shall rest, and will arise to your inheritance at the end of the days."

(NKJV)

1 Thessalonians 4 (NKJV)

Plea for Purity

4 Finally then, brethren, we urge and exhort in the Lord Jesus that you should abound more and more, just as you received from us how you ought to walk and to please God; ²for you know what commandments we gave you through the Lord Jesus.

³For this is the will of God, your sanctification: that you should abstain from sexual immorality; ⁴that each of you should know how to possess his own vessel in sanctification and honor, ⁵not in passion of lust, like the Gentiles who do not know God; ⁶that no one should take advantage of and defraud his brother in this matter, because the Lord *is* the avenger of all such, as we also forewarned you and testified. ⁷For God did not call us to uncleanness, but in holiness. ⁸Therefore he who rejects *this* does not reject man, but God, who has also given[a] us His Holy Spirit.

A Brotherly and Orderly Life

⁹But concerning brotherly love you have no need that I should write to you, for you yourselves are taught by God to love one another; ¹⁰and indeed you do so toward all the brethren who are in all Macedonia. But we urge you, brethren, that you increase more and more; ¹¹that you also aspire to lead a quiet life, to mind your own business, and to work with your own hands, as we commanded you, ¹²that you may walk properly toward those who are outside, and *that* you may lack nothing.

The Comfort of Christ's Coming

¹³But I do not want you to be ignorant, brethren, concerning those who have fallen asleep, lest you sorrow as others who have no hope. ¹⁴For if we believe that Jesus died and rose again, even so God will bring with Him those who sleep in Jesus.[b]

¹⁵ For this we say to you by the word of the Lord, that we who are alive *and* remain until the coming of the Lord will by no means precede those who are asleep. ¹⁶ For the Lord Himself will descend from heaven with a shout, with the voice of an archangel, and with the trumpet of God. And the dead in Christ will rise first. ¹⁷ Then we who are alive *and* remain shall be caught up together with them in the clouds to meet the Lord in the air. And thus we shall always be with the Lord. ¹⁸ Therefore comfort one another with these words.

Footnotes:

   a. 1 Thessalonians 4:8 NU-Text reads *who also gives.*
   b. 1 Thessalonians 4:14 Or *those who through Jesus sleep*

(NKJV)

1 Corinthians 15 (NKJV)

The Risen Christ, Faith's Reality

15 Moreover, brethren, I declare to you the gospel which I preached to you, which also you received and in which you stand, ² by which also you are saved, if you hold fast that word which I preached to you—unless you believed in vain.

³ For I delivered to you first of all that which I also received: that Christ died for our sins according to the Scriptures, ⁴ and that He was buried, and that He rose again the third day according to the Scriptures, ⁵ and that He was seen by Cephas, then by the twelve. ⁶ After that He was seen by over five hundred brethren at once, of whom the greater part remain to the present, but some have fallen asleep. ⁷ After that He was seen by James, then by all the apostles. ⁸ Then last of all He was seen by me also, as by one born out of due time.

⁹ For I am the least of the apostles, who am not worthy to be called an apostle, because I persecuted the church of God. ¹⁰ But by the grace of God I am what I am, and His grace toward me was not in vain; but I labored more abundantly than they all, yet not I, but the grace of God *which was* with me. ¹¹ Therefore, whether *it was* I or they, so we preach and so you believed.

The Risen Christ, Our Hope

¹² Now if Christ is preached that He has been raised from the dead, how do some among you say that there is no resurrection of the dead? ¹³ But if there is no resurrection of the dead, then Christ is not risen. ¹⁴ And if Christ is not risen, then our preaching *is* empty and your faith *is* also empty. ¹⁵ Yes, and we are found false witnesses of God, because we have testified of God that He raised up Christ, whom He did not raise up—if in fact the dead do not rise. ¹⁶ For if *the* dead do not rise, then Christ is not risen. ¹⁷ And if Christ is not

risen, your faith *is* futile; you are still in your sins! [18] Then also those who have fallen asleep in Christ have perished. [19] If in this life only we have hope in Christ, we are of all men the most pitiable.

The Last Enemy Destroyed

[20] But now Christ is risen from the dead, *and* has become the firstfruits of those who have fallen asleep. [21] For since by man *came* death, by Man also *came* the resurrection of the dead. [22] For as in Adam all die, even so in Christ all shall be made alive. [23] But each one in his own order: Christ the firstfruits, afterward those *who are* Christ's at His coming. [24] Then *comes* the end, when He delivers the kingdom to God the Father, when He puts an end to all rule and all authority and power. [25] For He must reign till He has put all enemies under His feet. [26] The last enemy *that* will be destroyed *is* death. [27] For "He has put all things under His feet."[a] But when He says "all things are put under *Him*," *it is* evident that He who put all things under Him is excepted. [28] Now when all things are made subject to Him, then the Son Himself will also be subject to Him who put all things under Him, that God may be all in all.

Effects of Denying the Resurrection

[29] Otherwise, what will they do who are baptized for the dead, if the dead do not rise at all? Why then are they baptized for the dead? [30] And why do we stand in jeopardy every hour? [31] I affirm, by the boasting in you which I have in Christ Jesus our Lord, I die daily. [32] If, in the manner of men, I have fought with beasts at Ephesus, what advantage *is it* to me? If *the* dead do not rise, "Let us eat and drink, for tomorrow we die!"[b]

[33] Do not be deceived: "Evil company corrupts good habits." [34] Awake to righteousness, and do not sin; for some do not have the knowledge of God. I speak *this* to your shame.

A Glorious Body

³⁵ But someone will say, "How are the dead raised up? And with what body do they come?" ³⁶ Foolish one, what you sow is not made alive unless it dies. ³⁷ And what you sow, you do not sow that body that shall be, but mere grain—perhaps wheat or some other *grain.* ³⁸ But God gives it a body as He pleases, and to each seed its own body.

³⁹ All flesh *is* not the same flesh, but *there is* one *kind of* flesh[c] of men, another flesh of animals, another of fish, *and* another of birds.

⁴⁰ *There are* also celestial bodies and terrestrial bodies; but the glory of the celestial *is* one, and the *glory* of the terrestrial *is* another. ⁴¹ *There is* one glory of the sun, another glory of the moon, and another glory of the stars; for *one* star differs from *another* star in glory.

⁴² So also *is* the resurrection of the dead. *The body* is sown in corruption, it is raised in incorruption. ⁴³ It is sown in dishonor, it is raised in glory. It is sown in weakness, it is raised in power. ⁴⁴ **It is sown a natural body, it is raised a spiritual body. There is a natural body, and there is a spiritual body. ⁴⁵ And so it is written, "The first man Adam became a living being."[d] The last Adam *became* a life-giving spirit.**

⁴⁶ However, the spiritual is not first, but the natural, and afterward the spiritual. ⁴⁷ The first man *was* of the earth, *made* of dust; the second Man *is* the Lord[e] from heaven. ⁴⁸ As *was* the *man* of dust, so also *are* those *who are made* of dust; and as *is* the heavenly *Man,* so also *are* those *who are* heavenly. ⁴⁹ And as we have borne the image of the *man* of dust, we shall also bear[f] the image of the heavenly *Man.*

Our Final Victory

⁵⁰ **Now this I say, brethren, that flesh and blood cannot inherit the kingdom of God; nor does corruption inherit incorruption. ⁵¹ Behold, I tell you a mystery: We shall not all sleep, but we**

shall all be changed— [52] in a moment, in the twinkling of an eye, at the last trumpet. For the trumpet will sound, and the dead will be raised incorruptible, and we shall be changed. [53] For this corruptible must put on incorruption, and this mortal *must* put on immortality. [54] So when this corruptible has put on incorruption, and this mortal has put on immortality, then shall be brought to pass the saying that is written: "Death is swallowed up in victory."[g]

[55] "O Death, where *is* your sting?[h]
O Hades, where *is* your victory?"[i]

[56] The sting of death *is* sin, and the strength of sin *is* the law. [57] But thanks *be* to God, who gives us the victory through our Lord Jesus Christ.

[58] Therefore, my beloved brethren, be steadfast, immovable, always abounding in the work of the Lord, knowing that your labor is not in vain in the Lord.

Footnotes:

a. 1 Corinthians 15:27 Psalm 8:6
b. 1 Corinthians 15:32 Isaiah 22:13
c. 1 Corinthians 15:39 NU-Text and M-Text omit *of flesh.*
d. 1 Corinthians 15:45 Genesis 2:7
e. 1 Corinthians 15:47 NU-Text omits *the Lord.*
f. 1 Corinthians 15:49 M-Text reads *let us also bear.*
g. 1 Corinthians 15:54 Isaiah 25:8
h. 1 Corinthians 15:55 Hosea 13:14
i. 1 Corinthians 15:55 NU-Text reads *O Death, where is your victory? O Death, where is your sting?*

(NKJV)

John 5 (NKJV)

A Man Healed at the Pool of Bethesda

5 After this there was a feast of the Jews, and Jesus went up to Jerusalem. ² Now there is in Jerusalem by the Sheep *Gate* a pool, which is called in Hebrew, Bethesda,[a] having five porches. ³ In these lay a great multitude of sick people, blind, lame, paralyzed, waiting for the moving of the water. ⁴ For an angel went down at a certain time into the pool and stirred up the water; then whoever stepped in first, after the stirring of the water, was made well of whatever disease he had.[b] ⁵ Now a certain man was there who had an infirmity thirty-eight years. ⁶ When Jesus saw him lying there, and knew that he already had been *in that condition* a long time, He said to him, "Do you want to be made well?"

⁷ The sick man answered Him, "Sir, I have no man to put me into the pool when the water is stirred up; but while I am coming, another steps down before me."

⁸ Jesus said to him, "Rise, take up your bed and walk." ⁹ And immediately the man was made well, took up his bed, and walked.

And that day was the Sabbath. ¹⁰ The Jews therefore said to him who was cured, "It is the Sabbath; it is not lawful for you to carry your bed."

¹¹ He answered them, "He who made me well said to me, 'Take up your bed and walk.'"

¹² Then they asked him, "Who is the Man who said to you, 'Take up your bed and walk'?" ¹³ But the one who was healed did not know who it was, for Jesus had withdrawn, a multitude being in *that* place. ¹⁴ Afterward Jesus found him in the temple, and said to him, "See, you have been made well. Sin no more, lest a worse thing come upon you."

[15] The man departed and told the Jews that it was Jesus who had made him well.

Honor the Father and the Son

[16] For this reason the Jews persecuted Jesus, and sought to kill Him,[c] because He had done these things on the Sabbath. [17] But Jesus answered them, "My Father has been working until now, and I have been working."

[18] Therefore the Jews sought all the more to kill Him, because He not only broke the Sabbath, but also said that God was His Father, making Himself equal with God. [19] Then Jesus answered and said to them, "Most assuredly, I say to you, the Son can do nothing of Himself, but what He sees the Father do; for whatever He does, the Son also does in like manner. [20] For the Father loves the Son, and shows Him all things that He Himself does; and He will show Him greater works than these, that you may marvel. [21] For as the Father raises the dead and gives life to *them,* even so the Son gives life to whom He will. [22] For the Father judges no one, but has committed all judgment to the Son, [23] that all should honor the Son just as they honor the Father. He who does not honor the Son does not honor the Father who sent Him.

Life and Judgment Are Through the Son

[24] "Most assuredly, I say to you, he who hears My word and believes in Him who sent Me has everlasting life, and shall not come into judgment, but has passed from death into life. [25] Most assuredly, I say to you, the hour is coming, and now is, when the dead will hear the voice of the Son of God; and those who hear will live. [26] For as the Father has life in Himself, so He has granted the Son to have life in Himself, [27] and has given Him authority to execute judgment also, because He is the Son of Man. [28] Do not marvel at this; for the hour is coming in which all who are in the

graves will hear His voice [29] and come forth—those who have done good, to the resurrection of life, and those who have done evil, to the resurrection of condemnation. [30] I can of Myself do nothing. As I hear, I judge; and My judgment is righteous, because I do not seek My own will but the will of the Father who sent Me.

The Fourfold Witness

[31] "If I bear witness of Myself, My witness is not true. [32] There is another who bears witness of Me, and I know that the witness which He witnesses of Me is true. [33] You have sent to John, and he has borne witness to the truth. [34] Yet I do not receive testimony from man, but I say these things that you may be saved. [35] He was the burning and shining lamp, and you were willing for a time to rejoice in his light. [36] But I have a greater witness than John's; for the works which the Father has given Me to finish—the very works that I do—bear witness of Me, that the Father has sent Me. [37] And the Father Himself, who sent Me, has testified of Me. You have neither heard His voice at any time, nor seen His form. [38] But you do not have His word abiding in you, because whom He sent, Him you do not believe. [39] You search the Scriptures, for in them you think you have eternal life; and these are they which testify of Me. [40] But you are not willing to come to Me that you may have life.

[41] "I do not receive honor from men. [42] But I know you, that you do not have the love of God in you. [43] I have come in My Father's name, and you do not receive Me; if another comes in his own name, him you will receive. [44] How can you believe, who receive honor from one another, and do not seek the honor that *comes* from the only God? [45] Do not think that I shall accuse you to the Father; there is *one* who accuses you—Moses, in whom you trust. [46] For if you believed Moses, you would believe Me; for he wrote about Me. [47] But if you do not believe his writings, how will you believe My words?"

Footnotes:

a. John 5:2 NU-Text reads *Bethzatha.*

117

James Robert Waugh

b. <u>John 5:4</u> NU-Text omits *waiting for the moving of the water* at the end of verse 3, and all of verse 4.

c. <u>John 5:16</u> NU-Text omits *and sought to kill Him.*

(NKJV)

Scripture taken from the New King James Version®. Copyright © 1982 by Thomas Nelson. Used by permission. All rights reserved.

Revelation 18 (NKJV)

The Fall of Babylon the Great

18 After these things I saw another angel coming down from heaven, having great authority, and the earth was illuminated with his glory. [2] And he cried mightily[a] with a loud voice, saying, "Babylon the great is fallen, is fallen, and has become a dwelling place of demons, a prison for every foul spirit, and a cage for every unclean and hated bird! [3] For all the nations have drunk of the wine of the wrath of her fornication, the kings of the earth have committed fornication with her, and the merchants of the earth have become rich through the abundance of her luxury."

[4] And I heard another voice from heaven saying, "Come out of her, my people, lest you share in her sins, and lest you receive of her plagues. [5] For her sins have reached[b] to heaven, and God has remembered her iniquities. [6] Render to her just as she rendered to you,[c] and repay her double according to her works; in the cup which she has mixed, mix double for her. [7] In the measure that she glorified herself and lived luxuriously, in the same measure give her torment and sorrow; for she says in her heart, 'I sit *as* queen, and am no widow, and will not see sorrow.' [8] Therefore her plagues will come in one day—death and mourning and famine. And she will be utterly burned with fire, for strong *is* the Lord God who judges[d] her.

The World Mourns Babylon's Fall

[9] "The kings of the earth who committed fornication and lived luxuriously with her will weep and lament for her, when they see the smoke of her burning, [10] standing at a distance for fear of her torment, saying, 'Alas, alas, that great city Babylon, that mighty city! For in one hour your judgment has come.'

[11] "And the merchants of the earth will weep and mourn over her, for no one buys their merchandise anymore: [12] merchandise of gold

and silver, precious stones and pearls, fine linen and purple, silk and scarlet, every kind of citron wood, every kind of object of ivory, every kind of object of most precious wood, bronze, iron, and marble; [13] and cinnamon and incense, fragrant oil and frankincense, wine and oil, fine flour and wheat, cattle and sheep, horses and chariots, and bodies and souls of men. [14] The fruit that your soul longed for has gone from you, and all the things which are rich and splendid have gone from you,[e] and you shall find them no more at all. [15] The merchants of these things, who became rich by her, will stand at a distance for fear of her torment, weeping and wailing, [16] and saying, 'Alas, alas, that great city that was clothed in fine linen, purple, and scarlet, and adorned with gold and precious stones and pearls! [17] For in one hour such great riches came to nothing.' Every shipmaster, all who travel by ship, sailors, and as many as trade on the sea, stood at a distance [18] and cried out when they saw the smoke of her burning, saying, 'What *is* like this great city?'

[19] "They threw dust on their heads and cried out, weeping and wailing, and saying, 'Alas, alas, that great city, in which all who had ships on the sea became rich by her wealth! For in one hour she is made desolate.'

[20] "Rejoice over her, O heaven, and *you* holy apostles[f] and prophets, for God has avenged you on her!"

Finality of Babylon's Fall

[21] Then a mighty angel took up a stone like a great millstone and threw *it* into the sea, saying, "Thus with violence the great city Babylon shall be thrown down, and shall not be found anymore. [22] The sound of harpists, musicians, flutists, and trumpeters shall not be heard in you anymore. No craftsman of any craft shall be found in you anymore, and the sound of a millstone shall not be heard in you anymore. [23] The light of a lamp shall not shine in you anymore, and the voice of bridegroom and bride shall not be heard in you anymore. For your merchants were the great men of the earth, for by your sorcery all the nations were deceived. [24] And in her was

found the blood of prophets and saints, and of all who were slain on the earth."

Footnotes:

a. Revelation 18:2 NU-Text and M-Text omit *mightily.*
b. Revelation 18:5 NU-Text and M-Text read *have been heaped up.*
c. Revelation 18:6 NU-Text and M-Text omit *to you.*
d. Revelation 18:8 NU-Text and M-Text read *has judged.*
e. Revelation 18:14 NU-Text and M-Text read *been lost to you.*
f. Revelation 18:20 NU-Text and M-Text read *saints and apostles.*

(NKJV)

Revelation 19 (NKJV)

Heaven Exults over Babylon

19 After these things I heard[a] a loud voice of a great multitude in heaven, saying, "Alleluia! Salvation and glory and honor and power *belong* **to the Lord[b] our God!** [2] For true and righteous *are* His judgments, because He has judged the great harlot who corrupted the earth with her fornication; and He has avenged on her the blood of His servants *shed* by her." [3] Again they said, "Alleluia! Her smoke rises up forever and ever!" [4] And the twenty-four elders and the four living creatures fell down and worshiped God who sat on the throne, saying, "Amen! Alleluia!" [5] Then a voice came from the throne, saying, "Praise our God, all you His servants and those who fear Him, both[c] small and great!"

[6] **And I heard, as it were, the voice of a great multitude, as the sound of many waters and as the sound of mighty thunderings, saying, "Alleluia! For the[d] Lord God Omnipotent reigns!** [7] Let us be glad and rejoice and give Him glory, for the marriage of the Lamb has come, and His wife has made herself ready." [8] And to her it was granted to be arrayed in fine linen, clean and bright, for the fine linen is the righteous acts of the saints.

[9] Then he said to me, "Write: 'Blessed *are* those who are called to the marriage supper of the Lamb!'" And he said to me, "These are the true sayings of God." [10] And I fell at his feet to worship him. But he said to me, "See *that you do* not *do that!* I am your fellow servant, and of your brethren who have the testimony of Jesus. Worship God! For the testimony of Jesus is the spirit of prophecy."

Christ on a White Horse

[11] Now I saw heaven opened, and behold, a white horse. And He who sat on him *was* called Faithful and True, and in righteousness He judges and makes war. [12] His eyes *were* like a flame of fire, and

on His head *were* many crowns. He had[e] a name written that no one knew except Himself. [13] He *was* clothed with a robe dipped in blood, and His name is called The Word of God. [14] And the armies in heaven, clothed in fine linen, white and clean,[f] followed Him on white horses. [15] Now out of His mouth goes a sharp[g] sword, that with it He should strike the nations. And He Himself will rule them with a rod of iron. He Himself treads the winepress of the fierceness and wrath of Almighty God. [16] And He has on *His* robe and on His thigh a name written:

KING OF KINGS AND LORD OF LORDS.

The Beast and His Armies Defeated

[17] Then I saw an angel standing in the sun; and he cried with a loud voice, saying to all the birds that fly in the midst of heaven, "Come and gather together for the supper of the great God,[h] [18] that you may eat the flesh of kings, the flesh of captains, the flesh of mighty men, the flesh of horses and of those who sit on them, and the flesh of all *people,* free[i] and slave, both small and great."

[19] And I saw the beast, the kings of the earth, and their armies, gathered together to make war against Him who sat on the horse and against His army. [20] Then the beast was captured, and with him the false prophet who worked signs in his presence, by which he deceived those who received the mark of the beast and those who worshiped his image. These two were cast alive into the lake of fire burning with brimstone. [21] And the rest were killed with the sword which proceeded from the mouth of Him who sat on the horse. And all the birds were filled with their flesh.

Footnotes:

   a. Revelation 19:1 NU-Text and M-Text add *something like.*
   b. Revelation 19:1 NU-Text and M-Text omit *the Lord.*
   c. Revelation 19:5 NU-Text and M-Text omit *both.*
   d. Revelation 19:6 NU-Text and M-Text read *our.*

e. <u>Revelation 19:12</u> M-Text adds *names written, and.*
f. <u>Revelation 19:14</u> NU-Text and M-Text read *pure white linen.*
g. <u>Revelation 19:15</u> M-Text adds *two-edged.*
h. <u>Revelation 19:17</u> NU-Text and M-Text read *the great supper of God.*
i. <u>Revelation 19:18</u> NU-Text and M-Text read *both free.*

(NKJV)

Revelation 7 (NKJV)

The Sealed of Israel

7 After these things I saw four angels standing at the four corners of the earth, holding the four winds of the earth, that the wind should not blow on the earth, on the sea, or on any tree. [2] Then I saw another angel ascending from the east, having the seal of the living God. And he cried with a loud voice to the four angels to whom it was granted to harm the earth and the sea, [3] saying, "Do not harm the earth, the sea, or the trees till we have sealed the servants of our God on their foreheads." [4] And I heard the number of those who were sealed. One hundred *and* forty-four thousand of all the tribes of the children of Israel *were* sealed:

[5] of the tribe of Judah twelve thousand *were* sealed;[a]
of the tribe of Reuben twelve thousand *were* sealed;
of the tribe of Gad twelve thousand *were* sealed;
[6] of the tribe of Asher twelve thousand *were* sealed;
of the tribe of Naphtali twelve thousand *were* sealed;
of the tribe of Manasseh twelve thousand *were* sealed;
[7] of the tribe of Simeon twelve thousand *were* sealed;
of the tribe of Levi twelve thousand *were* sealed;
of the tribe of Issachar twelve thousand *were* sealed;
[8] of the tribe of Zebulun twelve thousand *were* sealed;
of the tribe of Joseph twelve thousand *were* sealed;
of the tribe of Benjamin twelve thousand *were* sealed.

A Multitude from the Great Tribulation

[9] **After these things I looked, and behold, a great multitude which no one could number, of all nations, tribes, peoples, and tongues, standing before the throne and before the Lamb, clothed with white robes, with palm branches in their hands, [10] and crying out with a loud voice, saying, "Salvation *belongs* to our God who sits**

on the throne, and to the Lamb!" [11] All the angels stood around the throne and the elders and the four living creatures, and fell on their faces before the throne and worshiped God, [12] saying:

"Amen! Blessing and glory and wisdom,
Thanksgiving and honor and power and might,
Be to our God forever and ever.
Amen."

[13] Then one of the elders answered, saying to me, "Who are these arrayed in white robes, and where did they come from?"

[14] And I said to him, "Sir,[b] you know."

So he said to me, "These are the ones who come out of the great tribulation, and washed their robes and made them white in the blood of the Lamb. [15] Therefore they are before the throne of God, and serve Him day and night in His temple. And He who sits on the throne will dwell among them. [16] They shall neither hunger anymore nor thirst anymore; the sun shall not strike them, nor any heat; [17] for the Lamb who is in the midst of the throne will shepherd them and lead them to living fountains of waters.[c] And God will wipe away every tear from their eyes."

Footnotes:

a. Revelation 7:5 In NU-Text and M-Text *were sealed* is stated only in verses 5a and 8c; the words are understood in the remainder of the passage.
b. Revelation 7:14 NU-Text and M-Text read *My lord.*
c. Revelation 7:17 NU-Text and M-Text read *to fountains of the waters of life.*

(NKJV)

(2) The Invisible World

2 Corinthians 4 – New Testament
Colossians 1 – New Testament
1 John 2 – New Testament

2 Corinthians 4 (NKJV)

The Light of Christ's Gospel

4 Therefore, since we have this ministry, as we have received mercy, we do not lose heart. ² But we have renounced the hidden things of shame, not walking in craftiness nor handling the word of God deceitfully, but by manifestation of the truth commending ourselves to every man's conscience in the sight of God. ³ But even if our gospel is veiled, it is veiled to those who are perishing, ⁴ whose minds the god of this age has blinded, who do not believe, lest the light of the gospel of the glory of Christ, who is the image of God, should shine on them. ⁵ For we do not preach ourselves, but Christ Jesus the Lord, and ourselves your bondservants for Jesus' sake. ⁶ For it is the God who commanded light to shine out of darkness, who has shone in our hearts to *give* the light of the knowledge of the glory of God in the face of Jesus Christ.

Cast Down but Unconquered

⁷ But we have this treasure in earthen vessels, that the excellence of the power may be of God and not of us. ⁸ *We are* hard-pressed on every side, yet not crushed; *we are* perplexed, but not in despair; ⁹ persecuted, but not forsaken; struck down, but not destroyed— ¹⁰ always carrying about in the body the dying of the Lord Jesus, that the life of Jesus also may be manifested in our body. ¹¹ For we who live are always delivered to death for Jesus' sake, that the life of Jesus also may be manifested in our mortal flesh. ¹² So then death is working in us, but life in you.

¹³ And since we have the same spirit of faith, according to what is written, "I believed and therefore I spoke,"[a] we also believe and therefore speak, ¹⁴ knowing that He who raised up the Lord Jesus will also raise us up with Jesus, and will present *us* with you. ¹⁵ For all things *are* for your sakes, that grace, having spread through the many, may cause thanksgiving to abound to the glory of God.

Seeing the Invisible

[16]Therefore we do not lose heart. Even though our outward *man* is perishing, yet the inward man is being renewed day by day. [17]For our light affliction, which is but for a moment, is working for us a far more exceeding *and* eternal weight of glory, [18]while we do not look at the things which are seen, but at the things which are not seen. For the things which are seen *are* temporary, but the things which *are* not seen are eternal.

Footnotes:

a. 2 Corinthians 4:13 Psalm 116:10

(NKJV)

Colossians 1 (NKJV)

Greeting

1 Paul, an apostle of Jesus Christ by the will of God, and Timothy our brother,

[2] To the saints and faithful brethren in Christ *who are* in Colosse:

Grace to you and peace from God our Father and the Lord Jesus Christ.[a]

Their Faith in Christ

[3] We give thanks to the God and Father of our Lord Jesus Christ, praying always for you, [4] since we heard of your faith in Christ Jesus and of your love for all the saints; [5] because of the hope which is laid up for you in heaven, of which you heard before in the word of the truth of the gospel, [6] which has come to you, as *it has* also in all the world, and is bringing forth fruit,[b] as *it is* also among you since the day you heard and knew the grace of God in truth; [7] as you also learned from Epaphras, our dear fellow servant, who is a faithful minister of Christ on your behalf, [8] who also declared to us your love in the Spirit.

Preeminence of Christ

[9] For this reason we also, since the day we heard it, do not cease to pray for you, and to ask that you may be filled with the knowledge of His will in all wisdom and spiritual understanding; [10] that you may walk worthy of the Lord, fully pleasing *Him,* being fruitful in every good work and increasing in the knowledge of God; [11] strengthened with all might, according to His glorious power, for all patience and longsuffering with joy; [12] giving thanks to the Father who has qualified us to be partakers of the inheritance of the saints in the light. [13] He has delivered us from the power of darkness and

conveyed *us* into the kingdom of the Son of His love, [14] in whom we have redemption through His blood,[c] the forgiveness of sins.

[15] **He is the image of the invisible God, the firstborn over all creation. [16] For by Him all things were created that are in heaven and that are on earth, visible and invisible, whether thrones or dominions or principalities or powers. All things were created through Him and for Him. [17] And He is before all things, and in Him all things consist. [18] And He is the head of the body, the church, who is the beginning, the firstborn from the dead, that in all things He may have the preeminence.**

Reconciled in Christ

[19] For it pleased *the Father that* in Him all the fullness should dwell, [20] and by Him to reconcile all things to Himself, by Him, whether things on earth or things in heaven, having made peace through the blood of His cross.

[21] And you, who once were alienated and enemies in your mind by wicked works, yet now He has reconciled [22] in the body of His flesh through death, to present you holy, and blameless, and above reproach in His sight— [23] if indeed you continue in the faith, grounded and steadfast, and are not moved away from the hope of the gospel which you heard, which was preached to every creature under heaven, of which I, Paul, became a minister.

Sacrificial Service for Christ

[24] I now rejoice in my sufferings for you, and fill up in my flesh what is lacking in the afflictions of Christ, for the sake of His body, which is the church, [25] of which I became a minister according to the stewardship from God which was given to me for you, to fulfill the word of God, [26] the mystery which has been hidden from ages and from generations, but now has been revealed to His saints. [27] To them God willed to make known what are the riches of the glory of this mystery among the Gentiles: which[d] is Christ in you, the hope

of glory. [28] Him we preach, warning every man and teaching every man in all wisdom, that we may present every man perfect in Christ Jesus. [29] To this *end* I also labor, striving according to His working which works in me mightily.

Footnotes:

a. Colossians 1:2 NU-Text omits *and the Lord Jesus Christ.*
b. Colossians 1:6 NU-Text and M-Text add *and growing.*
c. Colossians 1:14 NU-Text and M-Text omit *through His blood.*
d. Colossians 1:27 M-Text reads *who.*

(NKJV)

1 John 2 (NKJV)

2 My little children, these things I write to you, so that you may not sin. And if anyone sins, we have an Advocate with the Father, Jesus Christ the righteous. [2] And He Himself is the propitiation for our sins, and not for ours only but also for the whole world.

The Test of Knowing Him

[3] Now by this we know that we know Him, if we keep His commandments. [4] He who says, "I know Him," and does not keep His commandments, is a liar, and the truth is not in him. [5] But whoever keeps His word, truly the love of God is perfected in him. By this we know that we are in Him. [6] He who says he abides in Him ought himself also to walk just as He walked.

[7] Brethren,[a] I write no new commandment to you, but an old commandment which you have had from the beginning. The old commandment is the word which you heard from the beginning.[b] [8] Again, a new commandment I write to you, which thing is true in

Him and in you, because the darkness is passing away, and the true light is already shining.

⁹ He who says he is in the light, and hates his brother, is in darkness until now. ¹⁰ He who loves his brother abides in the light, and there is no cause for stumbling in him. ¹¹ But he who hates his brother is in darkness and walks in darkness, and does not know where he is going, because the darkness has blinded his eyes.

Their Spiritual State

¹² I write to you, little children,
Because your sins are forgiven you for His name's sake.
¹³ I write to you, fathers,
Because you have known Him *who is* from the beginning.
I write to you, young men,
Because you have overcome the wicked one.
I write to you, little children,
Because you have known the Father.
¹⁴ I have written to you, fathers,
Because you have known Him *who is* from the beginning.
I have written to you, young men,
Because you are strong, and the word of God abides in you,
And you have overcome the wicked one.

Do Not Love the World

¹⁵ Do not love the world or the things in the world. If anyone loves the world, the love of the Father is not in him. ¹⁶ For all that *is* in the world—the lust of the flesh, the lust of the eyes, and the pride of life—is not of the Father but is of the world. ¹⁷ And the world is passing away, and the lust of it; but he who does the will of God abides forever.

Deceptions of the Last Hour

[18] Little children, it is the last hour; and as you have heard that the[c] Antichrist is coming, even now many antichrists have come, by which we know that it is the last hour. [19] They went out from us, but they were not of us; for if they had been of us, they would have continued with us; but *they went out* that they might be made manifest, that none of them were of us.

[20] But you have an anointing from the Holy One, and you know all things.[d] [21] I have not written to you because you do not know the truth, but because you know it, and that no lie is of the truth.

[22] Who is a liar but he who denies that Jesus is the Christ? He is antichrist who denies the Father and the Son. [23] Whoever denies the Son does not have the Father either; he who acknowledges the Son has the Father also.

Let Truth Abide in You

[24] Therefore let that abide in you which you heard from the beginning. If what you heard from the beginning abides in you, you also will abide in the Son and in the Father. [25] And this is the promise that He has promised us—eternal life.

[26] These things I have written to you concerning those who *try to* deceive you. [27] But the anointing which you have received from Him abides in you, and you do not need that anyone teach you; but as the same anointing teaches you concerning all things, and is true, and is not a lie, and just as it has taught you, you will[e] abide in Him.

The Children of God

[28] And now, little children, abide in Him, that when[f] He appears, we may have confidence and not be ashamed before Him at His coming. [29] If you know that He is righteous, you know that everyone who practices righteousness is born of Him.

Footnotes:

1. <u>1 John 2:7</u> NU-Text reads *Beloved.*
2. <u>1 John 2:7</u> NU-Text omits *from the beginning.*
3. <u>1 John 2:18</u> NU-Text omits *the.*
4. <u>1 John 2:20</u> NU-Text reads *you all know.*
5. <u>1 John 2:27</u> NU-Text reads *you abide.*
6. <u>1 John 2:28</u> NU-Text reads *if.*

(NKJV)

(3) Perilous times in the last days

2 Timothy 3 – New Testament

2 Timothy 3 (NKJV)

Perilous Times and Perilous Men

3 But know this, that in the last days perilous times will come: [2] For men will be lovers of themselves, lovers of money, boasters, proud, blasphemers, disobedient to parents, unthankful, unholy, [3] unloving, unforgiving, slanderers, without self-control, brutal, despisers of good, [4] traitors, headstrong, haughty, lovers of pleasure rather than lovers of God, [5] having a form of godliness but denying its power. And from such people turn away! [6] For of this sort are those who creep into households and make captives of gullible women loaded down with sins, led away by various lusts, [7] always learning and never able to come to the knowledge of the truth. [8] Now as Jannes and Jambres resisted Moses, so do these also resist the truth: men of corrupt minds, disapproved concerning the faith; [9] but they will progress no further, for their folly will be manifest to all, as theirs also was.

The Man of God and the Word of God

[10] But you have carefully followed my doctrine, manner of life, purpose, faith, longsuffering, love, perseverance, [11] persecutions, afflictions, which happened to me at Antioch, at Iconium, at Lystra—what persecutions I endured. And out of *them* all the Lord delivered me. [12] Yes, and all who desire to live godly in Christ Jesus will suffer persecution. [13] But evil men and impostors will grow worse and worse, deceiving and being deceived. [14] But you must continue in the things which you have learned and been assured of, knowing from whom you have learned *them,* [15] and that from childhood you have known the Holy Scriptures, which are able to make you wise for salvation through faith which is in Christ Jesus.

[16] All Scripture *is* given by inspiration of God, and *is* profitable for doctrine, for reproof, for correction, for instruction in righteousness,

[17] that the man of God may be complete, thoroughly equipped for every good work.

(NKJV)

(4) Satan and his angels are cast down and then deceive the nations

---

Revelation 12 – New Testament
Revelation 20 – New Testament

James Robert Waugh

Revelation 12 (NKJV)

The Woman, the Child, and the Dragon

12 Now a great sign appeared in heaven: a woman clothed with the sun, with the moon under her feet, and on her head a garland of twelve stars. [2] Then being with child, she cried out in labor and in pain to give birth.

[3] And another sign appeared in heaven: behold, a great, fiery red dragon having seven heads and ten horns, and seven diadems on his heads. [4] His tail drew a third of the stars of heaven and threw them to the earth. And the dragon stood before the woman who was ready to give birth, to devour her Child as soon as it was born. [5] She bore a male Child who was to rule all nations with a rod of iron. And her Child was caught up to God and His throne. [6] Then the woman fled into the wilderness, where she has a place prepared by God, that they should feed her there one thousand two hundred and sixty days.

Satan Thrown Out of Heaven

[7] And war broke out in heaven: Michael and his angels fought with the dragon; and the dragon and his angels fought, [8] but they did not prevail, nor was a place found for them[a] in heaven any longer. [9] So the great dragon was cast out, that serpent of old, called the Devil and Satan, who deceives the whole world; he was cast to the earth, and his angels were cast out with him.

[10] Then I heard a loud voice saying in heaven, "Now salvation, and strength, and the kingdom of our God, and the power of His Christ have come, for the accuser of our brethren, who accused them before our God day and night, has been cast down. [11] And they overcame him by the blood of the Lamb and by the word of their testimony, and they did not love their lives to the death. [12] Therefore rejoice, O heavens, and you who dwell in them! Woe

to the inhabitants of the earth and the sea! For the devil has come down to you, having great wrath, because he knows that he has a short time."

The Woman Persecuted

¹³ Now when the dragon saw that he had been cast to the earth, he persecuted the woman who gave birth to the male *Child.* ¹⁴ But the woman was given two wings of a great eagle, that she might fly into the wilderness to her place, where she is nourished for a time and times and half a time, from the presence of the serpent. ¹⁵ So the serpent spewed water out of his mouth like a flood after the woman, that he might cause her to be carried away by the flood. ¹⁶ But the earth helped the woman, and the earth opened its mouth and swallowed up the flood which the dragon had spewed out of his mouth. ¹⁷ And the dragon was enraged with the woman, and he went to make war with the rest of her offspring, who keep the commandments of God and have the testimony of Jesus Christ.[b]

Footnotes:

a. Revelation 12:8 M-Text reads *him.*
b. Revelation 12:17 NU-Text and M-Text omit *Christ.*

(NKJV)

Revelation 20 (NKJV)

Satan Bound 1,000 Years

20 Then I saw an angel coming down from heaven, having the key to the bottomless pit and a great chain in his hand. ² He laid hold of the dragon, that serpent of old, who is *the* Devil and Satan, and bound him for a thousand years; ³ **and he cast him into the bottomless pit, and shut him up, and set a seal on him, so that he should deceive the nations no more till the thousand years were finished. But after these things he must be released for a little while.**

The Saints Reign with Christ 1,000 Years

⁴ And I saw thrones, and they sat on them, and judgment was committed to them. Then *I saw* the souls of those who had been beheaded for their witness to Jesus and for the word of God, who had not worshiped the beast or his image, and had not received *his* mark on their foreheads or on their hands. And they lived and reigned with Christ for a[a] thousand years. ⁵ But the rest of the dead did not live again until the thousand years were finished. This *is* the first resurrection. ⁶ Blessed and holy *is* he who has part in the first resurrection. Over such the second death has no power, but they shall be priests of God and of Christ, and shall reign with Him a thousand years.

Satanic Rebellion Crushed

⁷ Now when the thousand years have expired, Satan will be released from his prison ⁸ and will go out to deceive the nations which are in the four corners of the earth, Gog and Magog, to gather them together to battle, whose number *is* as the sand of the sea. ⁹ They went up on the breadth of the earth and surrounded the camp of the saints and the beloved city. And fire came down from God out

of heaven and devoured them. [10] The devil, who deceived them, was cast into the lake of fire and brimstone where[b] the beast and the false prophet *are*. And they will be tormented day and night forever and ever.

The Great White Throne Judgment

[11] Then I saw a great white throne and Him who sat on it, from whose face the earth and the heaven fled away. And there was found no place for them. [12] And I saw the dead, small and great, standing before God,[c] and books were opened. And another book was opened, which is *the Book* of Life. And the dead were judged according to their works, by the things which were written in the books. [13] The sea gave up the dead who were in it, and Death and Hades delivered up the dead who were in them. And they were judged, each one according to his works. [14] Then Death and Hades were cast into the lake of fire. This is the second death.[d] [15] And anyone not found written in the Book of Life was cast into the lake of fire.

Footnotes:

a. Revelation 20:4 M-Text reads *the*.
b. Revelation 20:10 NU-Text and M-Text add *also*.
c. Revelation 20:12 NU-Text and M-Text read *the throne*.
d. Revelation 20:14 NU-Text and M-Text add *the lake of fire*.

(NKJV)

(5) The Rise of the Anti-Christ

Daniel 8 – Old Testament
Revelation 13 – New Testament

Daniel 8 (NKJV)

Vision of a Ram and a Goat

8 In the third year of the reign of King Belshazzar a vision appeared *to* me—to me, Daniel—after the one that appeared to me the first time. ² I saw in the vision, and it so happened while I was looking, that I *was* in Shushan, the citadel, which *is* in the province of Elam; and I saw in the vision that I was by the River Ulai. ³ Then I lifted my eyes and saw, and there, standing beside the river, was a ram which had two horns, and the two horns *were* high; but one *was* higher than the other, and the higher *one* came up last. ⁴ I saw the ram pushing westward, northward, and southward, so that no animal could withstand him; nor *was there any* that could deliver from his hand, but he did according to his will and became great.

⁵ And as I was considering, suddenly a male goat came from the west, across the surface of the whole earth, without touching the ground; and the goat *had* a notable horn between his eyes. ⁶ Then he came to the ram that had two horns, which I had seen standing beside the river, and ran at him with furious power. ⁷ And I saw him confronting the ram; he was moved with rage against him, attacked the ram, and broke his two horns. There was no power in the ram to withstand him, but he cast him down to the ground and trampled him; and there was no one that could deliver the ram from his hand.

⁸ Therefore the male goat grew very great; but when he became strong, the large horn was broken, and in place of it four notable ones came up toward the four winds of heaven. ⁹ And out of one of them came a little horn which grew exceedingly great toward the south, toward the east, and toward the Glorious *Land.* ¹⁰ And it grew up to the host of heaven; and it cast down *some* of the host and *some* of the stars to the ground, and trampled them. ¹¹ He even exalted *himself* as high as the Prince of the host; and by him the daily *sacrifices* were taken away, and the place of His sanctuary was cast down. ¹² Because of transgression, an army was given over *to the horn*

to oppose the daily *sacrifices;* and he cast truth down to the ground. He did *all this* and prospered.

¹³ Then I heard a holy one speaking; and *another* holy one said to that certain *one* who was speaking, "How long *will* the vision *be, concerning* the daily *sacrifices* and the transgression of desolation, the giving of both the sanctuary and the host to be trampled underfoot?"

¹⁴ And he said to me, "For two thousand three hundred days;[a] then the sanctuary shall be cleansed."

Gabriel Interprets the Vision

¹⁵ Then it happened, when I, Daniel, had seen the vision and was seeking the meaning, that suddenly there stood before me one having the appearance of a man. ¹⁶ And I heard a man's voice between *the banks of* the Ulai, who called, and said, "Gabriel, make this *man* understand the vision." ¹⁷ So he came near where I stood, and when he came I was afraid and fell on my face; but he said to me, "Understand, son of man, that the vision *refers* to the time of the end."

¹⁸ Now, as he was speaking with me, I was in a deep sleep with my face to the ground; but he touched me, and stood me upright. ¹⁹ And he said, "Look, I am making known to you what shall happen in the latter time of the indignation; for at the appointed time the end *shall be.* ²⁰ The ram which you saw, having the two horns—*they are* the kings of Media and Persia. ²¹ And the male goat *is* the kingdom[b] of Greece. The large horn that *is* between its eyes *is* the first king. ²² As for the broken *horn* and the four that stood up in its place, four kingdoms shall arise out of that nation, but not with its power.

²³ **"And in the latter time of their kingdom,**
When the transgressors have reached their fullness,
A king shall arise,
Having fierce features,
Who understands sinister schemes.

²⁴ His power shall be mighty, but not by his own power;
He shall destroy fearfully,
And shall prosper and thrive;
He shall destroy the mighty, and *also* the holy people.

²⁵ "Through his cunning
He shall cause deceit to prosper under his rule;[c]
And he shall exalt *himself* in his heart.
He shall destroy many in *their* prosperity.
He shall even rise against the Prince of princes;
But he shall be broken without *human* means.[d]

²⁶ "And the vision of the evenings and mornings
Which was told is true;
Therefore seal up the vision,
For *it refers* to many days *in the future.*"

²⁷ And I, Daniel, fainted and was sick for days; afterward I arose and went about the king's business. I was astonished by the vision, but no one understood it.

Footnotes:

a. Daniel 8:14 Literally *evening-mornings*
b. Daniel 8:21 Literally *king,* representing his kingdom (compare 7:17, 23)
c. Daniel 8:25 Literally *hand*
d. Daniel 8:25 Literally *hand*

(NKJV)

Revelation 13 (NKJV)

The Beast from the Sea

13 Then I[a] stood on the sand of the sea. And I saw a beast rising up out of the sea, having seven heads and ten horns,[b] and on his horns ten crowns, and on his heads a blasphemous name. **² Now the beast which I saw was like a leopard, his feet were like *the feet of* a bear, and his mouth like the mouth of a lion. The dragon gave him his power, his throne, and great authority. ³ And I saw one of his heads as if it had been mortally wounded, and his deadly wound was healed. And all the world marveled and followed the beast. ⁴ So they worshiped the dragon who gave authority to the beast; and they worshiped the beast, saying, "Who *is* like the beast? Who is able to make war with him?"**

⁵ And he was given a mouth speaking great things and blasphemies, and he was given authority to continue[c] for forty-two months. ⁶ Then he opened his mouth in blasphemy against God, to blaspheme His name, His tabernacle, and those who dwell in heaven. ⁷ It was granted to him to make war with the saints and to overcome them. And authority was given him over every tribe,[d] tongue, and nation. ⁸ All who dwell on the earth will worship him, whose names have not been written in the Book of Life of the Lamb slain from the foundation of the world.

⁹ If anyone has an ear, let him hear. ¹⁰ He who leads into captivity shall go into captivity; he who kills with the sword must be killed with the sword. Here is the patience and the faith of the saints.

The Beast from the Earth

¹¹ Then I saw another beast coming up out of the earth, and he had two horns like a lamb and spoke like a dragon. ¹² And he exercises all the authority of the first beast in his presence, and causes the earth and those who dwell in it to worship the first beast, whose deadly

wound was healed. [13] He performs great signs, so that he even makes fire come down from heaven on the earth in the sight of men. [14] And he deceives those[e] who dwell on the earth by those signs which he was granted to do in the sight of the beast, telling those who dwell on the earth to make an image to the beast who was wounded by the sword and lived. [15] He was granted *power* to give breath to the image of the beast, that the image of the beast should both speak and cause as many as would not worship the image of the beast to be killed. [16] He causes all, both small and great, rich and poor, free and slave, to receive a mark on their right hand or on their foreheads, [17] and that no one may buy or sell except one who has the mark or[f] the name of the beast, or the number of his name.

[18] Here is wisdom. Let him who has understanding calculate the number of the beast, for it is the number of a man: His number *is* 666.

Footnotes:

a. Revelation 13:1 NU-Text reads *he.*
b. Revelation 13:1 NU-Text and M-Text read *ten horns and seven heads.*
c. Revelation 13:5 M-Text reads *make war.*
d. Revelation 13:7 NU-Text and M-Text add *and people.*
e. Revelation 13:14 M-Text reads *my own people.*
f. Revelation 13:17 NU-Text and M-Text omit *or.*

(NKJV)

(6) Mark of the Beast

Revelation 13 – New Testament
Revelation 14 – New Testament

Revelation 13 (NKJV)

The Beast from the Sea

13 Then I[a] stood on the sand of the sea. And I saw a beast rising up out of the sea, having seven heads and ten horns,[b] and on his horns ten crowns, and on his heads a blasphemous name. [2] Now the beast which I saw was like a leopard, his feet were like *the feet of* a bear, and his mouth like the mouth of a lion. The dragon gave him his power, his throne, and great authority. [3] And I saw one of his heads as if it had been mortally wounded, and his deadly wound was healed. And all the world marveled and followed the beast. [4] So they worshiped the dragon who gave authority to the beast; and they worshiped the beast, saying, "Who *is* like the beast? Who is able to make war with him?"

[5] And he was given a mouth speaking great things and blasphemies, and he was given authority to continue[c] for forty-two months. [6] Then he opened his mouth in blasphemy against God, to blaspheme His name, His tabernacle, and those who dwell in heaven. [7] It was granted to him to make war with the saints and to overcome them. And authority was given him over every tribe,[d] tongue, and nation. [8] All who dwell on the earth will worship him, whose names have not been written in the Book of Life of the Lamb slain from the foundation of the world.

[9] If anyone has an ear, let him hear. [10] He who leads into captivity shall go into captivity; he who kills with the sword must be killed with the sword. Here is the patience and the faith of the saints.

The Beast from the Earth

[11] Then I saw another beast coming up out of the earth, and he had two horns like a lamb and spoke like a dragon. [12] And he exercises all the authority of the first beast in his presence, and causes the earth and those who dwell in it to worship the first beast, whose deadly

wound was healed. [13] He performs great signs, so that he even makes fire come down from heaven on the earth in the sight of men. [14] And he deceives those[e] who dwell on the earth by those signs which he was granted to do in the sight of the beast, telling those who dwell on the earth to make an image to the beast who was wounded by the sword and lived. [15] He was granted *power* to give breath to the image of the beast, that the image of the beast should both speak and cause as many as would not worship the image of the beast to be killed. [16] **He causes all, both small and great, rich and poor, free and slave, to receive a mark on their right hand or on their foreheads,** [17] **and that no one may buy or sell except one who has the mark or[f] the name of the beast, or the number of his name.**

[18] **Here is wisdom. Let him who has understanding calculate the number of the beast, for it is the number of a man: His number *is* 666.**

Footnotes:

  a. Revelation 13:1 NU-Text reads *he.*
  b. Revelation 13:1 NU-Text and M-Text read *ten horns and seven heads.*
  c. Revelation 13:5 M-Text reads *make war.*
  d. Revelation 13:7 NU-Text and M-Text add *and people.*
  e. Revelation 13:14 M-Text reads *my own people.*
  f. Revelation 13:17 NU-Text and M-Text omit *or.*

(NKJV)

Revelation 14 (NKJV)

The Lamb and the 144,000

14 Then I looked, and behold, a[a] Lamb standing on Mount Zion, and with Him one hundred *and* forty-four thousand, having[b] His Father's name written on their foreheads. [2] And I heard a voice from heaven, like the voice of many waters, and like the voice of loud thunder. And I heard the sound of harpists playing their harps. [3] They sang as it were a new song before the throne, before the four living creatures, and the elders; and no one could learn that song except the hundred *and* forty-four thousand who were redeemed from the earth. [4] These are the ones who were not defiled with women, for they are virgins. These are the ones who follow the Lamb wherever He goes. These were redeemed[c] from *among* men, *being* firstfruits to God and to the Lamb. [5] And in their mouth was found no deceit,[d] for they are without fault before the throne of God.[e]

The Proclamations of Three Angels

[6] Then I saw another angel flying in the midst of heaven, having the everlasting gospel to preach to those who dwell on the earth—to every nation, tribe, tongue, and people— [7] saying with a loud voice, "Fear God and give glory to Him, for the hour of His judgment has come; and worship Him who made heaven and earth, the sea and springs of water."

[8] And another angel followed, saying, "Babylon[f] is fallen, is fallen, that great city, because she has made all nations drink of the wine of the wrath of her fornication."

[9] **Then a third angel followed them, saying with a loud voice, "If anyone worships the beast and his image, and receives *his* mark on his forehead or on his hand, [10] he himself shall also drink of the wine of the wrath of God, which is poured out full strength into**

the cup of His indignation. He shall be tormented with fire and brimstone in the presence of the holy angels and in the presence of the Lamb. ¹¹ And the smoke of their torment ascends forever and ever; and they have no rest day or night, who worship the beast and his image, and whoever receives the mark of his name."

¹² Here is the patience of the saints; here *are* those[g] who keep the commandments of God and the faith of Jesus.

¹³ Then I heard a voice from heaven saying to me,[h] "Write: 'Blessed *are* the dead who die in the Lord from now on.'"

"Yes," says the Spirit, "that they may rest from their labors, and their works follow them."

Reaping the Earth's Harvest

¹⁴ Then I looked, and behold, a white cloud, and on the cloud sat *One* like the Son of Man, having on His head a golden crown, and in His hand a sharp sickle. ¹⁵ And another angel came out of the temple, crying with a loud voice to Him who sat on the cloud, "Thrust in Your sickle and reap, for the time has come for You[i] to reap, for the harvest of the earth is ripe." ¹⁶ So He who sat on the cloud thrust in His sickle on the earth, and the earth was reaped.

Reaping the Grapes of Wrath

¹⁷ Then another angel came out of the temple which is in heaven, he also having a sharp sickle.

¹⁸ And another angel came out from the altar, who had power over fire, and he cried with a loud cry to him who had the sharp sickle, saying, "Thrust in your sharp sickle and gather the clusters of the vine of the earth, for her grapes are fully ripe." ¹⁹ So the angel thrust his sickle into the earth and gathered the vine of the earth, and threw *it* into the great winepress of the wrath of God. ²⁰ And the winepress was trampled outside the city, and blood came out of the

winepress, up to the horses' bridles, for one thousand six hundred furlongs.

Footnotes:

a. Revelation 14:1 NU-Text and M-Text read *the*.
b. Revelation 14:1 NU-Text and M-Text add *His name and*.
c. Revelation 14:4 M-Text adds *by Jesus*.
d. Revelation 14:5 NU-Text and M-Text read *falsehood*.
e. Revelation 14:5 NU-Text and M-Text omit *before the throne of God*.
f. Revelation 14:8 NU-Text reads *Babylon the great is fallen, is fallen, which has made;* M-Text reads *Babylon the great is fallen. She has made*.
g. Revelation 14:12 NU-Text and M-Text omit *here are those*.
h. Revelation 14:13 NU-Text and M-Text omit *to me*.
i. Revelation 14:15 NU-Text and M-Text omit *for You*.

(NKJV)

James Robert Waugh

(7) The Destruction of the Holy people (Saints and Prophets)

Daniel 8 – Old Testament
Daniel 12 – Old Testament
Revelation 17 – New Testament
Revelation 18 – New Testament
Revelation 19 – New Testament

Daniel 8 (NKJV)

Vision of a Ram and a Goat

8 In the third year of the reign of King Belshazzar a vision appeared *to* me—to me, Daniel—after the one that appeared to me the first time. ² I saw in the vision, and it so happened while I was looking, that I *was* in Shushan, the citadel, which *is* in the province of Elam; and I saw in the vision that I was by the River Ulai. ³ Then I lifted my eyes and saw, and there, standing beside the river, was a ram which had two horns, and the two horns *were* high; but one *was* higher than the other, and the higher *one* came up last. ⁴ I saw the ram pushing westward, northward, and southward, so that no animal could withstand him; nor *was there any* that could deliver from his hand, but he did according to his will and became great.

⁵ And as I was considering, suddenly a male goat came from the west, across the surface of the whole earth, without touching the ground; and the goat *had* a notable horn between his eyes. ⁶ Then he came to the ram that had two horns, which I had seen standing beside the river, and ran at him with furious power. ⁷ And I saw him confronting the ram; he was moved with rage against him, attacked the ram, and broke his two horns. There was no power in the ram to withstand him, but he cast him down to the ground and trampled him; and there was no one that could deliver the ram from his hand.

⁸ Therefore the male goat grew very great; but when he became strong, the large horn was broken, and in place of it four notable ones came up toward the four winds of heaven. ⁹ And out of one of them came a little horn which grew exceedingly great toward the south, toward the east, and toward the Glorious *Land.* ¹⁰ And it grew up to the host of heaven; and it cast down *some* of the host and *some* of the stars to the ground, and trampled them. ¹¹ He even exalted *himself* as high as the Prince of the host; and by him the daily *sacrifices* were taken away, and the place of His sanctuary was cast down. ¹² Because of transgression, an army was given over *to the horn*

to oppose the daily *sacrifices;* and he cast truth down to the ground. He did *all this* and prospered.

[13] Then I heard a holy one speaking; and *another* holy one said to that certain *one* who was speaking, "How long *will* the vision *be, concerning* the daily *sacrifices* and the transgression of desolation, the giving of both the sanctuary and the host to be trampled underfoot?"

[14] And he said to me, "For two thousand three hundred days;[a] then the sanctuary shall be cleansed."

Gabriel Interprets the Vision

[15] Then it happened, when I, Daniel, had seen the vision and was seeking the meaning, that suddenly there stood before me one having the appearance of a man. [16] And I heard a man's voice between *the banks of* the Ulai, who called, and said, "Gabriel, make this *man* understand the vision." [17] So he came near where I stood, and when he came I was afraid and fell on my face; but he said to me, "Understand, son of man, that the vision *refers* to the time of the end."

[18] Now, as he was speaking with me, I was in a deep sleep with my face to the ground; but he touched me, and stood me upright. [19] And he said, "Look, I am making known to you what shall happen in the latter time of the indignation; for at the appointed time the end *shall be.* [20] The ram which you saw, having the two horns—*they are* the kings of Media and Persia. [21] And the male goat *is* the kingdom[b] of Greece. The large horn that *is* between its eyes *is* the first king. [22] As for the broken *horn* and the four that stood up in its place, four kingdoms shall arise out of that nation, but not with its power.

[23] "And in the latter time of their kingdom,
When the transgressors have reached their fullness,
A king shall arise,
Having fierce features,
Who understands sinister schemes.

[24] His power shall be mighty, but not by his own power;
He shall destroy fearfully,
And shall prosper and thrive;
He shall destroy the mighty, and *also* the holy people.

[25] "Through his cunning
He shall cause deceit to prosper under his rule;[c]
And he shall exalt *himself* in his heart.
He shall destroy many in *their* prosperity.
He shall even rise against the Prince of princes;
But he shall be broken without *human* means.[d]

[26] "And the vision of the evenings and mornings
Which was told is true;
Therefore seal up the vision,
For *it refers* to many days *in the future.*"

[27] And I, Daniel, fainted and was sick for days; afterward I arose and went about the king's business. I was astonished by the vision, but no one understood it.

Footnotes:

  a. Daniel 8:14 Literally *evening-mornings*
  b. Daniel 8:21 Literally *king,* representing his kingdom (compare 7:17, 23)
  c. Daniel 8:25 Literally *hand*
  d. Daniel 8:25 Literally *hand*

(NKJV)

James Robert Waugh

Daniel 12 (NKJV)

Prophecy of the End Time

12 "At that time Michael shall stand up,
The great prince who stands *watch* over the sons of your people;
And there shall be a time of trouble,
Such as never was since there was a nation,
Even to that time.
And at that time your people shall be delivered,
Every one who is found written in the book.
[2] And many of those who sleep in the dust of the earth shall awake,
Some to everlasting life,
Some to shame *and* everlasting contempt.
[3] Those who are wise shall shine
Like the brightness of the firmament,
And those who turn many to righteousness
Like the stars forever and ever.

[4] "But you, Daniel, shut up the words, and seal the book until the time of the end; many shall run to and fro, and knowledge shall increase."

[5] Then I, Daniel, looked; and there stood two others, one on this riverbank and the other on that riverbank. [6] And *one* said to the man clothed in linen, who *was* above the waters of the river, "How long shall the fulfillment of these wonders *be*?"

[7] **Then I heard the man clothed in linen, who *was* above the waters of the river, when he held up his right hand and his left hand to heaven, and swore by Him who lives forever, that *it shall be* for a time, times, and half *a time*; and when the power of the holy people has been completely shattered, all these *things* shall be finished.**

160

[8] Although I heard, I did not understand. Then I said, "My lord, what *shall be* the end of these *things?"*

[9] And he said, "Go *your way*, Daniel, for the words *are* closed up and sealed till the time of the end. [10] Many shall be purified, made white, and refined, but the wicked shall do wickedly; and none of the wicked shall understand, but the wise shall understand.

[11] "And from the time *that* the daily *sacrifice* is taken away, and the abomination of desolation is set up, *there shall be* one thousand two hundred and ninety days. [12] Blessed *is* he who waits, and comes to the one thousand three hundred and thirty-five days.

[13] "But you, go *your way* till the end; for you shall rest, and will arise to your inheritance at the end of the days."

(NKJV)

Revelation 17 (NKJV)

The Scarlet Woman and the Scarlet Beast

17 Then one of the seven angels who had the seven bowls came and talked with me, saying to me,[a] "Come, I will show you the judgment of the great harlot who sits on many waters, 2 with whom the kings of the earth committed fornication, and the inhabitants of the earth were made drunk with the wine of her fornication."

3 So he carried me away in the Spirit into the wilderness. And I saw a woman sitting on a scarlet beast *which was* full of names of blasphemy, having seven heads and ten horns. 4 The woman was arrayed in purple and scarlet, and adorned with gold and precious stones and pearls, having in her hand a golden cup full of abominations and the filthiness of her fornication.[b] 5 And on her forehead a name *was* written:

MYSTERY, BABYLON THE GREAT,
THE MOTHER OF HARLOTS
AND OF THE ABOMINATIONS
OF THE EARTH.

6 I saw the woman, drunk with the blood of the saints and with the blood of the martyrs of Jesus. And when I saw her, I marveled with great amazement.

The Meaning of the Woman and the Beast

7 But the angel said to me, "Why did you marvel? I will tell you the mystery of the woman and of the beast that carries her, which has the seven heads and the ten horns. 8 The beast that you saw was, and is not, and will ascend out of the bottomless pit and go to perdition.

And those who dwell on the earth will marvel, whose names are not written in the Book of Life from the foundation of the world, when they see the beast that was, and is not, and yet is.[c]

9 "Here *is* the mind which has wisdom: The seven heads are seven mountains on which the woman sits. 10 There are also seven kings. Five have fallen, one is, *and* the other has not yet come. And when he comes, he must continue a short time. 11 The beast that was, and is not, is himself also the eighth, and is of the seven, and is going to perdition.

12 "The ten horns which you saw are ten kings who have received no kingdom as yet, but they receive authority for one hour as kings with the beast. 13 These are of one mind, and they will give their power and authority to the beast. 14 These will make war with the Lamb, and the Lamb will overcome them, for He is Lord of lords and King of kings; and those *who are* with Him *are* called, chosen, and faithful."

15 Then he said to me, "The waters which you saw, where the harlot sits, are peoples, multitudes, nations, and tongues. 16 And the ten horns which you saw on[d] the beast, these will hate the harlot, make her desolate and naked, eat her flesh and burn her with fire. 17 For God has put it into their hearts to fulfill His purpose, to be of one mind, and to give their kingdom to the beast, until the words of God are fulfilled. 18 And the woman whom you saw is that great city which reigns over the kings of the earth."

Footnotes:

a. Revelation 17:1 NU-Text and M-Text omit *to me.*
b. Revelation 17:4 M-Text reads *the filthiness of the fornication of the earth.*
c. Revelation 17:8 NU-Text and M-Text read *and shall be present.*
d. Revelation 17:16 NU-Text and M-Text read *saw, and the beast.*

(NKJV)

Revelation 18 (NKJV)

The Fall of Babylon the Great

18 After these things I saw another angel coming down from heaven, having great authority, and the earth was illuminated with his glory. [2] And he cried mightily[a] with a loud voice, saying, "Babylon the great is fallen, is fallen, and has become a dwelling place of demons, a prison for every foul spirit, and a cage for every unclean and hated bird! [3] For all the nations have drunk of the wine of the wrath of her fornication, the kings of the earth have committed fornication with her, and the merchants of the earth have become rich through the abundance of her luxury."

[4] And I heard another voice from heaven saying, "Come out of her, my people, lest you share in her sins, and lest you receive of her plagues. [5] For her sins have reached[b] to heaven, and God has remembered her iniquities. [6] Render to her just as she rendered to you,[c] and repay her double according to her works; in the cup which she has mixed, mix double for her. [7] In the measure that she glorified herself and lived luxuriously, in the same measure give her torment and sorrow; for she says in her heart, 'I sit *as* queen, and am no widow, and will not see sorrow.' [8] Therefore her plagues will come in one day—death and mourning and famine. And she will be utterly burned with fire, for strong *is* the Lord God who judges[d] her.

The World Mourns Babylon's Fall

[9] "The kings of the earth who committed fornication and lived luxuriously with her will weep and lament for her, when they see the smoke of her burning, [10] standing at a distance for fear of her torment, saying, 'Alas, alas, that great city Babylon, that mighty city! For in one hour your judgment has come.'

[11] "And the merchants of the earth will weep and mourn over her, for no one buys their merchandise anymore: [12] merchandise of gold

and silver, precious stones and pearls, fine linen and purple, silk and scarlet, every kind of citron wood, every kind of object of ivory, every kind of object of most precious wood, bronze, iron, and marble; [13] and cinnamon and incense, fragrant oil and frankincense, wine and oil, fine flour and wheat, cattle and sheep, horses and chariots, and bodies and souls of men. [14] The fruit that your soul longed for has gone from you, and all the things which are rich and splendid have gone from you,[e] and you shall find them no more at all. [15] The merchants of these things, who became rich by her, will stand at a distance for fear of her torment, weeping and wailing, [16] and saying, 'Alas, alas, that great city that was clothed in fine linen, purple, and scarlet, and adorned with gold and precious stones and pearls! [17] For in one hour such great riches came to nothing.' Every shipmaster, all who travel by ship, sailors, and as many as trade on the sea, stood at a distance [18] and cried out when they saw the smoke of her burning, saying, 'What *is* like this great city?'

[19] "They threw dust on their heads and cried out, weeping and wailing, and saying, 'Alas, alas, that great city, in which all who had ships on the sea became rich by her wealth! For in one hour she is made desolate.'

[20] **"Rejoice over her, O heaven, and *you* holy apostles[f] and prophets, for God has avenged you on her!"**

Finality of Babylon's Fall

[21] Then a mighty angel took up a stone like a great millstone and threw *it* into the sea, saying, "Thus with violence the great city Babylon shall be thrown down, and shall not be found anymore. [22] The sound of harpists, musicians, flutists, and trumpeters shall not be heard in you anymore. No craftsman of any craft shall be found in you anymore, and the sound of a millstone shall not be heard in you anymore. [23] The light of a lamp shall not shine in you anymore, and the voice of bridegroom and bride shall not be heard in you anymore. For your merchants were the great men of the earth, for by your sorcery all the nations were deceived. [24] And in her was

found the blood of prophets and saints, and of all who were slain on the earth."

Footnotes:

    a. <u>Revelation 18:2</u> NU-Text and M-Text omit *mightily.*
    b. <u>Revelation 18:5</u> NU-Text and M-Text read *have been heaped up.*
    c. <u>Revelation 18:6</u> NU-Text and M-Text omit *to you.*
    d. <u>Revelation 18:8</u> NU-Text and M-Text read *has judged.*
    e. <u>Revelation 18:14</u> NU-Text and M-Text read *been lost to you.*
    f. <u>Revelation 18:20</u> NU-Text and M-Text read *saints and apostles.*

(NKJV)

Revelation 19 (NKJV)

Heaven Exults over Babylon

19 After these things I heard[a] a loud voice of a great multitude in heaven, saying, "Alleluia! Salvation and glory and honor and power *belong* to the Lord[b] our God! ² For true and righteous *are* His judgments, because He has judged the great harlot who corrupted the earth with her fornication; **and He has avenged on her the blood of His servants** *shed* **by her.**" ³ Again they said, "Alleluia! Her smoke rises up forever and ever!" ⁴ And the twenty-four elders and the four living creatures fell down and worshiped God who sat on the throne, saying, "Amen! Alleluia!" ⁵ Then a voice came from the throne, saying, "Praise our God, all you His servants and those who fear Him, both[c] small and great!"

⁶ And I heard, as it were, the voice of a great multitude, as the sound of many waters and as the sound of mighty thunderings, saying, "Alleluia! For the[d] Lord God Omnipotent reigns! ⁷ Let us be glad and rejoice and give Him glory, for the marriage of the Lamb has come, and His wife has made herself ready." ⁸ And to her it was granted to be arrayed in fine linen, clean and bright, for the fine linen is the righteous acts of the saints.

⁹ Then he said to me, "Write: 'Blessed *are* those who are called to the marriage supper of the Lamb!'" And he said to me, "These are the true sayings of God." ¹⁰ And I fell at his feet to worship him. But he said to me, "See *that you do* not *do that!* I am your fellow servant, and of your brethren who have the testimony of Jesus. Worship God! For the testimony of Jesus is the spirit of prophecy."

Christ on a White Horse

¹¹ Now I saw heaven opened, and behold, a white horse. And He who sat on him *was* called Faithful and True, and in righteousness He judges and makes war. ¹² His eyes *were* like a flame of fire, and

on His head *were* many crowns. He had[e] a name written that no one knew except Himself. [13] He *was* clothed with a robe dipped in blood, and His name is called The Word of God. [14] And the armies in heaven, clothed in fine linen, white and clean,[f] followed Him on white horses. [15] Now out of His mouth goes a sharp[g] sword, that with it He should strike the nations. And He Himself will rule them with a rod of iron. He Himself treads the winepress of the fierceness and wrath of Almighty God. [16] And He has on *His* robe and on His thigh a name written:

KING OF KINGS AND
LORD OF LORDS.

The Beast and His Armies Defeated

[17] Then I saw an angel standing in the sun; and he cried with a loud voice, saying to all the birds that fly in the midst of heaven, "Come and gather together for the supper of the great God,[h] [18] that you may eat the flesh of kings, the flesh of captains, the flesh of mighty men, the flesh of horses and of those who sit on them, and the flesh of all *people,* free[i] and slave, both small and great."

[19] And I saw the beast, the kings of the earth, and their armies, gathered together to make war against Him who sat on the horse and against His army. [20] Then the beast was captured, and with him the false prophet who worked signs in his presence, by which he deceived those who received the mark of the beast and those who worshiped his image. These two were cast alive into the lake of fire burning with brimstone. [21] And the rest were killed with the sword which proceeded from the mouth of Him who sat on the horse. And all the birds were filled with their flesh.

Footnotes:

a. Revelation 19:1 NU-Text and M-Text add *something like.*
b. Revelation 19:1 NU-Text and M-Text omit *the Lord.*
c. Revelation 19:5 NU-Text and M-Text omit *both.*

d. <u>Revelation 19:6</u> NU-Text and M-Text read *our.*
e. <u>Revelation 19:12</u> M-Text adds *names written, and.*
f. <u>Revelation 19:14</u> NU-Text and M-Text read *pure white linen.*
g. <u>Revelation 19:15</u> M-Text adds *two-edged.*
h. <u>Revelation 19:17</u> NU-Text and M-Text read *the great supper of God.*
i. <u>Revelation 19:18</u> NU-Text and M-Text read *both free.*

(NKJV)

(8) Six things the Lord hates, seven are an abomination to Him

Proverbs 6 – Old Testament

Proverbs 6 (NKJV)

Dangerous Promises

6 My son, if you become surety for your friend,
If you have shaken hands in pledge for a stranger,
[2] You are snared by the words of your mouth;
You are taken by the words of your mouth.
[3] So do this, my son, and deliver yourself;
For you have come into the hand of your friend:
Go and humble yourself;
Plead with your friend.
[4] Give no sleep to your eyes,
Nor slumber to your eyelids.
[5] Deliver yourself like a gazelle from the hand *of the hunter,*
And like a bird from the hand of the fowler.[a]

The Folly of Indolence

[6] Go to the ant, you sluggard!
Consider her ways and be wise,
[7] Which, having no captain,
Overseer or ruler,
[8] Provides her supplies in the summer,
And gathers her food in the harvest.
[9] How long will you slumber, O sluggard?
When will you rise from your sleep?
[10] A little sleep, a little slumber,
A little folding of the hands to sleep—
[11] So shall your poverty come on you like a prowler,
And your need like an armed man.

The Wicked Man

[12] A worthless person, a wicked man,
Walks with a perverse mouth;

¹³ He winks with his eyes,
He shuffles his feet,
He points with his fingers;
¹⁴ Perversity *is* in his heart,
He devises evil continually,
He sows discord.
¹⁵ Therefore his calamity shall come suddenly;
Suddenly he shall be broken without remedy.

¹⁶ These six *things* the LORD hates,
Yes, seven *are* an abomination to Him:
¹⁷ A proud look,
A lying tongue,
Hands that shed innocent blood,
¹⁸ A heart that devises wicked plans,
Feet that are swift in running to evil,
¹⁹ A false witness *who* speaks lies,
And one who sows discord among brethren.

Beware of Adultery

²⁰ My son, keep your father's command,
And do not forsake the law of your mother.
²¹ Bind them continually upon your heart;
Tie them around your neck.
²² When you roam, they[b] will lead you;
When you sleep, they will keep you;
And *when* you awake, they will speak with you.
²³ For the commandment *is* a lamp,
And the law a light;
Reproofs of instruction *are* the way of life,
²⁴ To keep you from the evil woman,
From the flattering tongue of a seductress.
²⁵ Do not lust after her beauty in your heart,
Nor let her allure you with her eyelids.
²⁶ For by means of a harlot
A *man is reduced* to a crust of bread;

And an adulteress[c] will prey upon his precious life.
[27] Can a man take fire to his bosom,
And his clothes not be burned?
[28] Can one walk on hot coals,
And his feet not be seared?
[29] So *is* he who goes in to his neighbor's wife;
Whoever touches her shall not be innocent.

[30] *People* do not despise a thief
If he steals to satisfy himself when he is starving.
[31] Yet *when* he is found, he must restore sevenfold;
He may have to give up all the substance of his house.
[32] Whoever commits adultery with a woman lacks understanding;
He *who* does so destroys his own soul.
[33] Wounds and dishonor he will get,
And his reproach will not be wiped away.
[34] For jealousy *is* a husband's fury;
Therefore he will not spare in the day of vengeance.
[35] He will accept no recompense,
Nor will he be appeased though you give many gifts.

Footnotes:

a. Proverbs 6:5 That is, one who catches birds in a trap or snare
b. Proverbs 6:22 Literally *it*
c. Proverbs 6:26 Literally *a man's wife*, that is, of another

(NKJV)

James Robert Waugh

(9) A Country's Borders

Genesis 22 – Old Testament
Genesis 24 - Old Testament
Deuteronomy 28 – Old Testament

Genesis 22 (NKJV)

Abraham's Faith Confirmed

22 Now it came to pass after these things that God tested Abraham, and said to him, "Abraham!"

And he said, "Here I am."

[2] Then He said, "Take now your son, your only *son* Isaac, whom you love, and go to the land of Moriah, and offer him there as a burnt offering on one of the mountains of which I shall tell you."

[3] So Abraham rose early in the morning and saddled his donkey, and took two of his young men with him, and Isaac his son; and he split the wood for the burnt offering, and arose and went to the place of which God had told him. [4] Then on the third day Abraham lifted his eyes and saw the place afar off. [5] And Abraham said to his young men, "Stay here with the donkey; the lad[a] and I will go yonder and worship, and we will come back to you."

[6] So Abraham took the wood of the burnt offering and laid *it* on Isaac his son; and he took the fire in his hand, and a knife, and the two of them went together. [7] But Isaac spoke to Abraham his father and said, "My father!"

And he said, "Here I am, my son."

Then he said, "Look, the fire and the wood, but where *is* the lamb for a burnt offering?"

[8] And Abraham said, "My son, God will provide for Himself the lamb for a burnt offering." So the two of them went together.

[9] Then they came to the place of which God had told him. And Abraham built an altar there and placed the wood in order; and he

bound Isaac his son and laid him on the altar, upon the wood. ¹⁰ And Abraham stretched out his hand and took the knife to slay his son.

¹¹ But the Angel of the LORD called to him from heaven and said, "Abraham, Abraham!"

So he said, "Here I am."

¹² And He said, "Do not lay your hand on the lad, or do anything to him; for now I know that you fear God, since you have not withheld your son, your only *son,* from Me."

¹³ Then Abraham lifted his eyes and looked, and there behind *him was* a ram caught in a thicket by its horns. So Abraham went and took the ram, and offered it up for a burnt offering instead of his son. ¹⁴ And Abraham called the name of the place, The-LORD-Will-Provide;[b] as it is said *to* this day, "In the Mount of the LORD it shall be provided."

¹⁵ Then the Angel of the LORD called to Abraham a second time out of heaven, ¹⁶ and said: "By Myself I have sworn, says the LORD, because you have done this thing, and have not withheld your son, your only *son*— ¹⁷ **blessing I will bless you, and multiplying I will multiply your descendants as the stars of the heaven and as the sand which *is* on the seashore; and your descendants shall possess the gate of their enemies.** ¹⁸ In your seed all the nations of the earth shall be blessed, because you have obeyed My voice." ¹⁹ So Abraham returned to his young men, and they rose and went together to Beersheba; and Abraham dwelt at Beersheba.

The Family of Nahor

²⁰ Now it came to pass after these things that it was told Abraham, saying, "Indeed Milcah also has borne children to your brother Nahor: ²¹ Huz his firstborn, Buz his brother, Kemuel the father of Aram, ²² Chesed, Hazo, Pildash, Jidlaph, and Bethuel." ²³ And Bethuel begot Rebekah.[c] These eight Milcah bore to Nahor, Abraham's

brother. [24] His concubine, whose name was Reumah, also bore Tebah, Gaham, Thahash, and Maachah.

Footnotes:

a. Genesis 22:5 Or *young man*
b. Genesis 22:14 Hebrew *YHWH Yireh*
c. Genesis 22:23 Spelled *Rebecca* in Romans 9:10

(NKJV)

Genesis 24 (NKJV)

A Bride for Isaac

24 Now Abraham was old, well advanced in age; and the LORD had blessed Abraham in all things. [2] So Abraham said to the oldest servant of his house, who ruled over all that he had, "Please, put your hand under my thigh, [3] and I will make you swear by the LORD, the God of heaven and the God of the earth, that you will not take a wife for my son from the daughters of the Canaanites, among whom I dwell; [4] but you shall go to my country and to my family, and take a wife for my son Isaac."

[5] And the servant said to him, "Perhaps the woman will not be willing to follow me to this land. Must I take your son back to the land from which you came?"

[6] But Abraham said to him, "Beware that you do not take my son back there. [7] The LORD God of heaven, who took me from my father's house and from the land of my family, and who spoke to me and swore to me, saying, 'To your descendants[a] I give this land,' He will send His angel before you, and you shall take a wife for my son from there. [8] And if the woman is not willing to follow you, then you will be released from this oath; only do not take my son back there." [9] So the servant put his hand under the thigh of Abraham his master, and swore to him concerning this matter.

[10] Then the servant took ten of his master's camels and departed, for all his master's goods *were in* his hand. And he arose and went to Mesopotamia, to the city of Nahor. [11] And he made his camels kneel down outside the city by a well of water at evening time, the time when women go out to draw *water.* [12] Then he said, "O LORD God of my master Abraham, please give me success this day, and show kindness to my master Abraham. [13] Behold, *here* I stand by the well of water, and the daughters of the men of the city are coming out to draw water. [14] Now let it be that the young woman to whom I say, 'Please let down your pitcher that I may drink,' and she says, 'Drink,

and I will also give your camels a drink'—*let* her *be the one* You have appointed for Your servant Isaac. And by this I will know that You have shown kindness to my master."

[15] And it happened, before he had finished speaking, that behold, Rebekah, who was born to Bethuel, son of Milcah, the wife of Nahor, Abraham's brother, came out with her pitcher on her shoulder. [16] Now the young woman *was* very beautiful to behold, a virgin; no man had known her. And she went down to the well, filled her pitcher, and came up. [17] And the servant ran to meet her and said, "Please let me drink a little water from your pitcher."

[18] So she said, "Drink, my lord." Then she quickly let her pitcher down to her hand, and gave him a drink. [19] And when she had finished giving him a drink, she said, "I will draw *water* for your camels also, until they have finished drinking." [20] Then she quickly emptied her pitcher into the trough, ran back to the well to draw *water,* and drew for all his camels. [21] And the man, wondering at her, remained silent so as to know whether the LORD had made his journey prosperous or not.

[22] So it was, when the camels had finished drinking, that the man took a golden nose ring weighing half a shekel, and two bracelets for her wrists weighing ten *shekels* of gold, [23] and said, "Whose daughter *are* you? Tell me, please, is there room *in* your father's house for us to lodge?"

[24] So she said to him, "I *am* the daughter of Bethuel, Milcah's son, whom she bore to Nahor." [25] Moreover she said to him, "We have both straw and feed enough, and room to lodge."

[26] Then the man bowed down his head and worshiped the LORD. [27] And he said, "Blessed *be* the LORD God of my master Abraham, who has not forsaken His mercy and His truth toward my master. As for me, being on the way, the LORD led me to the house of my master's brethren." [28] So the young woman ran and told her mother's household these things.

²⁹ Now Rebekah had a brother whose name *was* Laban, and Laban ran out to the man by the well. ³⁰ So it came to pass, when he saw the nose ring, and the bracelets on his sister's wrists, and when he heard the words of his sister Rebekah, saying, "Thus the man spoke to me," that he went to the man. And there he stood by the camels at the well. ³¹ And he said, "Come in, O blessed of the LORD! Why do you stand outside? For I have prepared the house, and a place for the camels."

³² Then the man came to the house. And he unloaded the camels, and provided straw and feed for the camels, and water to wash his feet and the feet of the men who *were* with him. ³³ *Food* was set before him to eat, but he said, "I will not eat until I have told about my errand."

And he said, "Speak on."

³⁴ So he said, "I *am* Abraham's servant. ³⁵ The LORD has blessed my master greatly, and he has become great; and He has given him flocks and herds, silver and gold, male and female servants, and camels and donkeys. ³⁶ And Sarah my master's wife bore a son to my master when she was old; and to him he has given all that he has. ³⁷ Now my master made me swear, saying, 'You shall not take a wife for my son from the daughters of the Canaanites, in whose land I dwell; ³⁸ but you shall go to my father's house and to my family, and take a wife for my son.' ³⁹ And I said to my master, 'Perhaps the woman will not follow me.' ⁴⁰ But he said to me, 'The LORD, before whom I walk, will send His angel with you and prosper your way; and you shall take a wife for my son from my family and from my father's house. ⁴¹ You will be clear from this oath when you arrive among my family; for if they will not give *her* to you, then you will be released from my oath.'

⁴² "And this day I came to the well and said, 'O LORD God of my master Abraham, if You will now prosper the way in which I go, ⁴³ behold, I stand by the well of water; and it shall come to pass that when the virgin comes out to draw *water*, and I say to her, "Please give me a little water from your pitcher to drink," ⁴⁴ and she says

to me, "Drink, and I will draw for your camels also,"—*let* her *be* the woman whom the LORD has appointed for my master's son.'

⁴⁵ "But before I had finished speaking in my heart, there was Rebekah, coming out with her pitcher on her shoulder; and she went down to the well and drew *water.* And I said to her, 'Please let me drink.' ⁴⁶ And she made haste and let her pitcher down from her *shoulder,* and said, 'Drink, and I will give your camels a drink also.' So I drank, and she gave the camels a drink also. ⁴⁷ Then I asked her, and said, 'Whose daughter *are* you?' And she said, 'The daughter of Bethuel, Nahor's son, whom Milcah bore to him.' So I put the nose ring on her nose and the bracelets on her wrists. ⁴⁸ And I bowed my head and worshiped the LORD, and blessed the LORD God of my master Abraham, who had led me in the way of truth to take the daughter of my master's brother for his son. ⁴⁹ Now if you will deal kindly and truly with my master, tell me. And if not, tell me, that I may turn to the right hand or to the left."

⁵⁰ Then Laban and Bethuel answered and said, "The thing comes from the LORD; we cannot speak to you either bad or good. ⁵¹ Here *is* Rebekah before you; take *her* and go, and let her be your master's son's wife, as the LORD has spoken."

⁵² And it came to pass, when Abraham's servant heard their words, that he worshiped the LORD, *bowing himself* to the earth. ⁵³ Then the servant brought out jewelry of silver, jewelry of gold, and clothing, and gave *them* to Rebekah. He also gave precious things to her brother and to her mother.

⁵⁴ And he and the men who *were* with him ate and drank and stayed all night. Then they arose in the morning, and he said, "Send me away to my master."

⁵⁵ But her brother and her mother said, "Let the young woman stay with us *a few* days, at least ten; after that she may go."

⁵⁶ And he said to them, "Do not hinder me, since the L ORD has prospered my way; send me away so that I may go to my master."

⁵⁷ So they said, "We will call the young woman and ask her personally." ⁵⁸ Then they called Rebekah and said to her, "Will you go with this man?"

And she said, "I will go."

⁵⁹ So they sent away Rebekah their sister and her nurse, and Abraham's servant and his men. ⁶⁰ And they blessed Rebekah and said to her:

"Our sister, *may* you *become*
The mother of thousands of ten thousands;
And may your descendants possess
The gates of those who hate them."

⁶¹ Then Rebekah and her maids arose, and they rode on the camels and followed the man. So the servant took Rebekah and departed.

⁶² Now Isaac came from the way of Beer Lahai Roi, for he dwelt in the South. ⁶³ And Isaac went out to meditate in the field in the evening; and he lifted his eyes and looked, and there, the camels *were* coming. ⁶⁴ Then Rebekah lifted her eyes, and when she saw Isaac she dismounted from her camel; ⁶⁵ for she had said to the servant, "Who *is* this man walking in the field to meet us?"

The servant said, "It *is* my master." So she took a veil and covered herself.

⁶⁶ And the servant told Isaac all the things that he had done. ⁶⁷ Then Isaac brought her into his mother Sarah's tent; and he took Rebekah and she became his wife, and he loved her. So Isaac was comforted after his mother's *death.*

Footnotes:

a. <u>Genesis 24:7</u> Literally *seed*

(NKJV)

Deuteronomy 28 (NKJV)

Blessings on Obedience

28 "Now it shall come to pass, if you diligently obey the voice of the LORD your God, to observe carefully all His commandments which I command you today, that the LORD your God will set you high above all nations of the earth. ² And all these blessings shall come upon you and overtake you, because you obey the voice of the LORD your God:

³ "Blessed *shall* you *be* in the city, and blessed *shall* you *be* in the country.

⁴ "Blessed *shall be* the fruit of your body, the produce of your ground and the increase of your herds, the increase of your cattle and the offspring of your flocks.

⁵ "Blessed *shall be* your basket and your kneading bowl.

⁶ "Blessed *shall* you *be* when you come in, and blessed *shall* you *be* when you go out.

⁷ "The LORD will cause your enemies who rise against you to be defeated before your face; they shall come out against you one way and flee before you seven ways.

⁸ "The LORD will command the blessing on you in your storehouses and in all to which you set your hand, and He will bless you in the land which the LORD your God is giving you.

⁹ "The LORD will establish you as a holy people to Himself, just as He has sworn to you, if you keep the commandments of the LORD your God and walk in His ways. ¹⁰ Then all peoples of the earth shall see that you are called by the name of the LORD, and they shall be afraid of you. ¹¹ And the LORD will grant you plenty of goods, in the fruit of your body, in the increase of your livestock, and in the produce of your ground, in the land of which the LORD swore to your fathers

to give you. ¹² The Lord will open to you His good treasure, the heavens, to give the rain to your land in its season, and to bless all the work of your hand. **You shall lend to many nations, but you shall not borrow. ¹³ And the Lord will make you the head and not the tail; you shall be above only, and not be beneath, if you heed the commandments of the Lord your God, which I command you today, and are careful to observe** *them.* ¹⁴So you shall not turn aside from any of the words which I command you this day, *to* the right or the left, to go after other gods to serve them.

Curses on Disobedience

¹⁵ "But it shall come to pass, if you do not obey the voice of the Lord your God, to observe carefully all His commandments and His statutes which I command you today, that all these curses will come upon you and overtake you:

¹⁶ "Cursed *shall* you *be* in the city, and cursed *shall* you *be* in the country.

¹⁷ "Cursed *shall be* your basket and your kneading bowl.

¹⁸ "Cursed *shall be* the fruit of your body and the produce of your land, the increase of your cattle and the offspring of your flocks.

¹⁹ "Cursed *shall* you *be* when you come in, and cursed *shall* you *be* when you go out.

²⁰ "The Lord will send on you cursing, confusion, and rebuke in all that you set your hand to do, until you are destroyed and until you perish quickly, because of the wickedness of your doings in which you have forsaken Me. ²¹ The Lord will make the plague cling to you until He has consumed you from the land which you are going to possess. ²² The Lord will strike you with consumption, with fever, with inflammation, with severe burning fever, with the sword, with scorching, and with mildew; they shall pursue you until you perish. ²³ And your heavens which *are* over your head shall be bronze, and

the earth which is under you *shall be* iron. [24] The LORD will change the rain of your land to powder and dust; from the heaven it shall come down on you until you are destroyed.

[25] "The LORD will cause you to be defeated before your enemies; you shall go out one way against them and flee seven ways before them; and you shall become troublesome to all the kingdoms of the earth. [26] Your carcasses shall be food for all the birds of the air and the beasts of the earth, and no one shall frighten *them* away. [27] The LORD will strike you with the boils of Egypt, with tumors, with the scab, and with the itch, from which you cannot be healed. [28] The LORD will strike you with madness and blindness and confusion of heart. [29] And you shall grope at noonday, as a blind man gropes in darkness; you shall not prosper in your ways; you shall be only oppressed and plundered continually, and no one shall save *you*.

[30] "You shall betroth a wife, but another man shall lie with her; you shall build a house, but you shall not dwell in it; you shall plant a vineyard, but shall not gather its grapes. [31] Your ox *shall be* slaughtered before your eyes, but you shall not eat of it; your donkey *shall be* violently taken away from before you, and shall not be restored to you; your sheep *shall be* given to your enemies, and you shall have no one to rescue *them*. [32] Your sons and your daughters *shall be* given to another people, and your eyes shall look and fail *with longing* for them all day long; and *there shall be* no strength in your hand. [33] A nation whom you have not known shall eat the fruit of your land and the produce of your labor, and you shall be only oppressed and crushed continually. [34] So you shall be driven mad because of the sight which your eyes see. [35] The LORD will strike you in the knees and on the legs with severe boils which cannot be healed, and from the sole of your foot to the top of your head.

[36] "The LORD will bring you and the king whom you set over you to a nation which neither you nor your fathers have known, and there you shall serve other gods—wood and stone. [37] And you shall become an astonishment, a proverb, and a byword among all nations where the LORD will drive you.

³⁸ "You shall carry much seed out to the field but gather little in, for the locust shall consume it. ³⁹ You shall plant vineyards and tend *them,* but you shall neither drink *of* the wine nor gather the *grapes;* for the worms shall eat them. ⁴⁰ You shall have olive trees throughout all your territory, but you shall not anoint *yourself* with the oil; for your olives shall drop off. ⁴¹ You shall beget sons and daughters, but they shall not be yours; for they shall go into captivity. ⁴² Locusts shall consume all your trees and the produce of your land.

⁴³ "The alien who is among you shall rise higher and higher above you, and you shall come down lower and lower. ⁴⁴ He shall lend to you, but you shall not lend to him; he shall be the head, and you shall be the tail.

⁴⁵ "Moreover all these curses shall come upon you and pursue and overtake you, until you are destroyed, because you did not obey the voice of the LORD your God, to keep His commandments and His statutes which He commanded you. ⁴⁶ And they shall be upon you for a sign and a wonder, and on your descendants forever.

⁴⁷ "Because you did not serve the LORD your God with joy and gladness of heart, for the abundance of everything, ⁴⁸ therefore you shall serve your enemies, whom the LORD will send against you, in hunger, in thirst, in nakedness, and in need of everything; and He will put a yoke of iron on your neck until He has destroyed you. ⁴⁹ The LORD will bring a nation against you from afar, from the end of the earth, as swift as the eagle flies, a nation whose language you will not understand, ⁵⁰ a nation of fierce countenance, which does not respect the elderly nor show favor to the young. ⁵¹ And they shall eat the increase of your livestock and the produce of your land, until you are destroyed; they shall not leave you grain or new wine or oil, or the increase of your cattle or the offspring of your flocks, until they have destroyed you.

⁵² "They shall besiege you at all your gates until your high and fortified walls, in which you trust, come down throughout all your land; and they shall besiege you at all your gates throughout all your land which the LORD your God has given you. ⁵³ You shall

eat the fruit of your own body, the flesh of your sons and your daughters whom the LORD your God has given you, in the siege and desperate straits in which your enemy shall distress you. ⁵⁴ The sensitive and very refined man among you will be hostile toward his brother, toward the wife of his bosom, and toward the rest of his children whom he leaves behind, ⁵⁵ so that he will not give any of them the flesh of his children whom he will eat, because he has nothing left in the siege and desperate straits in which your enemy shall distress you at all your gates. ⁵⁶ The tender and delicate woman among you, who would not venture to set the sole of her foot on the ground because of her delicateness and sensitivity, will refuse[a] to the husband of her bosom, and to her son and her daughter, ⁵⁷ her placenta which comes out from between her feet and her children whom she bears; for she will eat them secretly for lack of everything in the siege and desperate straits in which your enemy shall distress you at all your gates.

⁵⁸ "If you do not carefully observe all the words of this law that are written in this book, that you may fear this glorious and awesome name, THE LORD YOUR GOD, ⁵⁹ then the LORD will bring upon you and your descendants extraordinary plagues—great and prolonged plagues—and serious and prolonged sicknesses. ⁶⁰ Moreover He will bring back on you all the diseases of Egypt, of which you were afraid, and they shall cling to you. ⁶¹ Also every sickness and every plague, which *is* not written in this Book of the Law, will the LORD bring upon you until you are destroyed. ⁶² You shall be left few in number, whereas you were as the stars of heaven in multitude, because you would not obey the voice of the LORD your God. ⁶³ And it shall be, *that* just as the LORD rejoiced over you to do you good and multiply you, so the LORD will rejoice over you to destroy you and bring you to nothing; and you shall be plucked from off the land which you go to possess.

⁶⁴ "Then the LORD will scatter you among all peoples, from one end of the earth to the other, and there you shall serve other gods, which neither you nor your fathers have known—wood and stone. ⁶⁵ And among those nations you shall find no rest, nor shall the sole of your foot have a resting place; but there the LORD will give you a

trembling heart, failing eyes, and anguish of soul. [66] Your life shall hang in doubt before you; you shall fear day and night, and have no assurance of life. [67] In the morning you shall say, 'Oh, that it were evening!' And at evening you shall say, 'Oh, that it were morning!' because of the fear which terrifies your heart, and because of the sight which your eyes see.

[68] "And the LORD will take you back to Egypt in ships, by the way of which I said to you, 'You shall never see it again.' And there you shall be offered for sale to your enemies as male and female slaves, but no one will buy *you.*"

Footnotes:

a. Deuteronomy 28:56 Literally *her eye shall be evil toward*

(NKJV)

(10) Elevating a Sin to Acceptable

Matthew 5 –New Testament

Matthew 5 (NKJV)

The Beatitudes

5 And seeing the multitudes, He went up on a mountain, and when He was seated His disciples came to Him. ² Then He opened His mouth and taught them, saying:

³ "Blessed *are* the poor in spirit,
For theirs is the kingdom of heaven.
⁴ Blessed *are* those who mourn,
For they shall be comforted.
⁵ Blessed *are* the meek,
For they shall inherit the earth.
⁶ Blessed *are* those who hunger and thirst for righteousness,
For they shall be filled.
⁷ Blessed *are* the merciful,
For they shall obtain mercy.
⁸ Blessed *are* the pure in heart,
For they shall see God.
⁹ Blessed *are* the peacemakers,
For they shall be called sons of God.
¹⁰ Blessed *are* those who are persecuted for righteousness' sake,
For theirs is the kingdom of heaven.

¹¹ "Blessed are you when they revile and persecute you, and say all kinds of evil against you falsely for My sake. ¹² Rejoice and be exceedingly glad, for great *is* your reward in heaven, for so they persecuted the prophets who were before you.

Believers Are Salt and Light

¹³ "You are the salt of the earth; but if the salt loses its flavor, how shall it be seasoned? It is then good for nothing but to be thrown out and trampled underfoot by men.

¹⁴ "You are the light of the world. A city that is set on a hill cannot be hidden. ¹⁵ Nor do they light a lamp and put it under a basket, but on a lampstand, and it gives light to all *who are* in the house. ¹⁶ Let your light so shine before men, that they may see your good works and glorify your Father in heaven.

Christ Fulfills the Law

¹⁷ **"Do not think that I came to destroy the Law or the Prophets. I did not come to destroy but to fulfill. ¹⁸ For assuredly, I say to you, till heaven and earth pass away, one jot or one tittle will by no means pass from the law till all is fulfilled. ¹⁹ Whoever therefore breaks one of the least of these commandments, and teaches men so, shall be called least in the kingdom of heaven; but whoever does and teaches *them*, he shall be called great in the kingdom of heaven. ²⁰ For I say to you, that unless your righteousness exceeds *the righteousness* of the scribes and Pharisees, you will by no means enter the kingdom of heaven.**

Murder Begins in the Heart

²¹ "You have heard that it was said to those of old, 'You shall not murder,[a] and whoever murders will be in danger of the judgment.' ²² But I say to you that whoever is angry with his brother without a cause[b] shall be in danger of the judgment. And whoever says to his brother, 'Raca!' shall be in danger of the council. But whoever says, 'You fool!' shall be in danger of hell fire. ²³ Therefore if you bring your gift to the altar, and there remember that your brother has something against you, ²⁴ leave your gift there before the altar, and go your way. First be reconciled to your brother, and then come and offer your gift. ²⁵ Agree with your adversary quickly, while you are on the way with him, lest your adversary deliver you to the judge, the judge hand you over to the officer, and you be thrown into prison. ²⁶ Assuredly, I say to you, you will by no means get out of there till you have paid the last penny.

Adultery in the Heart

27 "You have heard that it was said to those of old,[c] 'You shall not commit adultery.'[d] 28 But I say to you that whoever looks at a woman to lust for her has already committed adultery with her in his heart. 29 If your right eye causes you to sin, pluck it out and cast *it* from you; for it is more profitable for you that one of your members perish, than for your whole body to be cast into hell. 30 And if your right hand causes you to sin, cut it off and cast *it* from you; for it is more profitable for you that one of your members perish, than for your whole body to be cast into hell.

Marriage Is Sacred and Binding

31 "Furthermore it has been said, 'Whoever divorces his wife, let him give her a certificate of divorce.' 32 But I say to you that whoever divorces his wife for any reason except sexual immorality[e] causes her to commit adultery; and whoever marries a woman who is divorced commits adultery.

Jesus Forbids Oaths

33 "Again you have heard that it was said to those of old, 'You shall not swear falsely, but shall perform your oaths to the Lord.' 34 But I say to you, do not swear at all: neither by heaven, for it is God's throne; 35 nor by the earth, for it is His footstool; nor by Jerusalem, for it is the city of the great King. 36 Nor shall you swear by your head, because you cannot make one hair white or black. 37 But let your 'Yes' be 'Yes,' and your 'No,' 'No.' For whatever is more than these is from the evil one.

Go the Second Mile

38 "You have heard that it was said, 'An eye for an eye and a tooth for a tooth.'[f] 39 But I tell you not to resist an evil person. But whoever slaps you on your right cheek, turn the other to him also. 40 If anyone wants to sue you and take away your tunic, let him have *your* cloak

also. [41] And whoever compels you to go one mile, go with him two. [42] Give to him who asks you, and from him who wants to borrow from you do not turn away.

Love Your Enemies

[43] "You have heard that it was said, 'You shall love your neighbor[g] and hate your enemy.' [44] But I say to you, love your enemies, bless those who curse you, do good to those who hate you, and pray for those who spitefully use you and persecute you,[h] [45] that you may be sons of your Father in heaven; for He makes His sun rise on the evil and on the good, and sends rain on the just and on the unjust. [46] For if you love those who love you, what reward have you? Do not even the tax collectors do the same? [47] And if you greet your brethren[i] only, what do you do more *than others?* Do not even the tax collectors[j] do so? [48] Therefore you shall be perfect, just as your Father in heaven is perfect.

Footnotes:

a. Matthew 5:21 Exodus 20:13; Deuteronomy 5:17
b. Matthew 5:22 NU-Text omits *without a cause.*
c. Matthew 5:27 NU-Text and M-Text omit *to those of old.*
d. Matthew 5:27 Exodus 20:14; Deuteronomy 5:18
e. Matthew 5:32 Or *fornication*
f. Matthew 5:38 Exodus 21:24; Leviticus 24:20; Deuteronomy 19:21
g. Matthew 5:43 Compare Leviticus 19:18
h. Matthew 5:44 NU-Text omits three clauses from this verse, leaving, *"But I say to you, love your enemies and pray for those who persecute you."*
i. Matthew 5:47 M-Text reads *friends.*
j. Matthew 5:47 NU-Text reads *Gentiles.*

(NKJV)

(11) The Transgressors

Isaiah 1 – Old Testament
Isaiah 46 – Old Testament
Isaiah 48 – Old Testament
Isaiah 53 – Old Testament
Daniel 8 – Old Testament
Psalm 37 – Old Testament

Isaiah 1 (NKJV)

1 The vision of Isaiah the son of Amoz, which he saw concerning Judah and Jerusalem in the days of Uzziah, Jotham, Ahaz, *and* Hezekiah, kings of Judah.

The Wickedness of Judah

[2] Hear, O heavens, and give ear, O earth!
For the LORD has spoken:
"I have nourished and brought up children,
And they have rebelled against Me;
[3] The ox knows its owner
And the donkey its master's crib;
But Israel does not know,
My people do not consider."

[4] Alas, sinful nation,
A people laden with iniquity,
A brood of evildoers,
Children who are corrupters!
They have forsaken the LORD,
They have provoked to anger
The Holy One of Israel,
They have turned away backward.

[5] Why should you be stricken again?
You will revolt more and more.
The whole head is sick,
And the whole heart faints.
[6] From the sole of the foot even to the head,
There is no soundness in it,
But wounds and bruises and putrefying sores;
They have not been closed or bound up,
Or soothed with ointment.

⁷ Your country *is* desolate,
Your cities *are* burned with fire;
Strangers devour your land in your presence;
And *it is* desolate, as overthrown by strangers.
⁸ So the daughter of Zion is left as a booth in a vineyard,
As a hut in a garden of cucumbers,
As a besieged city.
⁹ Unless the LORD of hosts
Had left to us a very small remnant,
We would have become like Sodom,
We would have been made like Gomorrah.

¹⁰ Hear the word of the LORD,
You rulers of Sodom;
Give ear to the law of our God,
You people of Gomorrah:
¹¹ "To what purpose *is* the multitude of your sacrifices to Me?"
Says the LORD.
"I have had enough of burnt offerings of rams
And the fat of fed cattle.
I do not delight in the blood of bulls,
Or of lambs or goats.

¹² "When you come to appear before Me,
Who has required this from your hand,
To trample My courts?
¹³ Bring no more futile sacrifices;
Incense is an abomination to Me.
The New Moons, the Sabbaths, and the calling of assemblies—
I cannot endure iniquity and the sacred meeting.
¹⁴ Your New Moons and your appointed feasts
My soul hates;
They are a trouble to Me,
I am weary of bearing *them.*
¹⁵ When you spread out your hands,
I will hide My eyes from you;
Even though you make many prayers,

I will not hear.
Your hands are full of blood.

¹⁶ "Wash yourselves, make yourselves clean;
Put away the evil of your doings from before My eyes.
Cease to do evil,
¹⁷ Learn to do good;
Seek justice,
Rebuke the oppressor;[a]
Defend the fatherless,
Plead for the widow.

¹⁸ "Come now, and let us reason together,"
Says the LORD,
"Though your sins are like scarlet,
They shall be as white as snow;
Though they are red like crimson,
They shall be as wool.
¹⁹ If you are willing and obedient,
You shall eat the good of the land;
²⁰ But if you refuse and rebel,
You shall be devoured by the sword";
For the mouth of the LORD has spoken.

The Degenerate City

²¹ How the faithful city has become a harlot!
It was full of justice;
Righteousness lodged in it,
But now murderers.
²² Your silver has become dross,
Your wine mixed with water.
²³ Your princes *are* rebellious,
And companions of thieves;
Everyone loves bribes,
And follows after rewards.
They do not defend the fatherless,
Nor does the cause of the widow come before them.

²⁴ Therefore the Lord says,
The LORD of hosts, the Mighty One of Israel,
"Ah, I will rid Myself of My adversaries,
And take vengeance on My enemies.
²⁵ I will turn My hand against you,
And thoroughly purge away your dross,
And take away all your alloy.
²⁶ I will restore your judges as at the first,
And your counselors as at the beginning.
Afterward you shall be called the city of righteousness, the faithful city."

²⁷ Zion shall be redeemed with justice,
And her penitents with righteousness.
**²⁸ The destruction of transgressors and of sinners shall be together,
And those who forsake the LORD shall be consumed.
²⁹ For they[b] shall be ashamed of the terebinth trees
Which you have desired;
And you shall be embarrassed because of the gardens
Which you have chosen.
³⁰ For you shall be as a terebinth whose leaf fades,
And as a garden that has no water.
³¹ The strong shall be as tinder,
And the work of it as a spark;
Both will burn together,
And no one shall quench them.**

Footnotes:

a. Isaiah 1:17 Some ancient versions read *the oppressed.*
b. Isaiah 1:29 Following Masoretic Text, Septuagint, and Vulgate; some Hebrew manuscripts and Targum read *you.*

(NKJV)

James Robert Waugh

Isaiah 46 (NKJV)

Dead Idols and the Living God

46 Bel bows down, Nebo stoops;
Their idols were on the beasts and on the cattle.
Your carriages *were* heavily loaded,
A burden to the weary *beast.*
² They stoop, they bow down together;
They could not deliver the burden,
But have themselves gone into captivity.

³ "Listen to Me, O house of Jacob,
And all the remnant of the house of Israel,
Who have been upheld *by Me* from birth,
Who have been carried from the womb:
⁴ Even to *your* old age, I *am* He,
And *even* to gray hairs I will carry *you!*
I have made, and I will bear;
Even I will carry, and will deliver *you.*

⁵ "To whom will you liken Me, and make *Me* equal
And compare Me, that we should be alike?
⁶ They lavish gold out of the bag,
And weigh silver on the scales;
They hire a goldsmith, and he makes it a god;
They prostrate themselves, yes, they worship.
⁷ They bear it on the shoulder, they carry it
And set it in its place, and it stands;
From its place it shall not move.
Though *one* cries out to it, yet it cannot answer
Nor save him out of his trouble.

⁸ "Remember this, and show yourselves men;
Recall to mind, O you transgressors.
⁹ Remember the former things of old,

For I *am* God, and *there is* no other;
I am God, and *there is* none like Me,
[10] Declaring the end from the beginning,
And from ancient times *things* that are not *yet* done,
Saying, 'My counsel shall stand,
And I will do all My pleasure,'
[11] Calling a bird of prey from the east,
The man who executes My counsel, from a far country.
Indeed I have spoken *it;*
I will also bring it to pass.
I have purposed *it;*
I will also do it.

[12] "Listen to Me, you stubborn-hearted,
Who *are* far from righteousness:
[13] I bring My righteousness near, it shall not be far off;
My salvation shall not linger.
And I will place salvation in Zion,
For Israel My glory.

(NKJV)

Isaiah 48 (NKJV)

Israel Refined for God's Glory

48 "Hear this, O house of Jacob,
Who are called by the name of Israel,
And have come forth from the wellsprings of Judah;
Who swear by the name of the LORD,
And make mention of the God of Israel,
But not in truth or in righteousness;
² For they call themselves after the holy city,
And lean on the God of Israel;
The LORD of hosts *is* His name:

³ "I have declared the former things from the beginning;
They went forth from My mouth, and I caused them to hear it.
Suddenly I did *them,* and they came to pass.
⁴ Because I knew that you *were* obstinate,
And your neck *was* an iron sinew,
And your brow bronze,
⁵ Even from the beginning I have declared *it* to you;
Before it came to pass I proclaimed *it* to you,
Lest you should say, 'My idol has done them,
And my carved image and my molded image
Have commanded them.'

⁶ "You have heard;
See all this.
And will you not declare *it?*
I have made you hear new things from this time,
Even hidden things, and you did not know them.
⁷ They are created now and not from the beginning;
And before this day you have not heard them,
Lest you should say, 'Of course I knew them.'
⁸ **Surely you did not hear,**
Surely you did not know;

Surely from long ago your ear was not opened.
For I knew that you would deal very treacherously,
And were called a transgressor from the womb.

9 "For My name's sake I will defer My anger,
And *for* My praise I will restrain it from you,
So that I do not cut you off.
10 Behold, I have refined you, but not as silver;
I have tested you in the furnace of affliction.
11 For My own sake, for My own sake, I will do *it;*
For how should *My name* be profaned?
And I will not give My glory to another.

God's Ancient Plan to Redeem Israel

12 "Listen to Me, O Jacob,
And Israel, My called:
I *am* He, I *am* the First,
I *am* also the Last.
13 Indeed My hand has laid the foundation of the earth,
And My right hand has stretched out the heavens;
When I call to them,
They stand up together.

14 "All of you, assemble yourselves, and hear!
Who among them has declared these *things?*
The LORD loves him;
He shall do His pleasure on Babylon,
And His arm *shall be against* the Chaldeans.
15 I, *even* I, have spoken;
Yes, I have called him,
I have brought him, and his way will prosper.
16 "Come near to Me, hear this:
I have not spoken in secret from the beginning;
From the time that it was, I *was* there.
And now the Lord GOD and His Spirit
Have[a] sent Me."

[17] Thus says the LORD, your Redeemer,
The Holy One of Israel:
"I *am* the LORD your God,
Who teaches you to profit,
Who leads you by the way you should go.
[18] Oh, that you had heeded My commandments!
Then your peace would have been like a river,
And your righteousness like the waves of the sea.
[19] Your descendants also would have been like the sand,
And the offspring of your body like the grains of sand;
His name would not have been cut off
Nor destroyed from before Me."

[20] Go forth from Babylon!
Flee from the Chaldeans!
With a voice of singing,
Declare, proclaim this,
Utter it to the end of the earth;
Say, "The LORD has redeemed
His servant Jacob!"
[21] And they did not thirst
When He led them through the deserts;
He caused the waters to flow from the rock for them;
He also split the rock, and the waters gushed out.

[22] "*There is* no peace," says the LORD, "for the wicked."

Footnotes:

    a.   <u>Isaiah 48:16</u> The Hebrew verb is singular.

(NKJV)

Isaiah 53 (NKJV)

53 Who has believed our report?
And to whom has the arm of the LORD been revealed?
[2] For He shall grow up before Him as a tender plant,
And as a root out of dry ground.
He has no form or comeliness;
And when we see Him,
There is no beauty that we should desire Him.
[3] He is despised and rejected by men,
A Man of sorrows and acquainted with grief.
And we hid, as it were, *our* faces from Him;
He was despised, and we did not esteem Him.

[4] Surely He has borne our griefs
And carried our sorrows;
Yet we esteemed Him stricken,
Smitten by God, and afflicted.
[5] But He *was* wounded for our transgressions,
He was bruised for our iniquities;
The chastisement for our peace *was* upon Him,
And by His stripes we are healed.
[6] All we like sheep have gone astray;
We have turned, every one, to his own way;
And the LORD has laid on Him the iniquity of us all.

[7] He was oppressed and He was afflicted,
Yet He opened not His mouth;
He was led as a lamb to the slaughter,
And as a sheep before its shearers is silent,
So He opened not His mouth.
[8] He was taken from prison and from judgment,
And who will declare His generation?
For He was cut off from the land of the living;
For the transgressions of My people He was stricken.
[9] And they[a] made His grave with the wicked—
But with the rich at His death,

Because He had done no violence,
Nor *was any* deceit in His mouth.

[10] Yet it pleased the LORD to bruise Him;
He has put *Him* to grief.
When You make His soul an offering for sin,
He shall see *His* seed, He shall prolong *His* days,
And the pleasure of the LORD shall prosper in His hand.
[11] He shall see the labor of His soul,[b] *and* be satisfied.
By His knowledge My righteous Servant shall justify many,
For He shall bear their iniquities.
[12] Therefore I will divide Him a portion with the great,
And He shall divide the spoil with the strong,
Because He poured out His soul unto death,
And He was numbered with the transgressors,
And He bore the sin of many,
And made intercession for the transgressors.

Footnotes:

a. Isaiah 53:9 Literally *he* or *He*
b. Isaiah 53:11 Following Masoretic Text, Targum, and Vulgate; Dead Sea Scrolls and Septuagint read *From the labor of His soul He shall see light.*

(NKJV)

Daniel 8 (NKJV)

Vision of a Ram and a Goat

8 In the third year of the reign of King Belshazzar a vision appeared *to* me—to me, Daniel—after the one that appeared to me the first time. ²I saw in the vision, and it so happened while I was looking, that I *was* in Shushan, the citadel, which *is* in the province of Elam; and I saw in the vision that I was by the River Ulai. ³Then I lifted my eyes and saw, and there, standing beside the river, was a ram which had two horns, and the two horns *were* high; but one *was* higher than the other, and the higher *one* came up last. ⁴I saw the ram pushing westward, northward, and southward, so that no animal could withstand him; nor *was there any* that could deliver from his hand, but he did according to his will and became great.

⁵And as I was considering, suddenly a male goat came from the west, across the surface of the whole earth, without touching the ground; and the goat *had* a notable horn between his eyes. ⁶Then he came to the ram that had two horns, which I had seen standing beside the river, and ran at him with furious power. ⁷And I saw him confronting the ram; he was moved with rage against him, attacked the ram, and broke his two horns. There was no power in the ram to withstand him, but he cast him down to the ground and trampled him; and there was no one that could deliver the ram from his hand.

⁸Therefore the male goat grew very great; but when he became strong, the large horn was broken, and in place of it four notable ones came up toward the four winds of heaven. ⁹And out of one of them came a little horn which grew exceedingly great toward the south, toward the east, and toward the Glorious *Land.* ¹⁰And it grew up to the host of heaven; and it cast down *some* of the host and *some* of the stars to the ground, and trampled them. ¹¹He even exalted *himself* as high as the Prince of the host; and by him the daily *sacrifices* were taken away, and the place of His sanctuary was cast down. ¹²Because of transgression, an army was given over *to the horn*

to oppose the daily *sacrifices;* and he cast truth down to the ground. He did *all this* and prospered.

[13] Then I heard a holy one speaking; and *another* holy one said to that certain *one* who was speaking, "How long *will* the vision *be, concerning* the daily *sacrifices* and the transgression of desolation, the giving of both the sanctuary and the host to be trampled underfoot?"

[14] And he said to me, "For two thousand three hundred days;[a] then the sanctuary shall be cleansed."

Gabriel Interprets the Vision

[15] Then it happened, when I, Daniel, had seen the vision and was seeking the meaning, that suddenly there stood before me one having the appearance of a man. [16] And I heard a man's voice between *the banks of* the Ulai, who called, and said, "Gabriel, make this *man* understand the vision." [17] So he came near where I stood, and when he came I was afraid and fell on my face; but he said to me, "Understand, son of man, that the vision *refers* to the time of the end."

[18] Now, as he was speaking with me, I was in a deep sleep with my face to the ground; but he touched me, and stood me upright. [19] And he said, "Look, I am making known to you what shall happen in the latter time of the indignation; for at the appointed time the end *shall be.* [20] The ram which you saw, having the two horns—*they are* the kings of Media and Persia. [21] And the male goat *is* the kingdom[b] of Greece. The large horn that *is* between its eyes *is* the first king. [22] As for the broken *horn* and the four that stood up in its place, four kingdoms shall arise out of that nation, but not with its power.

[23] **"And in the latter time of their kingdom,**
When the transgressors have reached their fullness,
A king shall arise,
Having fierce features,
Who understands sinister schemes.

²⁴His power shall be mighty, but not by his own power;
He shall destroy fearfully,
And shall prosper and thrive;
He shall destroy the mighty, and *also* the holy people.

²⁵"Through his cunning
He shall cause deceit to prosper under his rule;[c]
And he shall exalt *himself* in his heart.
He shall destroy many in *their* prosperity.
He shall even rise against the Prince of princes;
But he shall be broken without *human* means.[d]

²⁶"And the vision of the evenings and mornings
Which was told is true;
Therefore seal up the vision,
For *it refers* to many days *in the future.*"

²⁷ And I, Daniel, fainted and was sick for days; afterward I arose and went about the king's business. I was astonished by the vision, but no one understood it.

Footnotes:

a. Daniel 8:14 Literally *evening-mornings*
b. Daniel 8:21 Literally *king,* representing his kingdom (compare 7:17, 23)
c. Daniel 8:25 Literally *hand*
d. Daniel 8:25 Literally *hand*

(NKJV)

Psalm 37 (NKJV)

The Heritage of the Righteous and the Calamity of the Wicked

A Psalm of David.

37 Do not fret because of evildoers,
Nor be envious of the workers of iniquity.
[2] For they shall soon be cut down like the grass,
And wither as the green herb.

[3] Trust in the LORD, and do good;
Dwell in the land, and feed on His faithfulness.
[4] Delight yourself also in the LORD,
And He shall give you the desires of your heart.

[5] Commit your way to the LORD,
Trust also in Him,
And He shall bring *it* to pass.
[6] He shall bring forth your righteousness as the light,
And your justice as the noonday.

[7] Rest in the LORD, and wait patiently for Him;
Do not fret because of him who prospers in his way,
Because of the man who brings wicked schemes to pass.
[8] Cease from anger, and forsake wrath;
Do not fret—*it* only *causes* harm.

[9] For evildoers shall be cut off;
But those who wait on the LORD,
They shall inherit the earth.
[10] For yet a little while and the wicked *shall be* no *more;*
Indeed, you will look carefully for his place,
But it *shall be* no *more.*

¹¹ But the meek shall inherit the earth,
And shall delight themselves in the abundance of peace.

¹² The wicked plots against the just,
And gnashes at him with his teeth.
¹³ The Lord laughs at him,
For He sees that his day is coming.
¹⁴ The wicked have drawn the sword
And have bent their bow,
To cast down the poor and needy,
To slay those who are of upright conduct.
¹⁵ Their sword shall enter their own heart,
And their bows shall be broken.

¹⁶ A little that a righteous man has
Is better than the riches of many wicked.
¹⁷ For the arms of the wicked shall be broken,
But the LORD upholds the righteous.

¹⁸ The LORD knows the days of the upright,
And their inheritance shall be forever.
¹⁹ They shall not be ashamed in the evil time,
And in the days of famine they shall be satisfied.
²⁰ But the wicked shall perish;
And the enemies of the LORD,
Like the splendor of the meadows, shall vanish.
Into smoke they shall vanish away.

²¹ The wicked borrows and does not repay,
But the righteous shows mercy and gives.
²² For *those* blessed by Him shall inherit the earth,
But *those* cursed by Him shall be cut off.

²³ The steps of a *good* man are ordered by the LORD,
And He delights in his way.
²⁴ Though he fall, he shall not be utterly cast down;
For the LORD upholds *him with* His hand.

211

²⁵ I have been young, and *now* am old;
Yet I have not seen the righteous forsaken,
Nor his descendants begging bread.
²⁶ *He is* ever merciful, and lends;
And his descendants *are* blessed.

²⁷ Depart from evil, and do good;
And dwell forevermore.
²⁸ For the LORD loves justice,
And does not forsake His saints;
They are preserved forever,
But the descendants of the wicked shall be cut off.
²⁹ The righteous shall inherit the land,
And dwell in it forever.

³⁰ The mouth of the righteous speaks wisdom,
And his tongue talks of justice.
³¹ The law of his God *is* in his heart;
None of his steps shall slide.

³² The wicked watches the righteous,
And seeks to slay him.
³³ The LORD will not leave him in his hand,
Nor condemn him when he is judged.

³⁴ Wait on the LORD,
And keep His way,
And He shall exalt you to inherit the land;
When the wicked are cut off, you shall see *it.*
³⁵ I have seen the wicked in great power,
And spreading himself like a native green tree.
³⁶ Yet he passed away,[a] and behold, he *was* no *more;*
Indeed I sought him, but he could not be found.

³⁷ **Mark the blameless *man,* and observe the upright;**
For the future of *that* man *is* peace.
³⁸ **But the transgressors shall be destroyed together;**
The future of the wicked shall be cut off.

³⁹ But the salvation of the righteous *is* from the LORD;
He is their strength in the time of trouble.
⁴⁰ And the LORD shall help them and deliver them;
He shall deliver them from the wicked,
And save them,
Because they trust in Him.

Footnotes:

a. <u>Psalm 37:36</u> Following Masoretic Text, Septuagint, and Targum; Syriac and Vulgate read *I passed by.*

(NKJV)

(12) No one comes to the Father except through Jesus.

John 14 – New Testament

John 14 (NKJV)

The Way, the Truth, and the Life

14 "Let not your heart be troubled; you believe in God, believe also in Me. ² In My Father's house are many mansions;[a] if *it were* not *so*, I would have told you. I go to prepare a place for you.[b] ³ And if I go and prepare a place for you, I will come again and receive you to Myself; that where I am, *there* you may be also. ⁴ And where I go you know, and the way you know."

⁵ Thomas said to Him, "Lord, we do not know where You are going, and how can we know the way?"

⁶ Jesus said to him, "I am the way, the truth, and the life. No one comes to the Father except through Me.

The Father Revealed

⁷ "If you had known Me, you would have known My Father also; and from now on you know Him and have seen Him."

⁸ Philip said to Him, "Lord, show us the Father, and it is sufficient for us."

⁹ Jesus said to him, "Have I been with you so long, and yet you have not known Me, Philip? He who has seen Me has seen the Father; so how can you say, 'Show us the Father'? ¹⁰ Do you not believe that I am in the Father, and the Father in Me? The words that I speak to you I do not speak on My own *authority;* but the Father who dwells in Me does the works. ¹¹ Believe Me that I *am* in the Father and the Father in Me, or else believe Me for the sake of the works themselves.

The Answered Prayer

¹² "Most assuredly, I say to you, he who believes in Me, the works that I do he will do also; and greater *works* than these he will do, because I go to My Father. ¹³ And whatever you ask in My name, that I will do, that the Father may be glorified in the Son. ¹⁴ If you ask[c] anything in My name, I will do *it*.

Jesus Promises Another Helper

¹⁵ "If you love Me, keep[d] My commandments. ¹⁶ And I will pray the Father, and He will give you another Helper, that He may abide with you forever— ¹⁷ the Spirit of truth, whom the world cannot receive, because it neither sees Him nor knows Him; but you know Him, for He dwells with you and will be in you. ¹⁸ I will not leave you orphans; I will come to you.

Indwelling of the Father and the Son

¹⁹ "A little while longer and the world will see Me no more, but you will see Me. Because I live, you will live also. ²⁰ At that day you will know that I *am* in My Father, and you in Me, and I in you. ²¹ He who has My commandments and keeps them, it is he who loves Me. And he who loves Me will be loved by My Father, and I will love him and manifest Myself to him."

²² Judas (not Iscariot) said to Him, "Lord, how is it that You will manifest Yourself to us, and not to the world?"

²³ Jesus answered and said to him, "If anyone loves Me, he will keep My word; and My Father will love him, and We will come to him and make Our home with him. ²⁴ He who does not love Me does not keep My words; and the word which you hear is not Mine but the Father's who sent Me.

The Gift of His Peace

25 "These things I have spoken to you while being present with you. 26 But the Helper, the Holy Spirit, whom the Father will send in My name, He will teach you all things, and bring to your remembrance all things that I said to you. 27 Peace I leave with you, My peace I give to you; not as the world gives do I give to you. Let not your heart be troubled, neither let it be afraid. 28 You have heard Me say to you, 'I am going away and coming *back* to you.' If you loved Me, you would rejoice because I said,[e] 'I am going to the Father,' for My Father is greater than I.

29 "And now I have told you before it comes, that when it does come to pass, you may believe. 30 I will no longer talk much with you, for the ruler of this world is coming, and he has nothing in Me. 31 But that the world may know that I love the Father, and as the Father gave Me commandment, so I do. Arise, let us go from here.

Footnotes:

   a.   John 14:2 Literally *dwellings*
   b.   John 14:2 NU-Text adds a word which would cause the text to read either *if it were not so, would I have told you that I go to prepare a place for you?* or *if it were not so I would have told you; for I go to prepare a place for you.*
   c.   John 14:14 NU-Text adds *Me.*
   d.   John 14:15 NU-Text reads *you will keep.*
   e.   John 14:28 NU-Text omits *I said.*

(NKJV)

James Robert Waugh

(13) A House Divided Warning

Matthew 12 – New Testament
Jude – New Testament

Matthew 12 (NKJV)

Jesus Is Lord of the Sabbath

12 At that time Jesus went through the grainfields on the Sabbath. And His disciples were hungry, and began to pluck heads of grain and to eat. [2] And when the Pharisees saw *it,* they said to Him, "Look, Your disciples are doing what is not lawful to do on the Sabbath!"

[3] But He said to them, "Have you not read what David did when he was hungry, he and those who were with him: [4] how he entered the house of God and ate the showbread which was not lawful for him to eat, nor for those who were with him, but only for the priests? [5] Or have you not read in the law that on the Sabbath the priests in the temple profane the Sabbath, and are blameless? [6] Yet I say to you that in this place there is *One* greater than the temple. [7] But if you had known what *this* means, 'I desire mercy and not sacrifice,'[a] you would not have condemned the guiltless. [8] For the Son of Man is Lord even[b] of the Sabbath."

Healing on the Sabbath

[9] Now when He had departed from there, He went into their synagogue. [10] And behold, there was a man who had a withered hand. And they asked Him, saying, "Is it lawful to heal on the Sabbath?"—that they might accuse Him.

[11] Then He said to them, "What man is there among you who has one sheep, and if it falls into a pit on the Sabbath, will not lay hold of it and lift *it* out? [12] Of how much more value then is a man than a sheep? Therefore it is lawful to do good on the Sabbath." [13] Then He said to the man, "Stretch out your hand." And he stretched *it* out, and it was restored as whole as the other. [14] Then the Pharisees went out and plotted against Him, how they might destroy Him.

James Robert Waugh

Behold, My Servant

[15] But when Jesus knew *it,* He withdrew from there. And great multitudes[c] followed Him, and He healed them all. [16] Yet He warned them not to make Him known, [17] that it might be fulfilled which was spoken by Isaiah the prophet, saying:

[18] "Behold! My Servant whom I have chosen,
My Beloved in whom My soul is well pleased!
I will put My Spirit upon Him,
And He will declare justice to the Gentiles.
[19] He will not quarrel nor cry out,
Nor will anyone hear His voice in the streets.
[20] A bruised reed He will not break,
And smoking flax He will not quench,
Till He sends forth justice to victory;
[21] And in His name Gentiles will trust."[d]

A House Divided Cannot Stand

[22] Then one was brought to Him who was demon-possessed, blind and mute; and He healed him, so that the blind and[e] mute man both spoke and saw. [23] And all the multitudes were amazed and said, "Could this be the Son of David?"

[24] Now when the Pharisees heard *it* they said, "This *fellow* does not cast out demons except by Beelzebub,[f] the ruler of the demons."

[25] But Jesus knew their thoughts, and said to them: "Every kingdom divided against itself is brought to desolation, and every city or house divided against itself will not stand. [26] If Satan casts out Satan, he is divided against himself. How then will his kingdom stand? [27] And if I cast out demons by Beelzebub, by whom do your sons cast *them* out? Therefore they shall be your judges. [28] But if I cast out demons by the Spirit of God, surely the kingdom of God has come upon you. [29] Or how can one enter a strong man's house and plunder his goods, unless he first binds the strong man? And

then he will plunder his house. [30] He who is not with Me is against Me, and he who does not gather with Me scatters abroad.

The Unpardonable Sin

[31] "Therefore I say to you, every sin and blasphemy will be forgiven men, but the blasphemy *against* the Spirit will not be forgiven men. [32] Anyone who speaks a word against the Son of Man, it will be forgiven him; but whoever speaks against the Holy Spirit, it will not be forgiven him, either in this age or in the *age* to come.

A Tree Known by Its Fruit

[33] "Either make the tree good and its fruit good, or else make the tree bad and its fruit bad; for a tree is known by *its* fruit. [34] Brood of vipers! How can you, being evil, speak good things? For out of the abundance of the heart the mouth speaks. [35] A good man out of the good treasure of his heart[g] brings forth good things, and an evil man out of the evil treasure brings forth evil things. [36] But I say to you that for every idle word men may speak, they will give account of it in the day of judgment. [37] For by your words you will be justified, and by your words you will be condemned."

The Scribes and Pharisees Ask for a Sign

[38] Then some of the scribes and Pharisees answered, saying, "Teacher, we want to see a sign from You."

[39] But He answered and said to them, "An evil and adulterous generation seeks after a sign, and no sign will be given to it except the sign of the prophet Jonah. [40] For as Jonah was three days and three nights in the belly of the great fish, so will the Son of Man be three days and three nights in the heart of the earth. [41] The men of Nineveh will rise up in the judgment with this generation and condemn it, because they repented at the preaching of Jonah; and

indeed a greater than Jonah *is* here. [42] The queen of the South will rise up in the judgment with this generation and condemn it, for she came from the ends of the earth to hear the wisdom of Solomon; and indeed a greater than Solomon *is* here.

An Unclean Spirit Returns

[43] "When an unclean spirit goes out of a man, he goes through dry places, seeking rest, and finds none. [44] Then he says, 'I will return to my house from which I came.' And when he comes, he finds *it* empty, swept, and put in order. [45] Then he goes and takes with him seven other spirits more wicked than himself, and they enter and dwell there; and the last *state* of that man is worse than the first. So shall it also be with this wicked generation."

Jesus' Mother and Brothers Send for Him

[46] While He was still talking to the multitudes, behold, His mother and brothers stood outside, seeking to speak with Him. [47] Then one said to Him, "Look, Your mother and Your brothers are standing outside, seeking to speak with You."

[48] But He answered and said to the one who told Him, "Who is My mother and who are My brothers?" [49] And He stretched out His hand toward His disciples and said, "Here are My mother and My brothers! [50] For whoever does the will of My Father in heaven is My brother and sister and mother."

Footnotes:

- a. Matthew 12:7 Hosea 6:6
- b. Matthew 12:8 NU-Text and M-Text omit *even.*
- c. Matthew 12:15 NU-Text brackets *multitudes* as disputed.
- d. Matthew 12:21 Isaiah 42:1–4

e. <u>Matthew 12:22</u> NU-Text omits *blind and.*
f. <u>Matthew 12:24</u> NU-Text and M-Text read *Beelzebul.*
g. <u>Matthew 12:35</u> NU-Text and M-Text omit *of his heart.*

(NKJV)

Jude (NKJV)

Greeting to the Called

[1] Jude, a bondservant of Jesus Christ, and brother of James, To those who are called, sanctified[a] by God the Father, and preserved in Jesus Christ:

[2] Mercy, peace, and love be multiplied to you.

Contend for the Faith

[3] Beloved, while I was very diligent to write to you concerning our common salvation, I found it necessary to write to you exhorting you to contend earnestly for the faith which was once for all delivered to the saints. [4] For certain men have crept in unnoticed, who long ago were marked out for this condemnation, ungodly men, who turn the grace of our God into lewdness and deny the only Lord God[b] and our Lord Jesus Christ.

Old and New Apostates

[5] But I want to remind you, though you once knew this, that the Lord, having saved the people out of the land of Egypt, afterward destroyed those who did not believe. [6] And the angels who did not keep their proper domain, but left their own abode, He has reserved in everlasting chains under darkness for the judgment of the great day; [7] as Sodom and Gomorrah, and the cities around them in a similar manner to these, having given themselves over to sexual immorality and gone after strange flesh, are set forth as an example, suffering the vengeance of eternal fire.

[8] Likewise also these dreamers defile the flesh, reject authority, and speak evil of dignitaries. [9] Yet Michael the archangel, in contending with the devil, when he disputed about the body of Moses, dared not bring against him a reviling accusation, but said, "The Lord rebuke you!" [10] But these speak evil of whatever they do not know;

and whatever they know naturally, like brute beasts, in these things they corrupt themselves. [11] Woe to them! For they have gone in the way of Cain, have run greedily in the error of Balaam for profit, and perished in the rebellion of Korah.

Apostates Depraved and Doomed

[12] These are spots in your love feasts, while they feast with you without fear, serving only themselves. They are clouds without water, carried about[c] by the winds; late autumn trees without fruit, twice dead, pulled up by the roots; [13] raging waves of the sea, foaming up their own shame; wandering stars for whom is reserved the blackness of darkness forever.

[14] Now Enoch, the seventh from Adam, prophesied about these men also, saying, "Behold, the Lord comes with ten thousands of His saints, [15] to execute judgment on all, to convict all who are ungodly among them of all their ungodly deeds which they have committed in an ungodly way, and of all the harsh things which ungodly sinners have spoken against Him."

Apostates Predicted

[16] These are grumblers, complainers, walking according to their own lusts; and they mouth great swelling words, flattering people to gain advantage. [17] But you, beloved, remember the words which were spoken before by the apostles of our Lord Jesus Christ: [18] how they told you that there would be mockers in the last time who would walk according to their own ungodly lusts. [19] These are sensual persons, who cause divisions, not having the Spirit.

Maintain Your Life with God

[20] But you, beloved, building yourselves up on your most holy faith, praying in the Holy Spirit, [21] keep yourselves in the love of God, looking for the mercy of our Lord Jesus Christ unto eternal life.

[22] And on some have compassion, making a distinction;[d] [23] but others save with fear, pulling them out of the fire,[e] hating even the garment defiled by the flesh.

Glory to God

[24] Now to Him who is able to keep you[f] from stumbling,
And to present you faultless
Before the presence of His glory with exceeding joy,
[25] To God our Savior,[g]
Who alone is wise,[h]
Be glory and majesty,
Dominion and power,[i]
Both now and forever.
Amen.

Footnotes:

a. Jude 1:1 NU-Text reads *beloved*.
b. Jude 1:4 NU-Text omits *God*.
c. Jude 1:12 NU-Text and M-Text read *along*.
d. Jude 1:22 NU-Text reads *who are doubting* (or *making distinctions*).
e. Jude 1:23 NU-Text adds *and on some have mercy with fear* and omits *with fear* in first clause.
f. Jude 1:24 M-Text reads *them*.
g. Jude 1:25 NU-Text reads *To the only God our Savior*.
h. Jude 1:25 NU-Text omits *Who . . . is wise* and adds *Through Jesus Christ our Lord*.
i. Jude 1:25 NU-Text adds *Before all time*.

(NKJV)

(14) The Ten Commandments

Exodus 20 – Old Testament

James Robert Waugh

Exodus 20 (NKJV)

The Ten Commandments

20 And God spoke all these words, saying:

2 "I *am* the LORD your God, who brought you out of the land of Egypt, out of the house of bondage.

3 "You shall have no other gods before Me.

4 "You shall not make for yourself a carved image—any likeness *of anything* that *is* in heaven above, or that *is* in the earth beneath, or that *is* in the water under the earth; 5 you shall not bow down to them nor serve them. For I, the LORD your God, *am* a jealous God, visiting the iniquity of the fathers upon the children to the third and fourth *generations* of those who hate Me, 6 but showing mercy to thousands, to those who love Me and keep My commandments.

7 "You shall not take the name of the LORD your God in vain, for the LORD will not hold *him* guiltless who takes His name in vain.

8 "Remember the Sabbath day, to keep it holy. 9 Six days you shall labor and do all your work, 10 but the seventh day *is* the Sabbath of the LORD your God. *In it* you shall do no work: you, nor your son, nor your daughter, nor your male servant, nor your female servant, nor your cattle, nor your stranger who *is* within your gates. 11 For *in* six days the LORD made the heavens and the earth, the sea, and all that *is* in them, and rested the seventh day. Therefore the LORD blessed the Sabbath day and hallowed it.

12 "Honor your father and your mother, that your days may be long upon the land which the LORD your God is giving you.

13 "You shall not murder.

14 "You shall not commit adultery.

15 "You shall not steal.

[16] "You shall not bear false witness against your neighbor.

[17] "You shall not covet your neighbor's house; you shall not covet your neighbor's wife, nor his male servant, nor his female servant, nor his ox, nor his donkey, nor anything that *is* your neighbor's."

The People Afraid of God's Presence

[18] Now all the people witnessed the thunderings, the lightning flashes, the sound of the trumpet, and the mountain smoking; and when the people saw *it,* they trembled and stood afar off. [19] Then they said to Moses, "You speak with us, and we will hear; but let not God speak with us, lest we die."

[20] And Moses said to the people, "Do not fear; for God has come to test you, and that His fear may be before you, so that you may not sin." [21] So the people stood afar off, but Moses drew near the thick darkness where God *was.*

The Law of the Altar

[22] Then the LORD said to Moses, "Thus you shall say to the children of Israel: 'You have seen that I have talked with you from heaven. [23] You shall not make *anything to be* with Me—gods of silver or gods of gold you shall not make for yourselves. [24] An altar of earth you shall make for Me, and you shall sacrifice on it your burnt offerings and your peace offerings, your sheep and your oxen. In every place where I record My name I will come to you, and I will bless you. [25] And if you make Me an altar of stone, you shall not build it of hewn stone; for if you use your tool on it, you have profaned it. [26] Nor shall you go up by steps to My altar, that your nakedness may not be exposed on it.'

(NKJV)

(15) Jesus to be born and Jesus to return

Isaiah 52 – Old Testament – Prophecy of a Messiah to be born
Isaiah 53 – Old Testament – Prophecy of a Messiah to be born.
Daniel 7 - Old Testament – Jesus coming with clouds
Revelation 1– New Testament – Jesus coming with clouds

Isaiah 52 (NKJV)

God Redeems Jerusalem

52 Awake, awake!
Put on your strength, O Zion;
Put on your beautiful garments,
O Jerusalem, the holy city!
For the uncircumcised and the unclean
Shall no longer come to you.
2 Shake yourself from the dust, arise;
Sit down, O Jerusalem!
Loose yourself from the bonds of your neck,
O captive daughter of Zion!

3 For thus says the LORD:

"You have sold yourselves for nothing,
And you shall be redeemed without money."

4 For thus says the Lord GOD:

"My people went down at first
Into Egypt to dwell there;
Then the Assyrian oppressed them without cause.
5 Now therefore, what have I here," says the LORD,
"That My people are taken away for nothing?
Those who rule over them
Make them wail,"[a] says the LORD,
"And My name *is* blasphemed continually every day.
6 Therefore My people shall know My name;
Therefore *they shall know* in that day
That I *am* He who speaks:
'Behold, *it is* I.'"

7 How beautiful upon the mountains
Are the feet of him who brings good news,

Who proclaims peace,
Who brings glad tidings of good *things,*
Who proclaims salvation,
Who says to Zion,
"Your God reigns!"
⁸ Your watchmen shall lift up *their* voices,
With their voices they shall sing together;
For they shall see eye to eye
When the LORD brings back Zion.
⁹ Break forth into joy, sing together,
You waste places of Jerusalem!
For the LORD has comforted His people,
He has redeemed Jerusalem.
¹⁰ The LORD has made bare His holy arm
In the eyes of all the nations;
And all the ends of the earth shall see
The salvation of our God.

¹¹ Depart! Depart! Go out from there,
Touch no unclean *thing;*
Go out from the midst of her,
Be clean,
You who bear the vessels of the LORD.
¹² For you shall not go out with haste,
Nor go by flight;
For the LORD will go before you,
And the God of Israel *will be* your rear guard.

The Sin-Bearing Servant

¹³ Behold, My Servant shall deal prudently;
He shall be exalted and extolled and be very high.
¹⁴ Just as many were astonished at you,
So His visage was marred more than any man,
And His form more than the sons of men;
¹⁵ So shall He sprinkle[b] many nations.

Kings shall shut their mouths at Him;
For what had not been told them they shall see,
And what they had not heard they shall consider.

Footnotes:

a.   Isaiah 52:5 Dead Sea Scrolls read *Mock;* Septuagint reads *Marvel and wail;* Targum reads *Boast themselves;* Vulgate reads *Treat them unjustly.*
b.   Isaiah 52:15 Or *startle*

(NKJV)

Scripture taken from the New King James Version®. Copyright © 1982 by Thomas Nelson. Used by permission. All rights reserved.

Isaiah 53 (NKJV)

53 Who has believed our report?
And to whom has the arm of the Lᴏʀᴅ been revealed?
²For He shall grow up before Him as a tender plant,
And as a root out of dry ground.
He has no form or comeliness;
And when we see Him,
There is no beauty that we should desire Him.
³He is despised and rejected by men,
A Man of sorrows and acquainted with grief.
And we hid, as it were, *our* faces from Him;
He was despised, and we did not esteem Him.

⁴Surely He has borne our griefs
And carried our sorrows;
Yet we esteemed Him stricken,
Smitten by God, and afflicted.
⁵But He *was* wounded for our transgressions,
He was bruised for our iniquities;
The chastisement for our peace *was* upon Him,
And by His stripes we are healed.
⁶All we like sheep have gone astray;
We have turned, every one, to his own way;
And the Lᴏʀᴅ has laid on Him the iniquity of us all.

⁷He was oppressed and He was afflicted,
Yet He opened not His mouth;
He was led as a lamb to the slaughter,
And as a sheep before its shearers is silent,
So He opened not His mouth.
⁸He was taken from prison and from judgment,
And who will declare His generation?
For He was cut off from the land of the living;
For the transgressions of My people He was stricken.
⁹And they[a] made His grave with the wicked—
But with the rich at His death,

Because He had done no violence,
Nor *was any* deceit in His mouth.

[10] Yet it pleased the LORD to bruise Him;
He has put *Him* to grief.
When You make His soul an offering for sin,
He shall see *His* seed, He shall prolong *His* days,
And the pleasure of the LORD shall prosper in His hand.
[11] He shall see the labor of His soul,[b] *and* be satisfied.
By His knowledge My righteous Servant shall justify many,
For He shall bear their iniquities.
[12] Therefore I will divide Him a portion with the great,
And He shall divide the spoil with the strong,
Because He poured out His soul unto death,
And He was numbered with the transgressors,
And He bore the sin of many,
And made intercession for the transgressors.

Footnotes:

a. Isaiah 53:9 Literally *he* or *He*
b. Isaiah 53:11 Following Masoretic Text, Targum, and Vulgate; Dead Sea Scrolls and Septuagint read *From the labor of His soul He shall see light.*

(NKJV)

James Robert Waugh

Daniel 7 (NKJV)

Vision of the Four Beasts

7 In the first year of Belshazzar king of Babylon, Daniel had a dream and visions of his head *while* on his bed. Then he wrote down the dream, telling the main facts.[a]

[2] Daniel spoke, saying, "I saw in my vision by night, and behold, the four winds of heaven were stirring up the Great Sea. [3] And four great beasts came up from the sea, each different from the other. [4] The first *was* like a lion, and had eagle's wings. I watched till its wings were plucked off; and it was lifted up from the earth and made to stand on two feet like a man, and a man's heart was given to it.

[5] "And suddenly another beast, a second, like a bear. It was raised up on one side, and *had* three ribs in its mouth between its teeth. And they said thus to it: 'Arise, devour much flesh!'

[6] "After this I looked, and there was another, like a leopard, which had on its back four wings of a bird. The beast also had four heads, and dominion was given to it.

[7] "After this I saw in the night visions, and behold, a fourth beast, dreadful and terrible, exceedingly strong. It had huge iron teeth; it was devouring, breaking in pieces, and trampling the residue with its feet. It *was* different from all the beasts that *were* before it, and it had ten horns. [8] I was considering the horns, and there was another horn, a little one, coming up among them, before whom three of the first horns were plucked out by the roots. And there, in this horn, *were* eyes like the eyes of a man, and a mouth speaking pompous words.

Vision of the Ancient of Days

[9] "I watched till thrones were put in place,
And the Ancient of Days was seated;
His garment *was* white as snow,
And the hair of His head *was* like pure wool.
His throne *was* a fiery flame,
Its wheels a burning fire;
[10] A fiery stream issued
And came forth from before Him.
A thousand thousands ministered to Him;
Ten thousand times ten thousand stood before Him.
The court[b] was seated,
And the books were opened.

[11] "I watched then because of the sound of the pompous words which the horn was speaking; I watched till the beast was slain, and its body destroyed and given to the burning flame. [12] As for the rest of the beasts, they had their dominion taken away, yet their lives were prolonged for a season and a time.

[13] **"I was watching in the night visions,**
And behold, *One* **like the Son of Man,**
Coming with the clouds of heaven!
He came to the Ancient of Days,
And they brought Him near before Him.
[14] **Then to Him was given dominion and glory and a kingdom,**
That all peoples, nations, and languages should serve Him.
His dominion *is* **an everlasting dominion,**
Which shall not pass away,
And His kingdom *the one*
Which shall not be destroyed.

Daniel's Visions Interpreted

[15] "I, Daniel, was grieved in my spirit within *my* body, and the visions of my head troubled me. [16] I came near to one of those who

stood by, and asked him the truth of all this. So he told me and made known to me the interpretation of these things: [17]'Those great beasts, which are four, *are* four kings[c] *which* arise out of the earth. [18] But the saints of the Most High shall receive the kingdom, and possess the kingdom forever, even forever and ever.'

[19] "Then I wished to know the truth about the fourth beast, which was different from all the others, exceedingly dreadful, *with* its teeth of iron and its nails of bronze, *which* devoured, broke in pieces, and trampled the residue with its feet; [20] and the ten horns that *were* on its head, and the other *horn* which came up, before which three fell, namely, that horn which had eyes and a mouth which spoke pompous words, whose appearance *was* greater than his fellows.

[21] "I was watching; and the same horn was making war against the saints, and prevailing against them, [22] until the Ancient of Days came, and a judgment was made *in favor* of the saints of the Most High, and the time came for the saints to possess the kingdom.

[23] "Thus he said:

'The fourth beast shall be
A fourth kingdom on earth,
Which shall be different from all *other* kingdoms,
And shall devour the whole earth,
Trample it and break it in pieces.
[24] The ten horns *are* ten kings
Who shall arise from this kingdom.
And another shall rise after them;
He shall be different from the first *ones,*
And shall subdue three kings.
[25] He shall speak *pompous* words against the Most High,
Shall persecute[d] the saints of the Most High,
And shall intend to change times and law.
Then *the saints* shall be given into his hand
For a time and times and half a time.

[26] 'But the court shall be seated,
And they shall take away his dominion,
To consume and destroy *it* forever.
[27] Then the kingdom and dominion,
And the greatness of the kingdoms under the whole heaven,
Shall be given to the people, the saints of the Most High.
His kingdom *is* an everlasting kingdom,
And all dominions shall serve and obey Him.'

[28] "This *is* the end of the account.[e] As for me, Daniel, my thoughts greatly troubled me, and my countenance changed; but I kept the matter in my heart."

Footnotes:

a. Daniel 7:1 Literally *the head* (or *chief*) *of the words*
b. Daniel 7:10 Or *judgment*
c. Daniel 7:17 Representing their kingdoms (compare verse 23)
d. Daniel 7:25 Literally *wear out*
e. Daniel 7:28 Literally *the word*

(NKJV)

Revelation 1 (NKJV)

Introduction and Benediction

1 The Revelation of Jesus Christ, which God gave Him to show His servants—things which must shortly take place. And He sent and signified *it* by His angel to His servant John, [2] who bore witness to the word of God, and to the testimony of Jesus Christ, to all things that he saw. [3] Blessed *is* he who reads and those who hear the words of this prophecy, and keep those things which are written in it; for the time *is* near.

Greeting the Seven Churches

[4] John, to the seven churches which are in Asia:

Grace to you and peace from Him who is and who was and who is to come, and from the seven Spirits who are before His throne, [5] and from Jesus Christ, the faithful witness, the firstborn from the dead, and the ruler over the kings of the earth.

To Him who loved us and washed[a] us from our sins in His own blood, [6] and has made us kings[b] and priests to His God and Father, to Him *be* glory and dominion forever and ever. Amen.

[7] **Behold, He is coming with clouds, and every eye will see Him, even they who pierced Him. And all the tribes of the earth will mourn because of Him. Even so, Amen.**

[8] "I am the Alpha and the Omega, *the* Beginning and *the* End,"[c] says the Lord,[d] "who is and who was and who is to come, the Almighty."

Vision of the Son of Man

[9] I, John, both[e] your brother and companion in the tribulation and kingdom and patience of Jesus Christ, was on the island that is

called Patmos for the word of God and for the testimony of Jesus Christ. [10] I was in the Spirit on the Lord's Day, and I heard behind me a loud voice, as of a trumpet, [11] saying, "I am the Alpha and the Omega, the First and the Last," and,[f] "What you see, write in a book and send *it* to the seven churches which are in Asia:[g] to Ephesus, to Smyrna, to Pergamos, to Thyatira, to Sardis, to Philadelphia, and to Laodicea."

[12] Then I turned to see the voice that spoke with me. And having turned I saw seven golden lampstands, [13] and in the midst of the seven lampstands *One* like the Son of Man, clothed with a garment down to the feet and girded about the chest with a golden band. [14] His head and hair *were* white like wool, as white as snow, and His eyes like a flame of fire; [15] His feet *were* like fine brass, as if refined in a furnace, and His voice as the sound of many waters; [16] He had in His right hand seven stars, out of His mouth went a sharp two-edged sword, and His countenance *was* like the sun shining in its strength. [17] And when I saw Him, I fell at His feet as dead. But He laid His right hand on me, saying to me,[h] "Do not be afraid; I am the First and the Last. [18] I *am* He who lives, and was dead, and behold, I am alive forevermore. Amen. And I have the keys of Hades and of Death. [19] Write[i] the things which you have seen, and the things which are, and the things which will take place after this. [20] The mystery of the seven stars which you saw in My right hand, and the seven golden lampstands: The seven stars are the angels of the seven churches, and the seven lampstands which you saw[j] are the seven churches.

Footnotes:

a. Revelation 1:5 NU-Text reads *loves us and freed;* M-Text reads *loves us and washed.*
b. Revelation 1:6 NU-Text and M-Text read *a kingdom.*
c. Revelation 1:8 NU-Text and M-Text omit *the Beginning and the End.*
d. Revelation 1:8 NU-Text and M-Text add *God.*
e. Revelation 1:9 NU-Text and M-Text omit *both.*

    f.   <u>Revelation 1:11</u> NU-Text and M-Text omit *I am* through third *and.*

    g. <u>Revelation 1:11</u> NU-Text and M-Text omit *which are in Asia.*

    h. <u>Revelation 1:17</u> NU-Text and M-Text omit *to me.*

    i.   <u>Revelation 1:19</u> NU-Text and M-Text read *Therefore, write.*

    j.   <u>Revelation 1:20</u> NU-Text and M-Text omit *which you saw.*

(NKJV)

(16) Fear Him who can destroy both body and soul

Matthew 10 – New Testament

Matthew 10 (NKJV)

The Twelve Apostles

10 And when He had called His twelve disciples to *Him,* He gave them power *over* unclean spirits, to cast them out, and to heal all kinds of sickness and all kinds of disease. ² Now the names of the twelve apostles are these: first, Simon, who is called Peter, and Andrew his brother; James the *son* of Zebedee, and John his brother; ³ Philip and Bartholomew; Thomas and Matthew the tax collector; James the *son* of Alphaeus, and Lebbaeus, whose surname was[a] Thaddaeus; ⁴ Simon the Cananite,[b] and Judas Iscariot, who also betrayed Him.

Sending Out the Twelve

⁵ These twelve Jesus sent out and commanded them, saying: "Do not go into the way of the Gentiles, and do not enter a city of the Samaritans. ⁶ But go rather to the lost sheep of the house of Israel. ⁷ And as you go, preach, saying, 'The kingdom of heaven is at hand.' ⁸ Heal the sick, cleanse the lepers, raise the dead,[c] cast out demons. Freely you have received, freely give. ⁹ Provide neither gold nor silver nor copper in your money belts, ¹⁰ nor bag for *your* journey, nor two tunics, nor sandals, nor staffs; for a worker is worthy of his food.

¹¹ "Now whatever city or town you enter, inquire who in it is worthy, and stay there till you go out. ¹² And when you go into a household, greet it. ¹³ If the household is worthy, let your peace come upon it. But if it is not worthy, let your peace return to you. ¹⁴ And whoever will not receive you nor hear your words, when you depart from that house or city, shake off the dust from your feet. ¹⁵ Assuredly, I say to you, it will be more tolerable for the land of Sodom and Gomorrah in the day of judgment than for that city!

Persecutions Are Coming

[16] "Behold, I send you out as sheep in the midst of wolves. Therefore be wise as serpents and harmless as doves. [17] But beware of men, for they will deliver you up to councils and scourge you in their synagogues. [18] You will be brought before governors and kings for My sake, as a testimony to them and to the Gentiles. [19] But when they deliver you up, do not worry about how or what you should speak. For it will be given to you in that hour what you should speak; [20] for it is not you who speak, but the Spirit of your Father who speaks in you.

[21] "Now brother will deliver up brother to death, and a father *his* child; and children will rise up against parents and cause them to be put to death. [22] And you will be hated by all for My name's sake. But he who endures to the end will be saved. [23] When they persecute you in this city, flee to another. For assuredly, I say to you, you will not have gone through the cities of Israel before the Son of Man comes.

[24] "A disciple is not above *his* teacher, nor a servant above his master. [25] It is enough for a disciple that he be like his teacher, and a servant like his master. If they have called the master of the house Beelzebub,[d] how much more *will they call* those of his household! [26] Therefore do not fear them. For there is nothing covered that will not be revealed, and hidden that will not be known.

Jesus Teaches the Fear of God

[27] **"Whatever I tell you in the dark, speak in the light; and what you hear in the ear, preach on the housetops. [28] And do not fear those who kill the body but cannot kill the soul.** But rather fear Him who is able to destroy both soul and body in hell. [29] Are not two sparrows sold for a copper coin? And not one of them falls to the ground apart from your Father's will. [30] But the very hairs of your head are all numbered. [31] Do not fear therefore; you are of more value than many sparrows.

Confess Christ Before Men

³² "Therefore whoever confesses Me before men, him I will also confess before My Father who is in heaven. ³³ But whoever denies Me before men, him I will also deny before My Father who is in heaven.

Christ Brings Division

³⁴ "Do not think that I came to bring peace on earth. I did not come to bring peace but a sword. ³⁵ For I have come to 'set a man against his father, a daughter against her mother, and a daughter-in-law against her mother-in-law'; ³⁶ and 'a man's enemies *will be* those of his *own* household.'[e] ³⁷ He who loves father or mother more than Me is not worthy of Me. And he who loves son or daughter more than Me is not worthy of Me. ³⁸ And he who does not take his cross and follow after Me is not worthy of Me. ³⁹ He who finds his life will lose it, and he who loses his life for My sake will find it.

A Cup of Cold Water

⁴⁰ "He who receives you receives Me, and he who receives Me receives Him who sent Me. ⁴¹ He who receives a prophet in the name of a prophet shall receive a prophet's reward. And he who receives a righteous man in the name of a righteous man shall receive a righteous man's reward. ⁴² And whoever gives one of these little ones only a cup of cold *water* in the name of a disciple, assuredly, I say to you, he shall by no means lose his reward."

Footnotes:

a. Matthew 10:3 NU-Text omits *Lebbaeus, whose surname was.*
b. Matthew 10:4 NU-Text reads *Cananaean.*
c. Matthew 10:8 NU-Text reads *raise the dead, cleanse the lepers;* M-Text omits *raise the dead.*

d. <u>Matthew 10:25</u> NU-Text and M-Text read *Beelzebul.*
e. <u>Matthew 10:36</u> <u>Micah 7:6</u>

(NKJV)

James Robert Waugh

(17) The unrighteous who will not inherit the Kingdom of Heaven.

---

1 Corinthians 6 – New Testament
1 Timothy 1 – New Testament
Revelation 21 – New Testament

1 Corinthians 6 (NKJV)

Do Not Sue the Brethren

6 Dare any of you, having a matter against another, go to law before the unrighteous, and not before the saints? [2] Do you not know that the saints will judge the world? And if the world will be judged by you, are you unworthy to judge the smallest matters? [3] Do you not know that we shall judge angels? How much more, things that pertain to this life? [4] If then you have judgments concerning things pertaining to this life, do you appoint those who are least esteemed by the church to judge? [5] I say this to your shame. Is it so, that there is not a wise man among you, not even one, who will be able to judge between his brethren? [6] But brother goes to law against brother, and that before unbelievers!

[7] Now therefore, it is already an utter failure for you that you go to law against one another. Why do you not rather accept wrong? Why do you not rather *let yourselves* be cheated? [8] No, you yourselves do wrong and cheat, and *you do* these things *to your* brethren! [9] **Do you not know that the unrighteous will not inherit the kingdom of God? Do not be deceived. Neither fornicators, nor idolaters, nor adulterers, nor homosexuals,[a] nor sodomites, [10] nor thieves, nor covetous, nor drunkards, nor revilers, nor extortioners will inherit the kingdom of God. [11] And such were some of you. But you were washed, but you were sanctified, but you were justified in the name of the Lord Jesus and by the Spirit of our God.**

Glorify God in Body and Spirit

[12] All things are lawful for me, but all things are not helpful. All things are lawful for me, but I will not be brought under the power of any. [13] Foods for the stomach and the stomach for foods, but God will destroy both it and them. Now the body *is* not for sexual immorality but for the Lord, and the Lord for the body. [14] And God both raised up the Lord and will also raise us up by His power.

¹⁵ Do you not know that your bodies are members of Christ? Shall I then take the members of Christ and make *them* members of a harlot? Certainly not! ¹⁶ Or do you not know that he who is joined to a harlot is one body *with her*? For "the two," He says, "shall become one flesh."[b] ¹⁷ But he who is joined to the Lord is one spirit *with Him*.

¹⁸ Flee sexual immorality. Every sin that a man does is outside the body, but he who commits sexual immorality sins against his own body. ¹⁹ Or do you not know that your body is the temple of the Holy Spirit *who is* in you, whom you have from God, and you are not your own? ²⁰ For you were bought at a price; therefore glorify God in your body[c] and in your spirit, which are God's.

Footnotes:

a. 1 Corinthians 6:9 That is, catamites
b. 1 Corinthians 6:16 Genesis 2:24
c. 1 Corinthians 6:20 NU-Text ends the verse at *body*.

(NKJV)

1 Timothy 1 (NKJV)

Greeting

1 Paul, an apostle of Jesus Christ, by the commandment of God our Savior and the Lord Jesus Christ, our hope,

² To Timothy, a true son in the faith:

Grace, mercy, *and* peace from God our Father and Jesus Christ our Lord.

No Other Doctrine

³ As I urged you when I went into Macedonia—remain in Ephesus that you may charge some that they teach no other doctrine, ⁴ nor give heed to fables and endless genealogies, which cause disputes rather than godly edification which is in faith. ⁵ Now the purpose of the commandment is love from a pure heart, *from* a good conscience, and *from* sincere faith, ⁶ from which some, having strayed, have turned aside to idle talk, ⁷ desiring to be teachers of the law, understanding neither what they say nor the things which they affirm.

⁸ **But we know that the law *is* good if one uses it lawfully, ⁹ knowing this: that the law is not made for a righteous person, but for *the* lawless and insubordinate, for *the* ungodly and for sinners, for *the* unholy and profane, for murderers of fathers and murderers of mothers, for manslayers, ¹⁰ for fornicators, for sodomites, for kidnappers, for liars, for perjurers, and if there is any other thing that is contrary to sound doctrine, ¹¹ according to the glorious gospel of the blessed God which was committed to my trust.**

Glory to God for His Grace

¹² And I thank Christ Jesus our Lord who has enabled me, because He counted me faithful, putting *me* into the ministry, ¹³ although I

was formerly a blasphemer, a persecutor, and an insolent man; but I obtained mercy because I did *it* ignorantly in unbelief. [14] And the grace of our Lord was exceedingly abundant, with faith and love which are in Christ Jesus. [15] This *is* a faithful saying and worthy of all acceptance, that Christ Jesus came into the world to save sinners, of whom I am chief. [16] However, for this reason I obtained mercy, that in me first Jesus Christ might show all longsuffering, as a pattern to those who are going to believe on Him for everlasting life. [17] Now to the King eternal, immortal, invisible, to God who alone is wise,[a] *be* honor and glory forever and ever. Amen.

Fight the Good Fight

[18] This charge I commit to you, son Timothy, according to the prophecies previously made concerning you, that by them you may wage the good warfare, [19] having faith and a good conscience, which some having rejected, concerning the faith have suffered shipwreck, [20] of whom are Hymenaeus and Alexander, whom I delivered to Satan that they may learn not to blaspheme.

Footnotes:

a. 1 Timothy 1:17 NU-Text reads *to the only God.*

(NKJV)

Revelation 21 (NKJV)

All Things Made New

21 Now I saw a new heaven and a new earth, for the first heaven and the first earth had passed away. Also there was no more sea. ²Then I, John,[a] saw the holy city, New Jerusalem, coming down out of heaven from God, prepared as a bride adorned for her husband. ³ And I heard a loud voice from heaven saying, "Behold, the tabernacle of God *is* with men, and He will dwell with them, and they shall be His people. God Himself will be with them *and be* their God. ⁴ And God will wipe away every tear from their eyes; there shall be no more death, nor sorrow, nor crying. There shall be no more pain, for the former things have passed away."

⁵ Then He who sat on the throne said, "Behold, I make all things new." And He said to me,[b] "Write, for these words are true and faithful."

⁶ And He said to me, "It is done![c] I am the Alpha and the Omega, the Beginning and the End. I will give of the fountain of the water of life freely to him who thirsts. ⁷ He who overcomes shall inherit all things,[d] and I will be his God and he shall be My son. ⁸ **But the cowardly, unbelieving,[e] abominable, murderers, sexually immoral, sorcerers, idolaters, and all liars shall have their part in the lake which burns with fire and brimstone, which is the second death.**"

The New Jerusalem

⁹ Then one of the seven angels who had the seven bowls filled with the seven last plagues came to me[f] and talked with me, saying, "Come, I will show you the bride, the Lamb's wife."[g] ¹⁰ And he carried me away in the Spirit to a great and high mountain, and showed me the great city, the holy[h] Jerusalem, descending out of heaven from God, ¹¹ having the glory of God. Her light *was* like a

most precious stone, like a jasper stone, clear as crystal. [12] Also she had a great and high wall with twelve gates, and twelve angels at the gates, and names written on them, which are *the names* of the twelve tribes of the children of Israel: [13] three gates on the east, three gates on the north, three gates on the south, and three gates on the west.

[14] Now the wall of the city had twelve foundations, and on them were the names[i] of the twelve apostles of the Lamb. [15] And he who talked with me had a gold reed to measure the city, its gates, and its wall. [16] The city is laid out as a square; its length is as great as its breadth. And he measured the city with the reed: twelve thousand furlongs. Its length, breadth, and height are equal. [17] Then he measured its wall: one hundred *and* forty-four cubits, *according* to the measure of a man, that is, of an angel. [18] The construction of its wall was *of* jasper; and the city *was* pure gold, like clear glass. [19] The foundations of the wall of the city *were* adorned with all kinds of precious stones: the first foundation *was* jasper, the second sapphire, the third chalcedony, the fourth emerald, [20] the fifth sardonyx, the sixth sardius, the seventh chrysolite, the eighth beryl, the ninth topaz, the tenth chrysoprase, the eleventh jacinth, and the twelfth amethyst. [21] The twelve gates *were* twelve pearls: each individual gate was of one pearl. And the street of the city *was* pure gold, like transparent glass.

The Glory of the New Jerusalem

[22] But I saw no temple in it, for the Lord God Almighty and the Lamb are its temple. [23] The city had no need of the sun or of the moon to shine in it,[j] for the glory[k] of God illuminated it. The Lamb *is* its light. [24] And the nations of those who are saved[l] shall walk in its light, and the kings of the earth bring their glory and honor into it.[m] [25] Its gates shall not be shut at all by day (there shall be no night there). [26] And they shall bring the glory and the honor of the nations into it.[n] [27] But there shall by no means enter it anything that defiles, or causes[o] an abomination or a lie, but only those who are written in the Lamb's Book of Life.

Footnotes:

a. <u>Revelation 21:2</u> NU-Text and M-Text omit *John.*
b. <u>Revelation 21:5</u> NU-Text and M-Text omit *to me.*
c. <u>Revelation 21:6</u> M-Text omits *It is done.*
d. <u>Revelation 21:7</u> M-Text reads *overcomes, I shall give him these things.*
e. <u>Revelation 21:8</u> M-Text adds *and sinners.*
f. <u>Revelation 21:9</u> NU-Text and M-Text omit *to me.*
g. <u>Revelation 21:9</u> M-Text reads *I will show you the woman, the Lamb's bride.*
h. <u>Revelation 21:10</u> NU-Text and M-Text omit *the great* and read *the holy city, Jerusalem.*
i. <u>Revelation 21:14</u> NU-Text and M-Text read *twelve names.*
j. <u>Revelation 21:23</u> NU-Text and M-Text omit *in it.*
k. <u>Revelation 21:23</u> M-Text reads *the very glory.*
l. <u>Revelation 21:24</u> NU-Text and M-Text omit *of those who are saved.*
m. <u>Revelation 21:24</u> M-Text reads *the glory and honor of the nations to Him.*
n. <u>Revelation 21:26</u> M-Text adds *that they may enter in.*
o. <u>Revelation 21:27</u> NU-Text and M-Text read *anything profane, nor one who causes.*

(NKJV)

(18) Unlawful sexual relationships; warning that land will vomit out its inhabitants.

Leviticus 18 – Old Testament

Leviticus 18 (NKJV)

Laws of Sexual Morality

18 Then the Lord spoke to Moses, saying, ²"Speak to the children of Israel, and say to them: 'I am the Lord your God. ³According to the doings of the land of Egypt, where you dwelt, you shall not do; and according to the doings of the land of Canaan, where I am bringing you, you shall not do; nor shall you walk in their ordinances. ⁴You shall observe My judgments and keep My ordinances, to walk in them: I *am* the Lord your God. ⁵You shall therefore keep My statutes and My judgments, which if a man does, he shall live by them: I *am* the Lord.

⁶'None of you shall approach anyone who is near of kin to him, to uncover his nakedness: I *am* the Lord. ⁷The nakedness of your father or the nakedness of your mother you shall not uncover. She *is* your mother; you shall not uncover her nakedness. ⁸The nakedness of your father's wife you shall not uncover; it *is* your father's nakedness. ⁹The nakedness of your sister, the daughter of your father, or the daughter of your mother, *whether* born at home or elsewhere, their nakedness you shall not uncover. ¹⁰The nakedness of your son's daughter or your daughter's daughter, their nakedness you shall not uncover; for theirs *is* your own nakedness. ¹¹The nakedness of your father's wife's daughter, begotten by your father—she *is* your sister—you shall not uncover her nakedness. ¹²You shall not uncover the nakedness of your father's sister; she *is* near of kin to your father. ¹³You shall not uncover the nakedness of your mother's sister, for she *is* near of kin to your mother. ¹⁴You shall not uncover the nakedness of your father's brother. You shall not approach his wife; she *is* your aunt. ¹⁵You shall not uncover the nakedness of your daughter-in-law—she *is* your son's wife—you shall not uncover her nakedness. ¹⁶You shall not uncover the nakedness of your brother's wife; it *is* your brother's nakedness. ¹⁷You shall not uncover the nakedness of a woman and her daughter, nor shall you take her son's daughter or her daughter's daughter, to uncover her nakedness. They *are*

near of kin to her. It *is* wickedness. ¹⁸ Nor shall you take a woman as a rival to her sister, to uncover her nakedness while the other is alive.

¹⁹ 'Also you shall not approach a woman to uncover her nakedness as long as she is in her *customary* impurity. ²⁰ Moreover you shall not lie carnally with your neighbor's wife, to defile yourself with her. ²¹ And you shall not let any of your descendants pass through *the fire* to Molech, nor shall you profane the name of your God: I *am* the LORD. ²² You shall not lie with a male as with a woman. It *is* an abomination. ²³ Nor shall you mate with any animal, to defile yourself with it. Nor shall any woman stand before an animal to mate with it. It *is* perversion.

²⁴ 'Do not defile yourselves with any of these things; for by all these the nations are defiled, which I am casting out before you. ²⁵ For the land is defiled; therefore I visit the punishment of its iniquity upon it, and the land vomits out its inhabitants. ²⁶ You shall therefore keep My statutes and My judgments, and shall not commit *any* of these abominations, *either* any of your own nation or any stranger who dwells among you ²⁷ (for all these abominations the men of the land have done, who *were* before you, and thus the land is defiled), ²⁸ lest the land vomit you out also when you defile it, as it vomited out the nations that *were* before you. ²⁹ For whoever commits any of these abominations, the persons who commit *them* shall be cut off from among their people.

³⁰ 'Therefore you shall keep My ordinance, so that *you* do not commit *any* of these abominable customs which were committed before you, and that you do not defile yourselves by them: I *am* the LORD your God.'"

(NKJV)

(19) Blood Moons

Joel 2 – Old Testament
Acts 2 – New Testament
Revelation 6 – New Testament

James Robert Waugh

Joel 2 (NKJV)

The Day of the LORD

2 Blow the trumpet in Zion,
And sound an alarm in My holy mountain!
Let all the inhabitants of the land tremble;
For the day of the LORD is coming,
For it is at hand:
[2] A day of darkness and gloominess,
A day of clouds and thick darkness,
Like the morning *clouds* spread over the mountains.
A people *come,* great and strong,
The like of whom has never been;
Nor will there ever be any *such* after them,
Even for many successive generations.

[3] A fire devours before them,
And behind them a flame burns;
The land *is* like the Garden of Eden before them,
And behind them a desolate wilderness;
Surely nothing shall escape them.
[4] Their appearance is like the appearance of horses;
And like swift steeds, so they run.
[5] With a noise like chariots
Over mountaintops they leap,
Like the noise of a flaming fire that devours the stubble,
Like a strong people set in battle array.

[6] Before them the people writhe in pain;
All faces are drained of color.[a]
[7] They run like mighty men,
They climb the wall like men of war;
Every one marches in formation,
And they do not break ranks.
[8] They do not push one another;

Every one marches in his own column.[b]
Though they lunge between the weapons,
They are not cut down.[c]
⁹ They run to and fro in the city,
They run on the wall;
They climb into the houses,
They enter at the windows like a thief.

¹⁰ The earth quakes before them,
The heavens tremble;
The sun and moon grow dark,
And the stars diminish their brightness.
¹¹ The LORD gives voice before His army,
For His camp is very great;
For strong *is the One* who executes His word.
For the day of the LORD *is* great and very terrible;
Who can endure it?

A Call to Repentance

¹² "Now, therefore," says the LORD,
"Turn to Me with all your heart,
With fasting, with weeping, and with mourning."
¹³ So rend your heart, and not your garments;
Return to the LORD your God,
For He *is* gracious and merciful,
Slow to anger, and of great kindness;
And He relents from doing harm.
¹⁴ Who knows *if* He will turn and relent,
And leave a blessing behind Him—
A grain offering and a drink offering
For the LORD your God?
¹⁵ Blow the trumpet in Zion,
Consecrate a fast,
Call a sacred assembly;
¹⁶ Gather the people,
Sanctify the congregation,

James Robert Waugh

Assemble the elders,
Gather the children and nursing babes;
Let the bridegroom go out from his chamber,
And the bride from her dressing room.
¹⁷ Let the priests, who minister to the Lord,
Weep between the porch and the altar;
Let them say, "Spare Your people, O Lord,
And do not give Your heritage to reproach,
That the nations should rule over them.
Why should they say among the peoples,
'Where *is* their God?'"

The Land Refreshed

¹⁸ Then the Lord will be zealous for His land,
And pity His people.
¹⁹ The Lord will answer and say to His people,
"Behold, I will send you grain and new wine and oil,
And you will be satisfied by them;
I will no longer make you a reproach among the nations.

²⁰ "But I will remove far from you the northern *army*,
And will drive him away into a barren and desolate land,
With his face toward the eastern sea
And his back toward the western sea;
His stench will come up,
And his foul odor will rise,
Because he has done monstrous things."

²¹ Fear not, O land;
Be glad and rejoice,
For the Lord has done marvelous things!
²² Do not be afraid, you beasts of the field;
For the open pastures are springing up,
And the tree bears its fruit;
The fig tree and the vine yield their strength.
²³ Be glad then, you children of Zion,

And rejoice in the LORD your God;
For He has given you the former rain faithfully,[d]
And He will cause the rain to come down for you—
The former rain,
And the latter rain in the first *month*.
²⁴ The threshing floors shall be full of wheat,
And the vats shall overflow with new wine and oil.

²⁵ "So I will restore to you the years that the swarming locust has eaten,
The crawling locust,
The consuming locust,
And the chewing locust,[e]
My great army which I sent among you.
²⁶ You shall eat in plenty and be satisfied,
And praise the name of the LORD your God,
Who has dealt wondrously with you;
And My people shall never be put to shame.
²⁷ Then you shall know that I *am* in the midst of Israel:
I *am* the LORD your God
And there is no other.
My people shall never be put to shame.

God's Spirit Poured Out

²⁸ "And it shall come to pass afterward
That I will pour out My Spirit on all flesh;
Your sons and your daughters shall prophesy,
Your old men shall dream dreams,
Your young men shall see visions.
²⁹ And also on *My* menservants and on *My* maidservants
I will pour out My Spirit in those days.

³⁰ "And I will show wonders in the heavens and in the earth:
Blood and fire and pillars of smoke.
³¹ The sun shall be turned into darkness,
And the moon into blood,

Before the coming of the great and awesome day of the L<small>ORD</small>.
³² And it shall come to pass
That whoever calls on the name of the L<small>ORD</small>
Shall be saved.
For in Mount Zion and in Jerusalem there shall be deliverance,
As the L<small>ORD</small> has said,
Among the remnant whom the L<small>ORD</small> calls.

Footnotes:

1. Joel 2:6 Septuagint, Targum, and Vulgate read *gather blackness.*
2. Joel 2:8 Literally *his own highway*
3. Joel 2:8 That is, *they are not halted by losses*
4. Joel 2:23 Or *the teacher of righteousness*
5. Joel 2:25 Compare 1:4

(NKJV)

Acts 2 (NKJV)

Coming of the Holy Spirit

2 When the Day of Pentecost had fully come, they were all with one accord[a] in one place. ² And suddenly there came a sound from heaven, as of a rushing mighty wind, and it filled the whole house where they were sitting. ³ Then there appeared to them divided tongues, as of fire, and *one* sat upon each of them. ⁴ And they were all filled with the Holy Spirit and began to speak with other tongues, as the Spirit gave them utterance.

The Crowd's Response

⁵ And there were dwelling in Jerusalem Jews, devout men, from every nation under heaven. ⁶ And when this sound occurred, the multitude came together, and were confused, because everyone heard them speak in his own language. ⁷ Then they were all amazed and marveled, saying to one another, "Look, are not all these who speak Galileans? ⁸ And how *is it that* we hear, each in our own language in which we were born? ⁹ Parthians and Medes and Elamites, those dwelling in Mesopotamia, Judea and Cappadocia, Pontus and Asia, ¹⁰ Phrygia and Pamphylia, Egypt and the parts of Libya adjoining Cyrene, visitors from Rome, both Jews and proselytes, ¹¹ Cretans and Arabs—we hear them speaking in our own tongues the wonderful works of God." ¹² So they were all amazed and perplexed, saying to one another, "Whatever could this mean?"

¹³ Others mocking said, "They are full of new wine."

Peter's Sermon

¹⁴ But Peter, standing up with the eleven, raised his voice and said to them, "Men of Judea and all who dwell in Jerusalem, let this be known to you, and heed my words. ¹⁵ For these are not drunk, as

you suppose, since it is *only* the third hour of the day. ¹⁶ But this is what was spoken by the prophet Joel:

¹⁷ 'And it shall come to pass in the last days, says God,
That I will pour out of My Spirit on all flesh;
Your sons and your daughters shall prophesy,
Your young men shall see visions,
Your old men shall dream dreams.
¹⁸ And on My menservants and on My maidservants
I will pour out My Spirit in those days;
And they shall prophesy.
¹⁹ I will show wonders in heaven above
And signs in the earth beneath:
Blood and fire and vapor of smoke.
²⁰ The sun shall be turned into darkness,
And the moon into blood,
Before the coming of the great and awesome day of the LORD.
²¹ And it shall come to pass
That whoever calls on the name of the LORD
Shall be saved.'[b]

²² "Men of Israel, hear these words: Jesus of Nazareth, a Man attested by God to you by miracles, wonders, and signs which God did through Him in your midst, as you yourselves also know— ²³ Him, being delivered by the determined purpose and foreknowledge of God, you have taken[c] by lawless hands, have crucified, and put to death; ²⁴ whom God raised up, having loosed the pains of death, because it was not possible that He should be held by it. ²⁵ For David says concerning Him:

'I foresaw the LORD always before my face,
For He is at my right hand, that I may not be shaken.
²⁶ Therefore my heart rejoiced, and my tongue was glad;
Moreover my flesh also will rest in hope.
²⁷ For You will not leave my soul in Hades,
Nor will You allow Your Holy One to see corruption.
²⁸ You have made known to me the ways of life;
You will make me full of joy in Your presence.'[d]

[29] "Men *and* brethren, let *me* speak freely to you of the patriarch David, that he is both dead and buried, and his tomb is with us to this day. [30] Therefore, being a prophet, and knowing that God had sworn with an oath to him that of the fruit of his body, according to the flesh, He would raise up the Christ to sit on his throne,[e] [31] he, foreseeing this, spoke concerning the resurrection of the Christ, that His soul was not left in Hades, nor did His flesh see corruption. [32] This Jesus God has raised up, of which we are all witnesses. [33] Therefore being exalted to the right hand of God, and having received from the Father the promise of the Holy Spirit, He poured out this which you now see and hear.

[34] "For David did not ascend into the heavens, but he says himself:

'The LORD said to my Lord,
"Sit at My right hand,
[35] Till I make Your enemies Your footstool."'[f]

[36] "Therefore let all the house of Israel know assuredly that God has made this Jesus, whom you crucified, both Lord and Christ."

[37] Now when they heard *this,* they were cut to the heart, and said to Peter and the rest of the apostles, "Men *and* brethren, what shall we do?"

[38] Then Peter said to them, "Repent, and let every one of you be baptized in the name of Jesus Christ for the remission of sins; and you shall receive the gift of the Holy Spirit. [39] For the promise is to you and to your children, and to all who are afar off, as many as the Lord our God will call."

A Vital Church Grows

[40] And with many other words he testified and exhorted them, saying, "Be saved from this perverse generation." [41] Then those who gladly[g] received his word were baptized; and that day about three thousand souls were added *to them.* [42] And they

continued steadfastly in the apostles' doctrine and fellowship, in the breaking of bread, and in prayers. [43] Then fear came upon every soul, and many wonders and signs were done through the apostles. [44] Now all who believed were together, and had all things in common, [45] and sold their possessions and goods, and divided them among all, as anyone had need.

[46] So continuing daily with one accord in the temple, and breaking bread from house to house, they ate their food with gladness and simplicity of heart, [47] praising God and having favor with all the people. And the Lord added to the church[h] daily those who were being saved.

Footnotes:

1. Acts 2:1 NU-Text reads *together.*
2. Acts 2:21 Joel 2:28–32
3. Acts 2:23 NU-Text omits *have taken.*
4. Acts 2:28 Psalm 16:8–11
5. Acts 2:30 NU-Text omits *according to the flesh, He would raise up the Christ* and completes the verse with *He would seat one on his throne.*
6. Acts 2:35 Psalm 110:1
7. Acts 2:41 NU-Text omits *gladly.*
8. Acts 2:47 NU-Text omits *to the church.*

(NKJV)

Revelation 6 (NKJV)

First Seal: The Conqueror

6 Now I saw when the Lamb opened one of the seals;[a] and I heard one of the four living creatures saying with a voice like thunder, "Come and see." ² And I looked, and behold, a white horse. He who sat on it had a bow; and a crown was given to him, and he went out conquering and to conquer.

Second Seal: Conflict on Earth

³ When He opened the second seal, I heard the second living creature saying, "Come and see."[b] ⁴ Another horse, fiery red, went out. And it was granted to the one who sat on it to take peace from the earth, and that *people* should kill one another; and there was given to him a great sword.

Third Seal: Scarcity on Earth

⁵ When He opened the third seal, I heard the third living creature say, "Come and see." So I looked, and behold, a black horse, and he who sat on it had a pair of scales in his hand. ⁶ And I heard a voice in the midst of the four living creatures saying, "A quart[c] of wheat for a denarius,[d] and three quarts of barley for a denarius; and do not harm the oil and the wine."

Fourth Seal: Widespread Death on Earth

⁷ When He opened the fourth seal, I heard the voice of the fourth living creature saying, "Come and see." ⁸ So I looked, and behold, a pale horse. And the name of him who sat on it was Death, and Hades followed with him. And power was given to them over a fourth of the earth, to kill with sword, with hunger, with death, and by the beasts of the earth.

Fifth Seal: The Cry of the Martyrs

⁹ When He opened the fifth seal, I saw under the altar the souls of those who had been slain for the word of God and for the testimony which they held. ¹⁰ And they cried with a loud voice, saying, "How long, O Lord, holy and true, until You judge and avenge our blood on those who dwell on the earth?" ¹¹ Then a white robe was given to each of them; and it was said to them that they should rest a little while longer, until both *the number of* their fellow servants and their brethren, who would be killed as they *were*, was completed.

Sixth Seal: Cosmic Disturbances

¹² I looked when He opened the sixth seal, and behold,[e] there was a great earthquake; and the sun became black as sackcloth of hair, and the moon[f] became like blood. ¹³ And the stars of heaven fell to the earth, as a fig tree drops its late figs when it is shaken by a mighty wind. ¹⁴ Then the sky receded as a scroll when it is rolled up, and every mountain and island was moved out of its place. ¹⁵ And the kings of the earth, the great men, the rich men, the commanders,[g] the mighty men, every slave and every free man, hid themselves in the caves and in the rocks of the mountains, ¹⁶ and said to the mountains and rocks, "Fall on us and hide us from the face of Him who sits on the throne and from the wrath of the Lamb! ¹⁷ For the great day of His wrath has come, and who is able to stand?"

Footnotes:

1. <u>Revelation 6:1</u> NU-Text and M-Text read *seven seals.*
2. <u>Revelation 6:3</u> NU-Text and M-Text omit *and see.*
3. <u>Revelation 6:6</u> Greek *choinix;* that is, approximately one quart
4. <u>Revelation 6:6</u> This was approximately one day's wage for a worker.
5. <u>Revelation 6:12</u> NU-Text and M-Text omit *behold.*
6. <u>Revelation 6:12</u> NU-Text and M-Text read *the whole moon.*
7. <u>Revelation 6:15</u> NU-Text and M-Text read *the commanders, the rich men.*

(NKJV)

(20) Curses for Not Behaving God's Laws

Deuteronomy 28 – Old Testament

Deuteronomy 28 (NKJV)

Blessings on Obedience

28 "Now it shall come to pass, if you diligently obey the voice of the Lord your God, to observe carefully all His commandments which I command you today, that the Lord your God will set you high above all nations of the earth. [2] And all these blessings shall come upon you and overtake you, because you obey the voice of the Lord your God:

[3] "Blessed *shall* you *be* in the city, and blessed *shall* you *be* in the country.

[4] "Blessed *shall be* the fruit of your body, the produce of your ground and the increase of your herds, the increase of your cattle and the offspring of your flocks.

[5] "Blessed *shall be* your basket and your kneading bowl.

[6] "Blessed *shall* you *be* when you come in, and blessed *shall* you *be* when you go out.

[7] "The Lord will cause your enemies who rise against you to be defeated before your face; they shall come out against you one way and flee before you seven ways.

[8] "The Lord will command the blessing on you in your storehouses and in all to which you set your hand, and He will bless you in the land which the Lord your God is giving you.

[9] "The Lord will establish you as a holy people to Himself, just as He has sworn to you, if you keep the commandments of the Lord your God and walk in His ways. [10] Then all peoples of the earth shall see that you are called by the name of the Lord, and they shall be afraid of you. [11] And the Lord will grant you plenty of goods, in the fruit of your body, in the increase of your livestock, and in the produce of your ground, in the land of which the Lord swore to your

fathers to give you. ¹² The LORD will open to you His good treasure, the heavens, to give the rain to your land in its season, and to bless all the work of your hand. You shall lend to many nations, but you shall not borrow. ¹³ And the LORD will make you the head and not the tail; you shall be above only, and not be beneath, if you heed the commandments of the LORD your God, which I command you today, and are careful to observe *them.* ¹⁴ So you shall not turn aside from any of the words which I command you this day, *to* the right or the left, to go after other gods to serve them.

Curses on Disobedience

¹⁵ "But it shall come to pass, if you do not obey the voice of the LORD your God, to observe carefully all His commandments and His statutes which I command you today, that all these curses will come upon you and overtake you:

¹⁶ "Cursed *shall* you *be* in the city, and cursed *shall* you *be* in the country.

¹⁷ "Cursed *shall be* your basket and your kneading bowl.

¹⁸ "Cursed *shall be* the fruit of your body and the produce of your land, the increase of your cattle and the offspring of your flocks.

¹⁹ "Cursed *shall* you *be* when you come in, and cursed *shall* you *be* when you go out.

²⁰ "The LORD will send on you cursing, confusion, and rebuke in all that you set your hand to do, until you are destroyed and until you perish quickly, because of the wickedness of your doings in which you have forsaken Me. ²¹ The LORD will make the plague cling to you until He has consumed you from the land which you are going to possess. ²² The LORD will strike you with consumption, with fever, with inflammation, with severe burning fever, with the sword, with scorching, and with mildew; they shall pursue you until you perish. ²³ And your heavens which *are* over your head shall be bronze, and

the earth which is under you *shall be* iron. [24] The LORD will change the rain of your land to powder and dust; from the heaven it shall come down on you until you are destroyed.

[25] "The LORD will cause you to be defeated before your enemies; you shall go out one way against them and flee seven ways before them; and you shall become troublesome to all the kingdoms of the earth. [26] Your carcasses shall be food for all the birds of the air and the beasts of the earth, and no one shall frighten *them* away. [27] The LORD will strike you with the boils of Egypt, with tumors, with the scab, and with the itch, from which you cannot be healed. [28] The LORD will strike you with madness and blindness and confusion of heart. [29] And you shall grope at noonday, as a blind man gropes in darkness; you shall not prosper in your ways; you shall be only oppressed and plundered continually, and no one shall save *you*.

[30] "You shall betroth a wife, but another man shall lie with her; you shall build a house, but you shall not dwell in it; you shall plant a vineyard, but shall not gather its grapes. [31] Your ox *shall be* slaughtered before your eyes, but you shall not eat of it; your donkey *shall be* violently taken away from before you, and shall not be restored to you; your sheep *shall be* given to your enemies, and you shall have no one to rescue *them*. [32] Your sons and your daughters *shall be* given to another people, and your eyes shall look and fail *with longing* for them all day long; and *there shall be* no strength in your hand. [33] A nation whom you have not known shall eat the fruit of your land and the produce of your labor, and you shall be only oppressed and crushed continually. [34] So you shall be driven mad because of the sight which your eyes see. [35] The LORD will strike you in the knees and on the legs with severe boils which cannot be healed, and from the sole of your foot to the top of your head.

[36] "The LORD will bring you and the king whom you set over you to a nation which neither you nor your fathers have known, and there you shall serve other gods—wood and stone. [37] And you shall become an astonishment, a proverb, and a byword among all nations where the LORD will drive you.

³⁸ "You shall carry much seed out to the field but gather little in, for the locust shall consume it. ³⁹ You shall plant vineyards and tend *them,* but you shall neither drink *of* the wine nor gather the *grapes;* for the worms shall eat them. ⁴⁰ You shall have olive trees throughout all your territory, but you shall not anoint *yourself* with the oil; for your olives shall drop off. ⁴¹ You shall beget sons and daughters, but they shall not be yours; for they shall go into captivity. ⁴² Locusts shall consume all your trees and the produce of your land.

⁴³ "The alien who *is* among you shall rise higher and higher above you, and you shall come down lower and lower. ⁴⁴ He shall lend to you, but you shall not lend to him; he shall be the head, and you shall be the tail.

⁴⁵ **"Moreover all these curses shall come upon you and pursue and overtake you, until you are destroyed, because you did not obey the voice of the LORD your God, to keep His commandments and His statutes which He commanded you. ⁴⁶ And they shall be upon you for a sign and a wonder, and on your descendants forever.**

⁴⁷ **"Because you did not serve the LORD your God with joy and gladness of heart, for the abundance of everything, ⁴⁸ therefore you shall serve your enemies, whom the LORD will send against you, in hunger, in thirst, in nakedness, and in need of everything; and He will put a yoke of iron on your neck until He has destroyed you. ⁴⁹ The LORD will bring a nation against you from afar, from the end of the earth, *as swift* as the eagle flies, a nation whose language you will not understand, ⁵⁰ a nation of fierce countenance, which does not respect the elderly nor show favor to the young. ⁵¹ And they shall eat the increase of your livestock and the produce of your land, until you are destroyed; they shall not leave you grain or new wine or oil, *or* the increase of your cattle or the offspring of your flocks, until they have destroyed you.**

⁵² "They shall besiege you at all your gates until your high and fortified walls, in which you trust, come down throughout all your land; and they shall besiege you at all your gates throughout all your land which the LORD your God has given you. ⁵³ You shall eat the

fruit of your own body, the flesh of your sons and your daughters whom the Lord your God has given you, in the siege and desperate straits in which your enemy shall distress you. [54] The sensitive and very refined man among you will be hostile toward his brother, toward the wife of his bosom, and toward the rest of his children whom he leaves behind, [55] so that he will not give any of them the flesh of his children whom he will eat, because he has nothing left in the siege and desperate straits in which your enemy shall distress you at all your gates. [56] The tender and delicate woman among you, who would not venture to set the sole of her foot on the ground because of her delicateness and sensitivity, will refuse[a] to the husband of her bosom, and to her son and her daughter, [57] her placenta which comes out from between her feet and her children whom she bears; for she will eat them secretly for lack of everything in the siege and desperate straits in which your enemy shall distress you at all your gates.

[58] "If you do not carefully observe all the words of this law that are written in this book, that you may fear this glorious and awesome name, THE LORD YOUR GOD, [59] then the Lord will bring upon you and your descendants extraordinary plagues—great and prolonged plagues—and serious and prolonged sicknesses. [60] Moreover He will bring back on you all the diseases of Egypt, of which you were afraid, and they shall cling to you. [61] Also every sickness and every plague, which *is* not written in this Book of the Law, will the Lord bring upon you until you are destroyed. [62] You shall be left few in number, whereas you were as the stars of heaven in multitude, because you would not obey the voice of the Lord your God. [63] And it shall be, *that* just as the Lord rejoiced over you to do you good and multiply you, so the Lord will rejoice over you to destroy you and bring you to nothing; and you shall be plucked from off the land which you go to possess.

[64] "Then the Lord will scatter you among all peoples, from one end of the earth to the other, and there you shall serve other gods, which neither you nor your fathers have known—wood and stone. [65] And among those nations you shall find no rest, nor shall the sole of your foot have a resting place; but there the Lord will give you a

trembling heart, failing eyes, and anguish of soul. ⁶⁶ Your life shall hang in doubt before you; you shall fear day and night, and have no assurance of life. ⁶⁷ In the morning you shall say, 'Oh, that it were evening!' And at evening you shall say, 'Oh, that it were morning!' because of the fear which terrifies your heart, and because of the sight which your eyes see.

⁶⁸ "And the LORD will take you back to Egypt in ships, by the way of which I said to you, 'You shall never see it again.' And there you shall be offered for sale to your enemies as male and female slaves, but no one will buy *you*."

Footnotes:

a.   Deuteronomy 28:56 Literally *her eye shall be evil toward*

(NKJV)

James Robert Waugh

(21) Commandment from God to Israel

Deuteronomy 6 – Old Testament

Deuteronomy 6 (NKJV)

The Greatest Commandment

6 "Now this *is* the commandment, *and these are* the statutes and judgments which the Lord your God has commanded to teach you, that you may observe *them* in the land which you are crossing over to possess, ² that you may fear the Lord your God, to keep all His statutes and His commandments which I command you, you and your son and your grandson, all the days of your life, and that your days may be prolonged. ³ Therefore hear, O Israel, and be careful to observe *it,* that it may be well with you, and that you may multiply greatly as the Lord God of your fathers has promised you—'a land flowing with milk and honey.'[a]

⁴ **"Hear, O Israel: The Lord our God, the Lord *is* one![b] ⁵ You shall love the Lord your God with all your heart, with all your soul, and with all your strength.**

⁶ "And these words which I command you today shall be in your heart. ⁷ You shall teach them diligently to your children, and shall talk of them when you sit in your house, when you walk by the way, when you lie down, and when you rise up. ⁸ You shall bind them as a sign on your hand, and they shall be as frontlets between your eyes. ⁹ You shall write them on the doorposts of your house and on your gates.

James Robert Waugh

Caution Against Disobedience

[10] "So it shall be, when the LORD your God brings you into the land of which He swore to your fathers, to Abraham, Isaac, and Jacob, to give you large and beautiful cities which you did not build, [11] houses full of all good things, which you did not fill, hewn-out wells which you did not dig, vineyards and olive trees which you did not plant— when you have eaten and are full— [12] *then* beware, lest you forget the LORD who brought you out of the land of Egypt, from the house of bondage. [13] You shall fear the LORD your God and serve Him, and shall take oaths in His name. [14] You shall not go after other gods, the gods of the peoples who *are* all around you [15] (for the LORD your God *is* a jealous God among you), lest the anger of the LORD your God be aroused against you and destroy you from the face of the earth.

[16] "You shall not tempt the LORD your God as you tempted *Him* in Massah. [17] You shall diligently keep the commandments of the LORD your God, His testimonies, and His statutes which He has commanded you. [18] And you shall do *what is* right and good in the sight of the LORD, that it may be well with you, and that you may go in and possess the good land of which the LORD swore to your fathers, [19] to cast out all your enemies from before you, as the LORD has spoken.

[20] "When your son asks you in time to come, saying, 'What *is the meaning of* the testimonies, the statutes, and the judgments which the LORD our God has commanded you?' [21] then you shall say to your son: 'We were slaves of Pharaoh in Egypt, and the LORD brought us out of Egypt with a mighty hand; [22] and the LORD showed signs and wonders before our eyes, great and severe, against Egypt, Pharaoh, and all his household. [23] Then He brought us out from there, that He might bring us in, to give us the land of which He swore to our fathers. [24] And the LORD commanded us to observe all these statutes, to fear the LORD our God, for our good always, that He might preserve us alive, as *it is* this day. [25] Then it will be righteousness for us, if we are careful to observe all these commandments before the LORD our God, as He has commanded us.'

Footnotes:

    a. <u>Deuteronomy 6:3</u> <u>Exodus 3:8</u>
    b. <u>Deuteronomy 6:4</u> Or *The Lord is our God, the Lord alone* (that is, the only one)

(NKJV)

(22) Homosexuality

Leviticus 18 – Old Testament
Leviticus 20 – Old Testament
Romans 1 – New Testament
Mark 10 - New Testament
1 Corinthians 6 – New Testament
1 Timothy 1 – New Testament
Revelation 21 – New Testament

Leviticus 18 (NKJV)

Laws of Sexual Morality

18 Then the Lord spoke to Moses, saying, ²"Speak to the children of Israel, and say to them: 'I am the Lord your God. ³According to the doings of the land of Egypt, where you dwelt, you shall not do; and according to the doings of the land of Canaan, where I am bringing you, you shall not do; nor shall you walk in their ordinances. ⁴You shall observe My judgments and keep My ordinances, to walk in them: I *am* the Lord your God. ⁵You shall therefore keep My statutes and My judgments, which if a man does, he shall live by them: I *am* the Lord.

⁶'None of you shall approach anyone who is near of kin to him, to uncover his nakedness: I *am* the Lord. ⁷The nakedness of your father or the nakedness of your mother you shall not uncover. She *is* your mother; you shall not uncover her nakedness. ⁸The nakedness of your father's wife you shall not uncover; it *is* your father's nakedness. ⁹The nakedness of your sister, the daughter of your father, or the daughter of your mother, *whether* born at home or elsewhere, their nakedness you shall not uncover. ¹⁰The nakedness of your son's daughter or your daughter's daughter, their nakedness you shall not uncover; for theirs *is* your own nakedness. ¹¹The nakedness of your father's wife's daughter, begotten by your father—she *is* your sister—you shall not uncover her nakedness. ¹²You shall not uncover the nakedness of your father's sister; she *is* near of kin to your father. ¹³You shall not uncover the nakedness of your mother's sister, for she *is* near of kin to your mother. ¹⁴You shall not uncover the nakedness of your father's brother. You shall not approach his wife; she *is* your aunt. ¹⁵You shall not uncover the nakedness of your daughter-in-law—she *is* your son's wife—you shall not uncover her nakedness. ¹⁶You shall not uncover the nakedness of your brother's wife; it *is* your brother's nakedness. ¹⁷You shall not uncover the nakedness of a woman and her daughter, nor shall you take her son's daughter or her daughter's daughter, to uncover her nakedness. They *are* near

of kin to her. It *is* wickedness. [18] Nor shall you take a woman as a rival to her sister, to uncover her nakedness while the other is alive.

[19] 'Also you shall not approach a woman to uncover her nakedness as long as she is in her *customary* impurity. [20] Moreover you shall not lie carnally with your neighbor's wife, to defile yourself with her. [21] And you shall not let any of your descendants pass through *the fire* to Molech, nor shall you profane the name of your God: I *am* the LORD. [22] You shall not lie with a male as with a woman. It *is* an abomination. [23] Nor shall you mate with any animal, to defile yourself with it. Nor shall any woman stand before an animal to mate with it. It *is* perversion.

[24] 'Do not defile yourselves with any of these things; for by all these the nations are defiled, which I am casting out before you. [25] For the land is defiled; therefore I visit the punishment of its iniquity upon it, and the land vomits out its inhabitants. [26] You shall therefore keep My statutes and My judgments, and shall not commit *any* of these abominations, *either* any of your own nation or any stranger who dwells among you [27] (for all these abominations the men of the land have done, who *were* before you, and thus the land is defiled), [28] lest the land vomit you out also when you defile it, as it vomited out the nations that *were* before you. [29] For whoever commits any of these abominations, the persons who commit *them* shall be cut off from among their people.

[30] 'Therefore you shall keep My ordinance, so that *you* do not commit *any* of these abominable customs which were committed before you, and that you do not defile yourselves by them: I *am* the LORD your God.'"

(NKJV)

Leviticus 20 (NKJV)

Penalties for Breaking the Law

20 Then the LORD spoke to Moses, saying, ² "Again, you shall say to the children of Israel: 'Whoever of the children of Israel, or of the strangers who dwell in Israel, who gives *any* of his descendants to Molech, he shall surely be put to death. The people of the land shall stone him with stones. ³ I will set My face against that man, and will cut him off from his people, because he has given *some* of his descendants to Molech, to defile My sanctuary and profane My holy name. ⁴ And if the people of the land should in any way hide their eyes from the man, when he gives *some* of his descendants to Molech, and they do not kill him, ⁵ then I will set My face against that man and against his family; and I will cut him off from his people, and all who prostitute themselves with him to commit harlotry with Molech.

⁶ 'And the person who turns to mediums and familiar spirits, to prostitute himself with them, I will set My face against that person and cut him off from his people. ⁷ Consecrate yourselves therefore, and be holy, for I *am* the LORD your God. ⁸ And you shall keep My statutes, and perform them: I *am* the LORD who sanctifies you.

⁹ 'For everyone who curses his father or his mother shall surely be put to death. He has cursed his father or his mother. His blood *shall be* upon him.

¹⁰ 'The man who commits adultery with *another* man's wife, *he* who commits adultery with his neighbor's wife, the adulterer and the adulteress, shall surely be put to death. ¹¹ The man who lies with his father's wife has uncovered his father's nakedness; both of them shall surely be put to death. Their blood *shall be* upon them. ¹² If a man lies with his daughter-in-law, both of them shall surely be put to death. They have committed perversion. Their blood *shall be* upon them. ¹³ **If a man lies with a male as he lies with a woman, both of them have committed an abomination. They shall surely be**

put to death. Their blood *shall be* upon them. [14] If a man marries a woman and her mother, it *is* wickedness. They shall be burned with fire, both he and they, that there may be no wickedness among you. [15] If a man mates with an animal, he shall surely be put to death, and you shall kill the animal. [16] If a woman approaches any animal and mates with it, you shall kill the woman and the animal. They shall surely be put to death. Their blood *is* upon them.

[17] 'If a man takes his sister, his father's daughter or his mother's daughter, and sees her nakedness and she sees his nakedness, it *is* a wicked thing. And they shall be cut off in the sight of their people. He has uncovered his sister's nakedness. He shall bear his guilt. [18] If a man lies with a woman during her sickness and uncovers her nakedness, he has exposed her flow, and she has uncovered the flow of her blood. Both of them shall be cut off from their people.

[19] 'You shall not uncover the nakedness of your mother's sister nor of your father's sister, for that would uncover his near of kin. They shall bear their guilt. [20] If a man lies with his uncle's wife, he has uncovered his uncle's nakedness. They shall bear their sin; they shall die childless. [21] If a man takes his brother's wife, it *is* an unclean thing. He has uncovered his brother's nakedness. They shall be childless.

[22] 'You shall therefore keep all My statutes and all My judgments, and perform them, that the land where I am bringing you to dwell may not vomit you out. [23] And you shall not walk in the statutes of the nation which I am casting out before you; for they commit all these things, and therefore I abhor them. [24] But I have said to you, "You shall inherit their land, and I will give it to you to possess, a land flowing with milk and honey." I *am* the LORD your God, who has separated you from the peoples. [25] You shall therefore distinguish between clean animals and unclean, between unclean birds and clean, and you shall not make yourselves abominable by beast or by bird, or by any kind of living thing that creeps on the ground, which I have separated from you as unclean. [26] And you shall be holy to Me, for I the LORD *am* holy, and have separated you from the peoples, that you should be Mine.

[27] 'A man or a woman who is a medium, or who has familiar spirits, shall surely be put to death; they shall stone them with stones. Their blood *shall be* upon them.'"

(NKJV)

Scripture taken from the New King James Version®. Copyright © 1982 by Thomas Nelson. Used by permission. All rights reserved.

Romans 1 (NKJV)

Greeting

1 Paul, a bondservant of Jesus Christ, called *to be* an apostle, separated to the gospel of God ² which He promised before through His prophets in the Holy Scriptures, ³ concerning His Son Jesus Christ our Lord, who was born of the seed of David according to the flesh, ⁴ *and* declared *to be* the Son of God with power according to the Spirit of holiness, by the resurrection from the dead. ⁵ Through Him we have received grace and apostleship for obedience to the faith among all nations for His name, ⁶ among whom you also are the called of Jesus Christ;

⁷ To all who are in Rome, beloved of God, called *to be* saints:

Grace to you and peace from God our Father and the Lord Jesus Christ.

Desire to Visit Rome

⁸ First, I thank my God through Jesus Christ for you all, that your faith is spoken of throughout the whole world. ⁹ For God is my witness, whom I serve with my spirit in the gospel of His Son, that without ceasing I make mention of you always in my prayers, ¹⁰ making request if, by some means, now at last I may find a way in the will of God to come to you. ¹¹ For I long to see you, that I may impart to you some spiritual gift, so that you may be established— ¹² that is, that I may be encouraged together with you by the mutual faith both of you and me.

¹³ Now I do not want you to be unaware, brethren, that I often planned to come to you (but was hindered until now), that I might have some fruit among you also, just as among the other Gentiles. ¹⁴ I am a debtor both to Greeks and to barbarians, both to wise and to unwise. ¹⁵ So, as much as is in me, *I am* ready to preach the gospel to you who are in Rome also.

James Robert Waugh

The Just Live by Faith

[16] For I am not ashamed of the gospel of Christ,[a] for it is the power of God to salvation for everyone who believes, for the Jew first and also for the Greek. [17] For in it the righteousness of God is revealed from faith to faith; as it is written, "The just shall live by faith."[b]

God's Wrath on Unrighteousness

¹⁸ For the wrath of God is revealed from heaven against all ungodliness and unrighteousness of men, who suppress the truth in unrighteousness, ¹⁹ because what may be known of God is manifest in them, for God has shown *it* to them. ²⁰ For since the creation of the world His invisible *attributes* are clearly seen, being understood by the things that are made, *even* His eternal power and Godhead, so that they are without excuse, ²¹ because, although they knew God, they did not glorify *Him* as God, nor were thankful, but became futile in their thoughts, and their foolish hearts were darkened. ²² Professing to be wise, they became fools, ²³ and changed the glory of the incorruptible God into an image made like corruptible man—and birds and four-footed animals and creeping things.

²⁴ Therefore God also gave them up to uncleanness, in the lusts of their hearts, to dishonor their bodies among themselves, ²⁵ who exchanged the truth of God for the lie, and worshiped and served the creature rather than the Creator, who is blessed forever. Amen.

²⁶ **For this reason God gave them up to vile passions. For even their women exchanged the natural use for what is against nature.** ²⁷ **Likewise also the men, leaving the natural use of the woman, burned in their lust for one another, men with men committing what is shameful, and receiving in themselves the penalty of their error which was due.**

²⁸ **And even as they did not like to retain God in** *their* **knowledge, God gave them over to a debased mind, to do those things which are not fitting;** ²⁹ **being filled with all unrighteousness, sexual immorality,[c] wickedness, covetousness, maliciousness; full of envy, murder, strife, deceit, evil-mindedness;** *they are* **whisperers,** ³⁰ **backbiters, haters of God, violent, proud, boasters, inventors of evil things, disobedient to parents,** ³¹ **undiscerning, untrustworthy, unloving, unforgiving,[d] unmerciful;** ³² **who, knowing the righteous judgment of God, that those who practice such things are deserving of death, not only do the same but also approve of those who practice them.**

James Robert Waugh

Footnotes:

a. Romans 1:16 NU-Text omits *of Christ.*
b. Romans 1:17 Habakkuk 2:4
c. Romans 1:29 NU-Text omits *sexual immorality.*
d. Romans 1:31 NU-Text omits *unforgiving.*

(NKJV)

Mark 10 (NKJV)

Marriage and Divorce

10 Then He arose from there and came to the region of Judea by the other side of the Jordan. And multitudes gathered to Him again, and as He was accustomed, He taught them again.

² The Pharisees came and asked Him, "Is it lawful for a man to divorce *his* wife?" testing Him.

³ And He answered and said to them, "What did Moses command you?"

⁴ They said, "Moses permitted *a man* to write a certificate of divorce, and to dismiss *her.*"

⁵ And Jesus answered and said to them, "Because of the hardness of your heart he wrote you this precept. ⁶ But from the beginning of the creation, God 'made them male and female.'[a] ⁷ 'For this reason a man shall leave his father and mother and be joined to his wife, ⁸ and the two shall become one flesh'; [b] so then they are no longer two, but one flesh. ⁹ Therefore what God has joined together, let not man separate."

¹⁰ In the house His disciples also asked Him again about the same *matter.* ¹¹ So He said to them, "Whoever divorces his wife and marries another commits adultery against her. ¹² And if a woman divorces her husband and marries another, she commits adultery."

James Robert Waugh

Jesus Blesses Little Children

[13] Then they brought little children to Him, that He might touch them; but the disciples rebuked those who brought *them*. [14] But when Jesus saw *it*, He was greatly displeased and said to them, "Let the little children come to Me, and do not forbid them; for of such is the kingdom of God. [15] Assuredly, I say to you, whoever does not receive the kingdom of God as a little child will by no means enter it." [16] And He took them up in His arms, laid *His* hands on them, and blessed them.

Jesus Counsels the Rich Young Ruler

[17] Now as He was going out on the road, one came running, knelt before Him, and asked Him, "Good Teacher, what shall I do that I may inherit eternal life?"

[18] So Jesus said to him, "Why do you call Me good? No one *is* good but One, *that is*, God. [19] You know the commandments: 'Do not commit adultery,' 'Do not murder,' 'Do not steal,' 'Do not bear false witness,' 'Do not defraud,' 'Honor your father and your mother.'"[c]

[20] And he answered and said to Him, "Teacher, all these things I have kept from my youth."

[21] Then Jesus, looking at him, loved him, and said to him, "One thing you lack: Go your way, sell whatever you have and give to the poor, and you will have treasure in heaven; and come, take up the cross, and follow Me."

[22] But he was sad at this word, and went away sorrowful, for he had great possessions.

With God All Things Are Possible

[23] Then Jesus looked around and said to His disciples, "How hard it is for those who have riches to enter the kingdom of God!" [24] And the disciples were astonished at His words. But Jesus answered again and said to them, "Children, how hard it is for those who trust in riches[d] to enter the kingdom of God! [25] It is easier for a camel to go through the eye of a needle than for a rich man to enter the kingdom of God."

[26] And they were greatly astonished, saying among themselves, "Who then can be saved?"

[27] But Jesus looked at them and said, "With men *it is* impossible, but not with God; for with God all things are possible."

[28] Then Peter began to say to Him, "See, we have left all and followed You."

[29] So Jesus answered and said, "Assuredly, I say to you, there is no one who has left house or brothers or sisters or father or mother or wife[e] or children or lands, for My sake and the gospel's, [30] who shall not receive a hundredfold now in this time—houses and brothers and sisters and mothers and children and lands, with persecutions—and in the age to come, eternal life. [31] But many *who are* first will be last, and the last first."

Jesus a Third Time Predicts His Death and Resurrection

[32] Now they were on the road, going up to Jerusalem, and Jesus was going before them; and they were amazed. And as they followed they were afraid. Then He took the twelve aside again and began to tell them the things that would happen to Him: [33] "Behold, we are going up to Jerusalem, and the Son of Man will be betrayed to the chief priests and to the scribes; and they will condemn Him to death and deliver Him to the Gentiles; [34] and they will mock Him, and scourge Him, and spit on Him, and kill Him. And the third day He will rise again."

James Robert Waugh

Greatness Is Serving

[35] Then James and John, the sons of Zebedee, came to Him, saying, "Teacher, we want You to do for us whatever we ask."

[36] And He said to them, "What do you want Me to do for you?"

[37] They said to Him, "Grant us that we may sit, one on Your right hand and the other on Your left, in Your glory."

[38] But Jesus said to them, "You do not know what you ask. Are you able to drink the cup that I drink, and be baptized with the baptism that I am baptized with?"

[39] They said to Him, "We are able."

So Jesus said to them, "You will indeed drink the cup that I drink, and with the baptism I am baptized with you will be baptized; [40] but to sit on My right hand and on My left is not Mine to give, but *it is for those* for whom it is prepared."

[41] And when the ten heard *it,* they began to be greatly displeased with James and John. [42] But Jesus called them to *Himself* and said to them, "You know that those who are considered rulers over the Gentiles lord it over them, and their great ones exercise authority over them. [43] Yet it shall not be so among you; but whoever desires to become great among you shall be your servant. [44] And whoever of you desires to be first shall be slave of all. [45] For even the Son of Man did not come to be served, but to serve, and to give His life a ransom for many."

Jesus Heals Blind Bartimaeus

[46] Now they came to Jericho. As He went out of Jericho with His disciples and a great multitude, blind Bartimaeus, the son of Timaeus, sat by the road begging. [47] And when he heard that it was Jesus of Nazareth, he began to cry out and say, "Jesus, Son of David, have mercy on me!"

[48] Then many warned him to be quiet; but he cried out all the more, "Son of David, have mercy on me!"

[49] So Jesus stood still and commanded him to be called.

Then they called the blind man, saying to him, "Be of good cheer. Rise, He is calling you."

[50] And throwing aside his garment, he rose and came to Jesus.

[51] So Jesus answered and said to him, "What do you want Me to do for you?"

The blind man said to Him, "Rabboni, that I may receive my sight."

[52] Then Jesus said to him, "Go your way; your faith has made you well." And immediately he received his sight and followed Jesus on the road.

Footnotes:

   a. <u>Mark 10:6</u> <u>Genesis 1:27</u>; <u>5:2</u>
   b. <u>Mark 10:8</u> <u>Genesis 2:24</u>
   c. <u>Mark 10:19</u> <u>Exodus 20:12–16</u>; <u>Deuteronomy 5:16–20</u>
   d. <u>Mark 10:24</u> NU-Text omits *for those who trust in riches.*
   e. <u>Mark 10:29</u> NU-Text omits *or wife.*

(NKJV)

1 Corinthians 6 (NKJV)

Do Not Sue the Brethren

6 Dare any of you, having a matter against another, go to law before the unrighteous, and not before the saints? [2] Do you not know that the saints will judge the world? And if the world will be judged by you, are you unworthy to judge the smallest matters? [3] Do you not know that we shall judge angels? How much more, things that pertain to this life? [4] If then you have judgments concerning things pertaining to this life, do you appoint those who are least esteemed by the church to judge? [5] I say this to your shame. Is it so, that there is not a wise man among you, not even one, who will be able to judge between his brethren? [6] But brother goes to law against brother, and that before unbelievers!

[7] Now therefore, it is already an utter failure for you that you go to law against one another. Why do you not rather accept wrong? Why do you not rather *let yourselves* be cheated? [8] No, you yourselves do wrong and cheat, and *you do* these things *to your* brethren! [9] **Do you not know that the unrighteous will not inherit the kingdom of God? Do not be deceived. Neither fornicators, nor idolaters, nor adulterers, nor homosexuals,[a] nor sodomites, [10] nor thieves, nor covetous, nor drunkards, nor revilers, nor extortioners will inherit the kingdom of God. [11] And such were some of you. But you were washed, but you were sanctified, but you were justified in the name of the Lord Jesus and by the Spirit of our God.**

Glorify God in Body and Spirit

[12] All things are lawful for me, but all things are not helpful. All things are lawful for me, but I will not be brought under the power of any. [13] Foods for the stomach and the stomach for foods, but God will destroy both it and them. Now the body *is* not for sexual immorality but for the Lord, and the Lord for the body. [14] And God both raised up the Lord and will also raise us up by His power.

[15] Do you not know that your bodies are members of Christ? Shall I then take the members of Christ and make *them* members of a harlot? Certainly not! [16] Or do you not know that he who is joined to a harlot is one body *with her?* For "the two," He says, "shall become one flesh."[b] [17] But he who is joined to the Lord is one spirit *with Him.*

[18] Flee sexual immorality. Every sin that a man does is outside the body, but he who commits sexual immorality sins against his own body. [19] Or do you not know that your body is the temple of the Holy Spirit *who is* in you, whom you have from God, and you are not your own? [20] For you were bought at a price; therefore glorify God in your body[c] and in your spirit, which are God's.

Footnotes:

a. 1 Corinthians 6:9 That is, catamites
b. 1 Corinthians 6:16 Genesis 2:24
c. 1 Corinthians 6:20 NU-Text ends the verse at *body.*

(NKJV)

1 Timothy 1 (NKJV)

Greeting

1 Paul, an apostle of Jesus Christ, by the commandment of God our Savior and the Lord Jesus Christ, our hope,

[2] To Timothy, a true son in the faith:

Grace, mercy, *and* peace from God our Father and Jesus Christ our Lord.

James Robert Waugh

No Other Doctrine

[3] As I urged you when I went into Macedonia—remain in Ephesus that you may charge some that they teach no other doctrine, [4] nor give heed to fables and endless genealogies, which cause disputes rather than godly edification which is in faith. [5] Now the purpose of the commandment is love from a pure heart, *from* a good conscience, and *from* sincere faith, [6] from which some, having strayed, have turned aside to idle talk, [7] desiring to be teachers of the law, understanding neither what they say nor the things which they affirm.

[8] But we know that the law *is* good if one uses it lawfully, [9] knowing this: that the law is not made for a righteous person, but for *the* lawless and insubordinate, for *the* ungodly and for sinners, for *the* unholy and profane, for murderers of fathers and murderers of mothers, for manslayers, [10] for fornicators, for sodomites, for kidnappers, for liars, for perjurers, and if there is any other thing that is contrary to sound doctrine, [11] according to the glorious gospel of the blessed God which was committed to my trust.

Glory to God for His Grace

[12] And I thank Christ Jesus our Lord who has enabled me, because He counted me faithful, putting *me* into the ministry, [13] although I was formerly a blasphemer, a persecutor, and an insolent man; but I obtained mercy because I did *it* ignorantly in unbelief. [14] And the grace of our Lord was exceedingly abundant, with faith and love which are in Christ Jesus. [15] This *is* a faithful saying and worthy of all acceptance, that Christ Jesus came into the world to save sinners, of whom I am chief. [16] However, for this reason I obtained mercy, that in me first Jesus Christ might show all longsuffering, as a pattern to those who are going to believe on Him for everlasting life. [17] Now to the King eternal, immortal, invisible, to God who alone is wise,[a] *be* honor and glory forever and ever. Amen.

James Robert Waugh

Fight the Good Fight

[18] This charge I commit to you, son Timothy, according to the prophecies previously made concerning you, that by them you may wage the good warfare, [19] having faith and a good conscience, which some having rejected, concerning the faith have suffered shipwreck, [20] of whom are Hymenaeus and Alexander, whom I delivered to Satan that they may learn not to blaspheme.

Footnotes:

    a.   1 Timothy 1:17 NU-Text reads *to the only God.*

(NKJV)

Revelation 21 (NKJV)

All Things Made New

21 Now I saw a new heaven and a new earth, for the first heaven and the first earth had passed away. Also there was no more sea. ²Then I, John,[a] saw the holy city, New Jerusalem, coming down out of heaven from God, prepared as a bride adorned for her husband. ³ And I heard a loud voice from heaven saying, "Behold, the tabernacle of God *is* with men, and He will dwell with them, and they shall be His people. God Himself will be with them *and be* their God. ⁴ And God will wipe away every tear from their eyes; there shall be no more death, nor sorrow, nor crying. There shall be no more pain, for the former things have passed away."

⁵ Then He who sat on the throne said, "Behold, I make all things new." And He said to me,[b] "Write, for these words are true and faithful."

⁶ And He said to me, "It is done![c] I am the Alpha and the Omega, the Beginning and the End. I will give of the fountain of the water of life freely to him who thirsts. ⁷ He who overcomes shall inherit all things,[d] and I will be his God and he shall be My son. ⁸ **But the cowardly, unbelieving,[e] abominable, murderers, sexually immoral, sorcerers, idolaters, and all liars shall have their part in the lake which burns with fire and brimstone, which is the second death."**

The New Jerusalem

[9] Then one of the seven angels who had the seven bowls filled with the seven last plagues came to me[f] and talked with me, saying, "Come, I will show you the bride, the Lamb's wife."[g] [10] And he carried me away in the Spirit to a great and high mountain, and showed me the great city, the holy[h] Jerusalem, descending out of heaven from God, [11] having the glory of God. Her light *was* like a most precious stone, like a jasper stone, clear as crystal. [12] Also she had a great and high wall with twelve gates, and twelve angels at the gates, and names written on them, which are *the names* of the twelve tribes of the children of Israel: [13] three gates on the east, three gates on the north, three gates on the south, and three gates on the west.

[14] Now the wall of the city had twelve foundations, and on them were the names[i] of the twelve apostles of the Lamb. [15] And he who talked with me had a gold reed to measure the city, its gates, and its wall. [16] The city is laid out as a square; its length is as great as its breadth. And he measured the city with the reed: twelve thousand furlongs. Its length, breadth, and height are equal. [17] Then he measured its wall: one hundred *and* forty-four cubits, *according* to the measure of a man, that is, of an angel. [18] The construction of its wall was *of* jasper; and the city *was* pure gold, like clear glass. [19] The foundations of the wall of the city *were* adorned with all kinds of precious stones: the first foundation *was* jasper, the second sapphire, the third chalcedony, the fourth emerald, [20] the fifth sardonyx, the sixth sardius, the seventh chrysolite, the eighth beryl, the ninth topaz, the tenth chrysoprase, the eleventh jacinth, and the twelfth amethyst. [21] The twelve gates *were* twelve pearls: each individual gate was of one pearl. And the street of the city *was* pure gold, like transparent glass.

The Glory of the New Jerusalem

[22] But I saw no temple in it, for the Lord God Almighty and the Lamb are its temple. [23] The city had no need of the sun or of the moon to shine in it,[j] for the glory[k] of God illuminated it. The Lamb *is* its light. [24] And the nations of those who are saved[l] shall walk in its light, and the kings of the earth bring their glory and honor into it.[m] [25] Its gates shall not be shut at all by day (there shall be no night there). [26] And they shall bring the glory and the honor of the nations into it.[n] [27] But there shall by no means enter it anything that defiles, or causes[o] an abomination or a lie, but only those who are written in the Lamb's Book of Life.

Footnotes:

a. <u>Revelation 21:2</u> NU-Text and M-Text omit *John.*
b. <u>Revelation 21:5</u> NU-Text and M-Text omit *to me.*
c. <u>Revelation 21:6</u> M-Text omits *It is done.*
d. <u>Revelation 21:7</u> M-Text reads *overcomes, I shall give him these things.*
e. <u>Revelation 21:8</u> M-Text adds *and sinners.*
f. <u>Revelation 21:9</u> NU-Text and M-Text omit *to me.*
g. <u>Revelation 21:9</u> M-Text reads *I will show you the woman, the Lamb's bride.*
h. <u>Revelation 21:10</u> NU-Text and M-Text omit *the great* and read *the holy city, Jerusalem.*
i. <u>Revelation 21:14</u> NU-Text and M-Text read *twelve names.*
j. <u>Revelation 21:23</u> NU-Text and M-Text omit *in it.*
k. <u>Revelation 21:23</u> M-Text reads *the very glory.*
l. <u>Revelation 21:24</u> NU-Text and M-Text omit *of those who are saved.*
m. <u>Revelation 21:24</u> M-Text reads *the glory and honor of the nations to Him.*
n. <u>Revelation 21:26</u> M-Text adds *that they may enter in.*
o. <u>Revelation 21:27</u> NU-Text and M-Text read *anything profane, nor one who causes.*

(NKJV)

ABOUT THE AUTHOR

DEDICATION

This book is dedicated to the author of my life, Jesus Christ, as I would not have a book worthy of reading, if it were not for the blessed signs Jesus has given me.

[SPECIAL NOTES TO THE READER OF THIS BOOK]:

I did physically type this book, but I asked the Holy Spirit to help me write it. Please note the following signs that occurred in making this book:

> The book came back initially from WestBow Press with the last numbered page being "316". (John 3:16)

> The JPG number of the author's picture for this book starts with the numbers "316". (John 3:16)

> (Please see the end of the book for these signs, on pages 315 and 316.)

> ALL GLORY TO THE FATHER, THE SON, AND THE HOLY GHOST!

John 3 (NKJV)

¹⁶ For God so loved the world that He gave His only begotten Son, that whoever believes in Him should not perish but have everlasting life. ¹⁷ For God did not send His Son into the world to condemn the world, but that the world through Him might be saved.

Printed in the United States
by Baker & Taylor Publisher Services